Religious
Leaders

Other titles in
Chambers Compact Reference
Great Inventions Through History
Great Modern Inventions
Great Scientific Discoveries
Masters of Jazz
Musical Masterpieces
Mythology
The Occult

To be published in 1992
Catastrophes and Disasters
Crimes and Criminals
50 Years of Rock Music
Key Movies
Modern British History 1914–90
Sacred Writings of World Religions
Saints
Space Exploration

Religious Leaders

Jacques Brosse

Chambers

Published 1991 by W & R Chambers Ltd,
43–45 Annandale Street, Edinburgh EH7 4AZ

First published in France as *Les maîtres spirituels*
© Bordas, Paris, 1988
© English text edition W & R Chambers 1991

British Library Cataloguing in Publication Data

A catalogue record for this book is available from the British
Library.

ISBN 0550 17006 5

Cover design Blue Peach Design Consultants Ltd
Printed in England by Clays Ltd, St Ives, plc

Acknowledgements

Translated from the French by Sara Newbery

Adapted for the English edition by Thérèse Duriez
Jane Pollock

Chambers Compact Reference Series Editor   Min Lee

Illustration credits

Contents

Synoptic and Chronological Table of Contents

Introduction

Today, the words 'religious leader' can easily be misconstrued. They have been used to describe the creators of certain 'sects' which, founded principally as a personality cult, have abused a very large number of people. This misguided phenomenon is to some extent a sign of the times. It bears witness to a real need which the institutionalized churches can no longer satisfy. This is why even a succinct overview of the world's greatest leaders and their teachings, from antiquity to the present day, can be a useful guide for those attracted to the search for religion. As an introduction to this work, it is therefore worth redefining what religious leaders are by specifying those criteria according to which true leader can be recognized. The first quality is absolute selflessness. A genuine leader cannot draw material reward from his teaching. If this rule had been always applied, imposters would have been disqualified by their own behaviour.

The true leader is unaware of his status. Most often his own master will have chosen him to be his successor, or he will have been recognized as such by the people who came to consult him. He will not have sought to be a leader. Having renounced the world and himself, he remains totally indifferent to the judgments passed on him by others and is more concerned about the quality of his disciples than their number. He becomes no more than an instrument of the 'Self' of Eternal Wisdom. It is therefore not surprising that some of the most important leaders' teachings only became influential after their death.

A religious leader should not be confused with a teacher, nor with a psychotherapist, nor even a spiritual advisor. His mission is to guide others along the path he has already trodden. He helps them to bring about the change in direction from the outer to the inner, without which there can be no spiritual life; he supervises their meditation and concentration exercises, enlightens them on the resultant revelations, warns them of the obstacles they will have to overcome and the dangers they will have to face. The leader never imposes the truths he has found; he merely encourages the disciple to discover them within himself.

While the leader is obliged to draw on his personal experiences, the doctrine he passes on is in no way personal. No matter how original his theories may be, he sees himself as a link in a chain; even when he appears to be independent, he associates himself with one of the great traditions. This is why the succession from one leader to another takes on such importance. Thus, the Muslim brotherhoods (*tariqa*) are said to stem from the Prophet himself, the different schools of Buddhism claim to originate in the Buddha, and the 'golden chain' links the orthodox leaders to the Church Fathers, the Apostles, and finally to Jesus.

Although they professed and remained faithful to one particular religion, most of the great leaders admitted the validity of other religious paths for, while they may differ or even oppose each other at the base, they converge at the summit, which is the return of the being to its original oneness and the search for the presence of God in the soul.

In theory, all the paths and all the schools are represented in this book, but a choice had to be made amongst the leaders. The choice was self-imposed: only those whose message remains alive today figure in this book. Are there still authentic religious leaders today? The reader might well ask himself such a question, but there is no precise answer. Undoubtedly, certain traditional lines have not died out in, for example, India, Tibetan Buddhism, Japanese Buddhism, and the Muslim (particularly Sufi) countries; but the true religious guides shy away from publicity or

1

even hide themselves, remaining anonymous like many of their predecessors. The current climate is far from being favourable to religious teaching. In some cases, some thinkers have found themselves taking on a role which they had never sought, but which resulted from their works. Such is the case of Jung, Guénon, and Teilhard de Chardin, although they all came from different academic and religious backgrounds.

On the whole, this work is made up of monographs outlining the life, the experience and personality, and the works and teachings of the greatest leaders, but it also contains a number of theoretical articles devoted to the different schools and religious currents with which the leaders were associated.

Acts of the Apostles

From Jesus to the Church

Relating the events which, after the Ascension and the Pentecost, led to the first Christian communities being formed, Acts was intended to reinforce the faith of new converts.

According to Saint Jerome, the fifth book of the New Testament was written in Greek while its author was living in Rome. We used to believe that Acts originated between AD 58 and 64 (therefore in Paul's lifetime) but it is now generally accepted that it dates from the later period of AD 80 to 90. The author presents Acts as the sequel to his first 'book', the Gospel of Luke. Luke is also believed to have been Paul's faithful companion, a theory confirmed by the text in which the author frequently uses the 'we' form when he narrates certain of his voyages. Paul, the Gentiles' Apostle, the former pagan doctor of probable Greek extraction, has left the imprint of his personality throughout this text.

The narrative opens with the Ascension of Jesus and his last instructions to the disciples. It goes on to describe how the Holy Spirit came down to the Apostles, thereby fulfilling the prophecy. There follows an account of the ensuing persecution and the martyrdom of Saint Stephen, and finally the expansion of Christianity into Antioch's pagan milieu leading up to Paul's mission there. The remainder of the work is dedicated to that mission, from his conversion and missionary voyages to his arrest and subsequent incarceration at Caesarea. The text goes on to tell us that Paul was transferred to Rome where, although still a prisoner, he was permitted to preach the Gospel. Here the text of Acts breaks off suddenly. In Acts, the life of the first Christian community, which was already qualified as *ecclesia*, is given as exemplary. The evangelical precepts are defined through mutual love, joy, and patience in the face of adversity.

The origins of Christianity

Although considered to be of dubious authenticity by 19th century historians, today the Acts of the Apostles is considered to be genuine. However, actual Church historians point out that Acts gives only one part of Christianity's earliest history and in fact, the author barely mentions the Armean branch of Judaeo-Christianity which was a thriving nucleus of the primitive Church, but to which he was overtly hostile. This in no way detracts from the book's historical value; it not only remains our most important primary source work but also evokes the changes which overcame the Apostles after the Pentecost and the powerful impetus which carried Jesus's message of Salvation to the 'ends of the Earth'.

The Acts of the Apostles is written in very clear language resulting in an interesting and charming narrative which emphasizes the stature of those characters whose words it so often reproduces.

The Holy Spirit

'But when the Holy Spirit descends upon you, you will receive power, and you will tell of me in Jerusalem, and all over Judea, and all over the world.'

Amida Worship

The cult of the Buddha of the Land of Purity

Amida Worship originated in China and is based on a particular invocation which allows the worshipper to be reborn in the 'Land of Purity' of Amida. This cult has an extensive following in Japan.

Amida is the Sino-Japanese transcription of the Sanskrit *Amitabha* ('Infinite Light') or *Amitayus* ('Infinite Life'). These are the names of one of the five great Jina of Mahayana, who stated: 'If I cannot come before him who believes in me and whose last wish will be to be reborn in my country, I refuse to become a Buddha.' Invoking Amida's name brings about rebirth in his paradise, the 'Land of Purity', where Buddhahood is joyfully awaited. Although Amida worship was not widespread in India, in China it gave birth to the 'Land of Purity' school, based on the *Sukhavati-Sutra* ('Spreading of the Land of Bliss') and founded by Hui Yuan. However, it was in Japan that Amida worship was to realize its full potential.

The Nembutsu

From the 10th century onwards, when political and social unrest were at their height. Amida worship became very popular, promising as it did the infinite compassion of Buddha the Saviour. A monk named Kuya (903–1017) published his *Ojoyoshu* (Essentials of Salvation or Birth in the Land of Purity) which was inspired by the teachings of the Chinese patria Chan-Tao (613–681). The first Ami sect, the *Yuzi Nembutsu shu* was founded Ryomin (1073–1132). But the true found of the School of the Land of Purity *Jodo-shu* in 1134, was Genku (1133–121 who is better known as Honen. Hon believed the way in which the Doctrine h been perverted rendered the final delive ance from the endless cycle of death a rebirth an impossibility. Only the chanti of *Nembutsu* (*Namu Amidu Butsu*), 'Adorati to the Buddha Amida', could guaran salvation. Honen gained so many followe from all walks of life that the monks fre other schools succeeded in having h banished in 1207.

His best-known disciple, Shinran Shor (1173–1262) who had also been banish in 1207, settled in the Eastern provin and married a nun, with whom he had fa children. He declared himself to be 'neith monk nor layman' and had many followe His theory was much more radical th Honen's. He insisted that simple chanti of *Nembutsu* could only be an expression gratitude and of unshakeable faith in Ar da, and that only Amida's mercy cou ensure salvation. This eventually ga birth to *Jodo Shin Shu* ('True Cult of t Land of Purity'). In Japan, *Jodo Shin S* had phenomenal success and is even tod more popular (15 million followers) th any other Buddhist school.

Honen

'The method of deliverance I preach does no depend in meditation or study, but on the simple conviction that if one chants *Nembuts* with the aim of being reborn in his paradise, one is certain to achieve that aim. That is all.

Angelus Silesius

1624 Breslau — Breslau 1677

The Cherubic Pilgrim

Today the work of the German mystic poet, Angelus Silesius, is widely considered to be one of the purest expressions of Western mysticism.

Born into a well-off Lutheran family, Johann Scheffler was educated in the classical tradition at Breslau and in 1643 went on to study medicine at Strasbourg, Leyden and Padua. As a doctor of philosophy and medicine he became personal physician to the Prince of Öls. Around this time he began to frequent mystic circles and came into contact with Abraham von Frankenberg who, as a disciple of Jakob Böhme, had adopted the practice of inter-confession. Von Frankenberg's influence over his disciple was great, and as a result, one year after the former's death, on 12 June 1653, Scheffler converted to Catholicism. Having taken the name Angelus Silesius (The Messenger from Silesia), he went into silent retreat for three years, though during this time he published several collections of poems. He was ordained in 1661 and, while continuing to write poetry, he produced a series of pamphlets denouncing Protestantism. He died, his health ruined by his severe asceticism.

His works

His works consist of several collections including: *The Holy Pleasure of the Soul* (1657–68) in which the author presents the Christian's love of Jesus as an idyll and the *Pilgrim of Truth* which was partially written prior to his conversion and completed after it, and which earned him posthumous fame.

The theory

Angelus Silesius added a personal and poetic expression to the great tradition of Eckhart, Tauler, and Böhme. If he exceeds standard confessional form, it is because God is Indefinable, at once All and Nothing, Being and Non-Being. Before our Creator, we are nothing and yet it is only in us as the image of God, that God can see Himself. We must therefore abandon ourselves totally, purify ourselves in order to become what we really are: a divine reflection and therefore eternal. Such a radical theory, close in essence to Neoplatonism, necessarily aroused the suspicions of the Church. On the other hand, Angelus Silesius's intense fervour and lyricism served as a model for piety (see **Spener**). 'The Pilgrim' influenced many German poets, including Schopenhauer, before gaining recognition as one of the most remarkable examples of a mysticism.

Being eternity

'I myself am eternity when I abandon time and return myself to God.'

Rendering the Spirit

'I know that without me, God cannot live an instant. If I am reduced to nothing, he has to render the Spirit.'

Ascetics and Asceticism

All spiritual life is ascetic in nature

Asceticism, which revolves around contempt for the body and encourages suffering as a necessary evil, has at times led its followers into dangerous excesses.

The word 'ascetic' comes from the Greek and was originally applied to the rigorous training of athletes but was later given a more moral meaning by Greek philosophers, the Pythagoreans then the Stoics. A comparison was made between the indispensable efforts to master the instincts and overcome the passions, and the drawn-out exercises of the athlete in the stadium. All spiritual life requires an effort for it aims at a profound transformation of the being. This change can only be achieved if the self becomes detached from sensory objects and material goods. For Pythagoreans, life has to be a process of purification in order to allow the divine spark to resurface. Plato considers that the immortal soul is denied life principally because of the flesh that surrounds it. Plotinus is even more extreme. In the *Enneades*, the body is depicted as a tomb in which the soul is imprisoned. To liberate the soul, the flesh must be mortified (the etymological meaning of mortified is 'caused to die'). With Plotinus we move from an ascetic way of life to asceticsm. In Christianity he found new justification for his beliefs: human nature was corrupted by original sin, but 'God became a man so that man might become God'; Christians then, must repent, rid themselves of their former impure charac-

ter in order to become 'new'. The most extreme manifestation of this contempt for the body, this battle against instinct, is perhaps the life of penitence led by the Fathers of the Desert, who were seen as role models and heroes, particularly by monks. Physical mortification offered as a sacrifice to Jesus was for a long time considered to be a step towards redemption, but at times this seeking of pain has led to rather suspicious excesses.

Oriental asceticism

Yet asceticism is not particular to Christianity; it exists in all religions. In Islam, many Sufis led lives of mortification. In their quest for freedom of the spirit, India's Sannyasin renounce the world and pursue asceticism through a rigorous and taxing programme of yoga. Buddha himself practised such extreme asceticism that he sometimes put his life at risk. He later gave it up as he found that this form of suffering did not bring him any closer to attaining his goal. He warned his disciples against this kind of excessiveness, but nevertheless the monk's life was one of extreme severity (see **Monachism**).

Today we may regard asceticism with hostility because of the extremes it has given rise to in the past, but an ascetic way of life (which is not the same as asceticism) remains a fundamental part of spirituality.

Monastic asceticism

'It cannot be construed as negative, it must be a positive act of love. The life of God is love. An ascetic way of life therefore is the purification of a meeting ground in preparation for the union with God.' (Jean Marcadet)

Ashram

In India a community dedicated to spiritual teaching

Disciples live in an ashram under the guidance of their guru.

Ashram comes from the Sanskrit *srama*, 'effort' in spiritual exercises; it denotes the followers of a particular spiritual discipline living communally under the direction of the guru. There are still ashrams in India. The disciples often wear ochre robes which symbolize their chastity and their renunciation of the material world. The disciples are under the spiritual guidance of a guru or leader who is believed to represent the divine presence. The guru passes on the esoteric teachings transmitted to him by *his* master. Guided by him, the novices recite the sacred texts, practise yoga and chant their own personal *mantra*, a sacred formula chosen for each individual by the guru. Laypersons may join the disciples for retreats of varying duration. On festival days, whole families from the neighbourhood bring offerings which the leader blesses and redistributes (Prasada). He then gives them his *darsan*, or blessing, which is often accompanied by the laying on of hands. In general, the guru makes a short speech which is followed by group chanting, though sometimes he does not speak but remains in the meditation position, and his *samadhi*, or state of blissful concentration, is supposed to communicate itself to his followers.

The most famous ashrams are: that of Ramakrishna near Calcutta, in the 19th century; Gandhi's Satyagrahashram at Sabarmati, near Ahmedabad, in the first half of the 20th century; Sri Aurobindo's at Pondicherry, Ramana Maharishi's at Tiruvannamalai in southern India, and Shivananda's at Rishikesh, which is especially known for its zealous practice of yoga. This Himalayan spiritual centre attracts many visitors today. In India ashrams are almost as common as convents and monasteries are rare; some are visited by European pilgrims.

Retreat and renunciation

Even in the oldest texts, the ashram is mentioned as an isolated, forest retreat, for those who had given up worldly things in order to live in a more ascetic manner, nourished only through the charity of their neighbours. Moreover, this retreat corresponded to the third stage in traditional Hindu life (see **Hinduism**), in which, having educated his family, the Hindu decided to give himself totally to a spiritual life of solitude. This is still common practice today.

Swāmi Sivānanda Sarvasti

'Nothing is more powerful for ridding the soul of impurities than serving a guru.'

Vivekānanda

'Let us workship our guru as we worship God, but let us not obey him blindly. Let us think for ourselves.'

Attar

c. 1120 Nishapur, Khorassan—Nishapur 1190

A Persian poet and mystic

*Attar brought the esoteric
teachings of the Sufis within easy
reach of everyone.*

Farid al-Din Muhammad ben Ibrahim is
better known by his pseudonym 'Attar'or
the 'Perfumer', which was also his profession (as it was his father's before him). It
would appear that he never left his native
town in the north-east of Persia where
Omar Khayyam, the poet and sage, died.
Although he did not belong to any particular religious group, Attar was a Shi'ite
Muslim and close to the Sufis, which led to
his persecution by the Sunni branch of the
religion (see **Islam**). One of his works was
burned and his house ransacked. This is all
we know of his life. Attar belongs to the
group of mystic Muslims who seek the truth
within themselves, have no living teacher
and are guided by an angel.

His works

Twenty-five works have been ascribed to
Attar but some are definitely of doubtful
authenticity. Two of his books are particularly well known: *Memorial of the Saints*, a
collection of biographies of 72 men of God
(most importantly of Hallaj), which was
the result of 40 years of research; and
Mantiq al-Tair (The Language of the Birds),
in which 30 birds depart on a pilgrimage to
find their king, the legendary bird Simorgh,
who is 'close to us and from whom we are

distanced'. At the end of the perilous
journey, they find Simorgh, in whom they
recognize their true essence which has
always been hidden in the deepest recesses
of their being. This long poem remains one
of the most popular expressions of Islamic
spirituality. Attar has also given us an
important collection of poems (*Diwan*); *The
Divine Book*, a poem on the superiority of all
things spiritual; and *The Book of Adversity*,
which describes the voyage of the soul
towards liberation, during which it comes
to understand that to seek God is to seek
one's own inner self through questioning
nature.

The theory

To Attar, human life can only have meaning after death, which represents deliverance. This is the concept that we must
understand because God is there even if we
are ignorant of his presence. When he set
down these truths, discovered through a
process of profound inner contemplation,
Attar showed true poetic genius. Not only
has all subsequent Persian poetry been
orientated towards this kind of expression
of personal spirituality, but he was and is, a
trustworthy guide, even outwith Islam, for
his theories are of universal value.

Attar and Rumi
'Attar has roamed through the seven cities of
love, while I am still at the corner of a side
street.' (Djalal ad-Din Rumi)

Augustine

354 Thagaste — Hippo 430

The first of the great Christian philosophers

Father of the Church, Augustine influenced a whole school in Western spirituality. A writer of genius, he is best known for his Confessions.

Aurelius Augustinus was born a Roman citizen in what is now Algeria. His father was pagan and his mother an extremely devout Christian. He had an education in the classics at Carthage which was then the metropolis of Africa. When he was 18, after reading Cicero, he became convinced of his philosophic vocation. In his youth Augustine married a girl of low birth, staying with her for 14 years until the final separation imposed by his mother, Monica. He also had a son Adeodat (*A deo datus*, 'given by God'), and it was to support his family that he opened a school at Thagaste, before becoming an orator in Carthage. Ten years later he taught rhetoric in Rome and then in Milan. Fascinated by the problem of evil, which became a life-long obsession, Augustine was firstly attracted to the Manichaeans, remaining attached to them in a passive capacity for nine years. Eventually, when he was 32 years old and had heard Saint Ambroise speak, he converted to Christianity, the religion he had known from birth but of which he had always been wary.

He returned to Thagaste and, cutting all ties with the outside world, from 388–391 he lived a monastic life accompanied by only a few followers. At the request of the citizens of Hippo, he took the office of bishop. He was to remain the driving force behind the African Church until his death. In this capacity, he preached against the Donatist schism and the Pelagian heresy, whose doctrine was condemned by the

Council of Carthage in 418. The bishop's twilight years were darkened by the invasion of the Vandals and he died at Hippo while they besieged the city. This ardent and emotional man, who was constantly in evolution and sometimes even contradictory in his teachings, has not lost his appeal over the centuries.

His works

His works number 113 polemic treatises covering dissidents and pagans, catechism and moral theology; 218 *Letters* and more than 500 *Sermons*. But the works which brought their author worldwide fame are the *Soliloquies*, written while he was a novice; the *Confessions* (c. 400), which is unique in ancient literature, being both the confession of his human weaknesses and a hymn of grace to the mysterious presence of God; *Of Christian Doctrine* (397–427); and finally *The City of God*, a Christian apologia and philosophy of the developing Christian society.

The theory

Augustine's philosophy does not deal with the pursuit undertaken by a solitary spirit, but is a fervent and ongoing dialogue between the creation and its creator, between man seeking for God and God coming

'I have looked for you, and what I have believed, I have wanted to see with the eyes of intelligence.'

The Immutable
'And so in the depth of the soul we have been able to grasp some degree of the Immutable in a flash . . . I have already touched the Immutable, why bother me again?'

to meet him, a spiritual journey which leads the finite being to infinity. If circumstances conspired to make him a person of action, he nevertheless retained his meditative and mystic nature. He was in continual pursuit of spiritual knowledge: 'We will look as if we were going to find, but we will never find without always looking.'

When dealing with the problem of knowing God, Augustine takes the presence of the divine image in the hearts of the human race as his starting point. He states that the divine image is the source of true wisdom, and that true wisdom is love, for if the soul loves God,' it will be wise, not through its own knowledge but through sharing the supreme knowledge of God; where the soul will be eternal, it will reign in bliss'. This wisdom, which is the union of human and divine, allows knowledge and perception of God, without completely demystifying Him. Having made this wisdom 'the object of it's contemplation', the soul attaches itself completely to this idea and at the same time detaches itself from the 'vain things' of the world. It experiences bliss when it joins with the Spirit and participates in divine nature. Augustine in his *Confessions* stated 'You have called, and clamoured, and broken my deafness; You have shone, and dazzled, and chased away my blindness; You have hung heavy in the air and I have inhaled and breathed you in; I have tasted and I am hungry and thirsty for You; You touched me and I burn for Your peace'.

This profoundly personal expression of faith has guided many mystics. Augustine's original way of thinking played a fundamental role in the development of Christianity, for it represents the most successful Western fusion of Christian doctrine and Graeco-Latin culture.

However, one of the theories exposed in *On the Predestination of Saints* has troubled and puzzled theologians. Against Pelagianism, Augustine maintained that since the Fall, humanity has become so deeply entrenched in sin that salvation can only come from God, and that God, acting in inexplicable wisdom, will arbitrarily refuse to some what he accords to others. This led him to formulate his theory of 'predestination': the chosen or elect experience the mercy of God while the rejected are exposed to His terrible wrath. This doctrine was never fully accepted by the Church, for it rendered useless good works and gave birth to innumerable controversies, from semi-Pelagianism in the 6th century, to the Reformation in the 16th century. Luther upholds the doctrine of predestination which Calvin later set down in more harsh terms. In the following century, in his *Augustinus*, Jansen, Bishop of Ypres, promoted Augustinian doctrine, which he stated, had been altered by the Jesuits. And yet the prestige of Saint Augustine was so great that even those who were opposed to his doctrines sometimes referred to his works. Taken out of a religious context, Augustine's works form a profound philosophical meditation on the destiny of the human race.

Saint Cyran

'Saint Augustine is the first of the Latin Fathers. His every word is the expression of his virtue and his passion.'

Luther

'I prefer Augustine above all others. He taught a pure doctrine and with Christian humility, submitted his books to the Holy Scriptures. He was the first Church Father to have dealt with Original Sin . . . All of Augustine is with me.'

Aurobindo

1872 Calcutta — Pondicherry 1950

Towards the New Person

Blending together tradition and change, East and West, Sri Aurobindo announced the birth of the New Person

Son of a Bengali doctor, Aurobindo Ghose was educated in England from 1879–93 and graduated from Cambridge University. On his return to India, he took up the study of his country's principal traditions of which he had previously known little. Although atheist in England, Aurobindo discovered God through Indian philosophy. His conviction that an independent India would rediscover her true identity led him to become an extreme nationalist, but he did not give up the yoga which brought him serenity and self-control. In 1909 he moved to Pondichery, which was then on French territory and devoted himself to the composition of his great works. Disciples came to live close to him and his companion, a French woman called Madame Richard, who became the 'Mother' of the ashram. In 1926 she took over the running of the ashram while Aurobindo went into retreat, appearing in public only once a year. 'Mother', who died in 1975, kept up his work, in creating a 'university centre' and then Auroville, which is populated by disciples from all over the world.

His works

Sri Aurobindo is the author of a number of works, the most important of which have been translated into many languages: *The Synthesis of Yogas* (1939); *The Guide to Yoga* (1951); *The Divine Life* (4 vols. 1955–9); and *The Secret of the Veda* (1975). He is also the author of commentaries on the *Bhagavadgita* (1962), and the *Three Upanishad* (1949), as well as on Heraclite.

The theory

Throughout his education, Sri Aurobindo was nourished on Western philosophy, but he later became very attached to Indian non-dualist thought, and concerned himself mainly with the effect of modern science on its future development. His work also attempts to express a 'new synthesis' which would be capable of reconciling Western science and Eastern wisdom, action and contemplation, and rationalism and mysticism. To Aurobindo, God, who is both transcendent and imminent, appears to humanity as Cosmic Conscience, manifesting itself in space and time.

As the world is the product of the 'cosmic game', which is the involution of spirit in matter, one must be able to re-establish, both internally and externally 'divine life', so as to be rid of all egotistical desires. This is to be achieved through tapping previously unused potential, in particular the faculty that Aurobindo calls the 'supramental', and through the practice of different yogas. This voluntary mutation should give birth to a new type of human, the true 'Superman'.

Sri
In India, 'Sri' is roughly equivalent to 'leader'.

The Absolute Being is 'the unknown, the omnipresent, the indispensable that the human conscience seeks perpetually through knowledge, sensitivity, perception and action.'

Avicenna

980 Afshena, near Bokhara — Hamadan 1037

Philosopher of the West and mystic of the East

Although Avicenna exercised considerable influence over Medieval European thought, in Muslim circles he is considered above all to be a great spiritual leader.

Avicenna is the transcription of Ibn Sina. Abu'Ali al-Hosayn Ibn Sina was born near the extreme eastern frontier of Persia and spent his whole life there. He was most likely Shi'ite and close to the Ishmaelis. As a precocious child, he was much admired for the extent of his knowledge. For a time he practised medicine and compiled a Canon, which became the guide to medicinal study in Europe for centuries after. Ibn Sina was much sought after by Princes, and held the position of Vizir on numerous occasions at Hamadan, then Isphahan. He may have spent his days in business, but his nights were dedicated to study and teaching. He died a true Believer.

His works

His works consist of more than 200 titles, of which, apart from his Canon of Medicine, the most famous are: *Kitab Ash Shifa,* (The Cure of the Error), an encyclopaedia of philosophical sciences in 18 volumes; and *Almahad* (The Return), which describes how, after its separation from the body, the soul returns to its simple pre-incarnatory state. Ibn Sina worked at length on an Oriental Philosophy which he considered his major work. We only know of frag-

ments, in particular the three mystic *Narratives,* in which he partially unveils the secret of his own personal experience, in the guise of an initiatory voyage towards the mystic East, in the company of the guiding Angel.

The theory

Ibn Sina's role in Islamic spirituality has been somewhat disguised by the encyclopaedic nature of his work, and the use made of it by medieval acadaemia. For him, philosophy and theology are inseparable; fused together they form a theosophy and even a gnosis. The human soul originates in the last of the ten angelic Intelligences emanating from divine thought. The soul, therefore, cannot really come to a state of self-recognition without first having recognized within itself the presence of the Angel, as only the Angel can reveal the divine secret. This doctrine, which contains elements of Neoplatonic thought, explains the influence Ibn Sina had on the mystic philosophy of Shi'ite Persia, especially on Sohrawardi and, in the 17th century, on Sadra Shirazi, author of a detailed commentary of *The Cure of the Error.*

'Gain knowledge of the self, and you will know your Maker.'

What will survive

'After death, the soul remains immortal in the heart of the universal intellect. On the other hand, its other faculties, like the animal or the vegetable which cannot act independently of the body, die with the body.'

Bardo Thodol

The Tibetan 'Book of the Dead'

*Devised as a guide to the liberation
of the spirit after death, the Bardo
Thodol is studied by Tibetan
Buddhists and read to the dying.*

In contrast to the Egyptian 'Book of the Dead', the *Bardo Thodol* is not an itinerary for the deceased, but a series of instructions given to those 'who want to go beyond death by changing its process into an act of liberation'. Its full title is 'The Great Liberation through Listening during the Bardo'. Although the oldest manuscripts only date from the 14th century, the work is listed as *terma*, that is to say, as a text found in a hiding place where it would have been kept at a time when its disclosure would have been unpropitious; it is therefore thought to predate the year of its discovery. The Bardo Thodol can be traced back to Padmasambhava, who introduced Tantric Buddhism to Tibet in the 8th century.

The Bardo

Buddhists aspire to avoid the interval which separates death from rebirth. The masters of Varjrayana do not consider death to be momentary but see it as a slow disintegration which begins with the agony of dying, and continues long after apparent death, until the last vestiges of conscious-ness have left the body. Reciting this text at the death bed is only a reminder of the essential ideals acquired in a lifetime. After outward death, the deceased crosses the *Chikai Bardo*, during which time he does not understand that he is dead, and is suspended in a sleep-like state. The first part of the book is recited in order to make him aware of his state, to spare him any regrets and to prepare him for the final liberation which manifests itself as a vision of the 'Clear Primordial Light.' If he does not take this chance to enter Nirvana because he is ill-prepared or frightened, then the deceased finds himself in the presence firstly of helpful divinities, then of terrifying ones, which are the manifes-tations of the content of his own *karma*. If he has faith in the compassion of the Buddhas and the Bodhisattvas, he may still escape, but if he does not, he will tumble into the *Sidpa Bardo*, a phase which begins on the 14th day following death. This phase is the most dangerous, for the deceased must be reborn in order to escape the terrifying visions which attack him. Nevertheless, the deceased will have been helped at every stage of his voyage by the words of warning issued by the priest in charge of reciting the text. This text is considered to be one of the most extraordinary in literature.

Illusion

'If I could only realize that any apparition is but the reflection of my own conscience.'

The ceremonial sacred dance which evokes the Bardo Thodol, *performed at the Stok monastery (Ladakh)*
The person wearing the mask in the shape of a stag's head represents Yama Raja, the Judge of the Dead

Basil of Caesarea

c. 330 Caesarea, Cappadocia — Caesarea 379

First of the great ecumenical doctors

Basil defended the principles of moral and social Christianity. He firmly established monachism as a model for Christian life.

Basil came from an old Christian family, which includes a surprising number of saints, from his grandmother to his sister Macrine; two of his brothers were bishops, Gregory at Nyssa and Peter at Sebasteia. Basil studied under the famous orator Libanios at Constantinople, then at Athens where he became friends with Gregory of Nazianze, whom he had met previously at Caesarea. On his father's death, Basil returned to his native town to teach rhetoric, but soon decided to dedicate his life to God. After his baptism, he went on a long journey which took him through Syria, Palestine, Mesopotamia, and Egypt. On his travels, he visited the most famous hermit saints, whose lifestyle he decided to emulate. When he returned to Caesarea, he gave away all his worldly goods to the poor and went into solitary retreat. He was joined by several disciples and within a few years, had founded a number of monasteries for which he wrote his *Rules*. His reputation was such that Eusebius, the Bishop of Caesarea, decided to have him

ordained in 364. Basil succeeded him in 370. A model pastor, he contributed to the fight against the Arian heresy.

His works

His writings consist of several polemic and theological works, including *Against Euno-mius* (an Arian bishop, c. 364), and the *Treatise of the Holy Spirit*; works of exegesis like the Hexameron (before 370), a collection of homilies on the six days of creation; and the *Exultation to the Young on the way to prophet from the Hellenic Letters*, which contributed to the continuing taste for classical literature; guiding *Letters*; and finally the *Four Rules* and the *Little Rules*.

The theory

Basil played an essential role in the collaborating of the dogma of the Trinity, in that he reconciled conflicting points of view which threatened to cause a schism in Christianity, but he was most influential as an orator and spiritual leader. If he defined the new morality as based on love for God and for one's neighbour, for Basil, true Christian life took place in the monastery, which he carefully described and tabulated in the *Rules*. The *Rules* contained all the elements of monastic life: prayer, regular confession, frequent communion, meditation on sacred texts, manual labour and good works, and was to become the standard reference book for monasteries not only in the West, where it was the inspiration for Saint Benedict's *Rule*, but also in the East where it is still used in the Orthodox Church. Finally, Basil created the liturgy which bears his name and is still used in the Greek Church today.

> **The Spirit**
> 'It leads the weak by the hand, perfects those who make progress, and lights up the purified.'

Benedict of Nursia

c. 480 Nursia — Monte Casino 547

The 'Patriarch of Western Monks'

Having given them the quest for intimate knowledge of God as their goal, Benedict made the monasteries 'schools in the service of the Lord'.

All we know about his life comes from Gregory the Great's *Dialogues*, which were written barely 50 years after Benedict's death. By this time, Benedict was already legendary. He was born into a family of the provincial nobility and studied in Rome. He was horrified by the violence of his era, caused by a wave of invasions, and decided to shun the world in order to take up an ascetic life in a Christian community at Enfida. Then, because of a miracle, he became the centre of attraction, and to escape he withdrew completely into solitary retreat at Subiaco. When they discovered his identity, the monks of the neighbouring abbey invited him to become their abbot, but he firmly refused. An attempt to poison him in retaliation almost succeeded. This did not discourage numerous postulants from placing themselves under his tutorage. After he was driven from Subiaco by the jealousy of a neighbouring priest, he settled on Monte Casino in 529. There he founded a large abbey where he was able to organize a strict monastic regime following the *Rule*, which he finished towards the end of his life.

In its heyday in the 12th century, the Benedictine order he had created in France numbered more than 2000 abbeys and 2000 priories. Throughout Europe there were more than 100 000 branches of the Benedictine order. Today there are about 23 000 Benedictines, 9600 monks and 13 800 nuns.

To the monks

'My words and my fatherly exhortation are addressed to you, whoever you are, so long as you belong to the race of the meek and the strong.'

The theory

According to modern studies, Saint Benedict's *Rule* is only a clear and more concise version of a more ancient *Rule of the Master*. Although Benedict rather than wanting to innovate, aimed at combining three centuries of monasticism with his own knowledge, his *Rule* became the definitive guide to Western monasticism for six centuries. This book has 73 remarkably precise chapters, dealing with liturgical prayer, the daily life of monks, discipline, the way to receive novices and to be sure of their vocation, and finally, the in-depth study of the Scriptures and Texts of the Church Fathers. The tone is reformatory, evangelical and solemn, but also kindly and humane. In every monastery each monk must 'pray and work' like a 'labourer of God', obeying Him absolutely under the direction of the abbot, who is Christ's representative.

Berdiaev, Nicholas

1874 Kiev — Clamart 1948

The prophet of a new Christianity

Influential both during his lifetime and after his death, Berdiaev announced the coming of a world mystic era which would profoundly change the nature of humanity.

Born into the Russian aristocracy, Berdiaev broke away from his social milieu very early. He was expelled from Kiev University and deported to the north of Russia (1898–1901) for his revolutionary sympathies. In St Petersburg from 1901–09, and then Moscow from 1909–22, he and Bulgakov played an active part in the revival of orthodox philosophy, while denouncing the conservative nature of the clergy. He described himself as a 'prophet dedicated to the development of a Christian anthropology'. Although the Bolsheviks totalitarian tendencies worried him, Berdiaev remained socialist and attempted to defend freedom of the spirit and religion. In 1922 he was finally expelled as an ideological enemy of the people. He settled first in Germany (1922–4), then in Clamart near

Paris where he stayed until his death. In 1924 the publication of *A New Middle Age* brought Berdiaev a wide European audience, which grew further with the appearance of his works devoted to the union of East and West.

His works

The Meaning of the Creative Act (1916) was Berdiaev's first important book. It defined the creative act as an active participation in divine Creation. In *The New Middle Ages*, the author affirms that in modern times humanism has come to represent the deifying of the self, which is all the more dangerous since mass culture has transformed people into irresponsible robots. In *Spirit and Reality* (1929), he makes a distinction between the spirit and the soul, while in *Of the Destination of Man* (1935), he lays down the foundations of a 'paradoxical ethic'. Finally, *Spiritual Autobiography* (written in 1940) retraces the steps which took him from social revolution to spiritual revolution.

The theory

Revolted by the injustice and mediocrity of a world in which an individual could not hope to reach his full potential, Berdiaev spent his life searching for ways to change it. He was first a social, and then a religious revolutionary, criticizing the Church, and Communism, which had not kept its promises. In mysticism, Berdiaev found the only possibility for anybody to change the outside world would be through changing himself. This quest, as passionate as it is intransigent, places Berdiaev with the foremost spiritual thinkers of his time.

Spiritual autobiography

'I am only a seeker of truth and of life in God . . . not a leader.'

'God is nothing like the image we create of Him, nothing at all.'

Bernard of Clairvaux

1090 The castle of Fontaine-lès-Dijon — Clairvaux 1153

A spirituality based on love

Bernard was tenderly and intensely devoted to Christ and the Virgin, and also loved nature in which he saw the hand of God

Born of a noble French family, Bernard received an education in the classics. During his adolescence his mother, an extremely virtuous woman, died and for a few years he led the dissolute life of a young lord. But in 1112 he was admitted to the abbey at Citeaux with 30 companions, including all his brothers in whom he had encouraged monastic ideals. The relatively new Citeaux abbey aimed at a return to the strictest of ascetic regimes but this was proving very difficult to accomplish. When he was sent to found a new monastery at Clairvaux, Bernard had such success that it gave a great boost to the Cistercian order, which at his death had some 350 branches. His fame spread throughout Christendom where, sometimes contrary to his own wishes, he was called upon to play an important role in world affairs. On one occasion, Bernard managed to avert the downfall of the papacy threatened by schism. He also condemned Abélard for his excesses and encouraged the Second Crusade in his sermons. This humble monk never hesitated to speak out against those in power, including the popes, who often asked for his advice. Most of all, Bernard, who was both ascetic and generous, energetic and sensitive, played a major role in medieval spirituality.

His works

His works consist of a dozen short pieces including the *Treatise of the Love of God* and *The Degrees of Humanity and Pride*, a spiritual guide to monastic life; 300 *Sermons*, and 450 *Letters*, which have shed some light on the many facets of his intriguing personality.

The theory

The first step to take on the path towards spirituality is to come to know oneself fully, a process which must disregard the superficial to capture what is truly essential. Then the soul, newly released from the chains of desire and envy, can proceed to rediscover the divine element it had lost earlier. Following Christ's example, the soul progresses from the carnal to the spiritual, and prepares itself to meet God and join with Him. If this state is but temporary, the fleeting moments shared with God allow the soul to bear His absence during the wait for the eternal day when this union will become permanent and, therefore, perfect.

Cistercian art

The spiritual trend which followed in the wake of Bernard's teachings gave birth in the 12th century to a new style in church architecture. The Cistercian church is characterized by its extreme sobriety, the emphasis being on the simple harmony of proportion and repartition of light.

> **'God** gave himself to deserve our love, he keeps himself back as our reward; he is nourishment for saintly souls, the victim sacrificed to buy back captivated souls'. (*Tract on the Love of God*)

Bhagavadgita

The 'Song of the Happy Lord'

The Bhagavadgita, a guide to spiritual life, has been venerated in India for 2000 years and has elicited commentaries from all the great spiritual leaders.

The Bhagavadgita forms part of the great Indian poem called the *Mahabharata* which is the longest epic poem in literature (90 000 lines). It recounts the conflict between two related clans, the Kaurava who represent the forces of evil, and the Pandava, descendants of the gods. An autonomous poem within a poem, the Bhagavadgita is considered to be one of the foremost Indian books, equalling the *Veda* (see **Hinduism**), and the *Upanishad*. The poem is presented in the form of a dialogue in verse, grouped into 18 chapters and 700 stanzas.

On the eve of battle, Arjuna the Pandava, revolted by the prospect of fratricide, is ready to lay down arms. However, his chariot driver, who is none other than a human manifestation of Vishnu the Supreme Being, persuades him to carry out his duty as a warrior. But he adds that if one cannot escape the duties imposed by social position, then by the same token, one must not deny the benefits of that same position, and by extension, the positive or negative consequences of *karma*. This detachment leads to love (*bhakti*), and to the imitation of the Lord, who is essentially action for if He ceased to act, then 'the world would cease to exist'. But God at the same time is only the spectator of His creation. The Supreme Being then reveals Himself in all His splendour to an amazed Arjuna. On this occasion He is shown as a personal Absolute, transcending, and yet imminent to, His creation.

The theory

The *Bhagavadgita* lifts the disciple from the human to the divine in three stages. First, as a necessary sacrifice to God, he must renounce desire and carry out certain acts which he must believe to be of his own volition. Then, he must come to realize that these acts are in fact the effect of universal power, or *Prakriti*, in him. Finally, he must identify the latter as a partial manifestation of the Supreme and Unchanging *Purusha*. Through his participation in divine transcendence he achieves perfect freedom, and gives himself in love to *Parusha*. These three stages correspond to the three branches of yoga, which are *karma, jnana* and *bhakti*, and to *samkhya*, or true knowledge of the self.

In the *Bhagavadgita*, the greatest trends in Hinduism are synthesized. It is considered the ultimate expression of Indian spirituality and enjoys undying popularity. All the great philosophers from Shankara in the 8th century to Ramakrishna in the 19th century and Sri Aurobindo in the 20th century, have devoted lengthy commentaries to it. Thanks to recent translations, readers in the West can now discover the universal nature of the philosophy contained within it.

> 'With all your being take refuge in the **Lord** who resides in your heart; through his mercy you will reach supreme peace and the state of eternity'. *Bhagavadgita*

Bible

The Holy Word

Providing the rules and guidelines for believers, the Bible has been an inexhaustible source of spiritual inspiration for both Christians and Jews for 2000 years.

The word Bible, which comes from the Greek *ta bibla* meaning 'the books', describes the collection of holy texts drawn from both Judaism and Christianity. To Jews, it represents the Law of the people of Israel, which God revealed to Moses. The Law comprising the first five books, is frequently called the *Pentateuch*. *Genesis* (from the Greek *genesis* meaning 'birth'), after a preamble in which the story of the Creation is told, goes on to relate the life of Adam and Eve and the Fall, then the Flood, and Abraham's vocation; it traces the fate of his progeny, and ends with Joseph's death in Egypt. *Exodus* tells of how the people of Israel were led out of Egypt by Moses and culminates with the giving of the Law on Mount Sinai. *Leviticus* lists the rules for the faith entrusted to the children of Levi. The book of *Numbers* primarily lists the peoples of the world, then gives the next episode in the history of the Israelites until their entry into the Promised Land. *Deuteronomy* (the 'Second Law') is a summation of the precepts given to Moses by Yahweh. It also describes the death of Moses.

If the *Pentateuch* as we know it dates from no earlier than the 12th–11th centuries BC and has been subject to frequent revision (*Deuteronomy* is an 8th century BC edition), the biblical assertion that Moses himself was the author cannot be doubted. In fact, texts such as the Covenant Code and the Ten Commandments constitute the true Law and have been preserved as such by tradition.

The Books of the Bible

With the passing of time, the Books of the *Prophets*, those inspired spiritual leaders who were the successors of Moses and entrusted with the task of transmitting Yahweh's instructions to his people, were added to the Pentateuch. In the Bible, *Prophets* are followed by the *Books of Wisdom* which differ in source, age, and spirit. Even if a great number of Psalms were written by David (11th–10th centuries BC), *Proverbs* and *Job*, which grippingly describes the suffering of the Just, and therefore the drama of the human condition, cannot have been written before the 5th century. *Ecclesiastes*, or *Qohelet*, a testimony of the disillusionment caused by the vanity of human efforts, and the *Song of Songs*, a burning love poem which can be seen as an allegory of the union of God with his people, could not have been composed before the end of the 3rd century BC; this is also true of two books of *Chronicles*, then *Edras* and *Nehemiah*. The books of *Tobias*, *Judith*, and the supplements to *Esther* and *Daniel*, were all written directly in Greek, which caused them to be banned from the synagogue. These books figure only partially in the Protestant Bible, but in their complete form in the Catholic. They also date from the 3rd century BC. Around the year 100 BC, *Maccabees*, the last historical

> **'So God created Man in His own image;** in the image of God He created him.' (*Genesis* 1, 27)

> **'My face you cannot see,** for no mortal may see me and live.' (*Exodus* 33, 20)

books, were added. These books relate the recent revolt of the Jewish people under the Greek king, Antiochus Epiphanes of Syria.

Although the Bible was compiled and codified by lawyers of the priestly school in the 1st century BC, it was only in the 1st century AD that it began to take the form we know today. At this time it had become necessary to give the Bible its own definitive shape, to distinguish it from the various other writings that poured from a growing number of Jewish sects.

The Jewish Bible

To Jews, the Bible is not simply an account of the history of Israel, but a monument to the Covenant drawn up between God and his people. It is the 'living Word of the living God', and as such, governs all aspects of Jewish daily life. After the destruction of the Temple of Jerusalem (AD 70), and the dispersion (*diaspora*) of the Jewish people, the Bible was vital to these communities living under frequently hostile conditions, in that it helped them to survive by giving them hope. Born of an oral tradition and passed down from generation to generation, the written Law or Torah has always been subject to interpretation. The Pharisees considered these interpretations to be the Spoken Law; with the rabbis who were to replace the Pharisees, these commentaries were to take on a more fundamental significance. They came to constitute the *Mishna* (teaching), which was divided into the *Halakha* (the Way) and the *Aggadah* (the Narration). The *Gemara*, the collected discussions and decisions of the experts of the Law, and the *Mishna* were edited together into the *Talmud*, of which there were two versions. The Jerusalem Talmud (2nd–4th centuries AD) was followed by the Babylonian Talmud (5th century AD), which became the more authoritative version for later Judaism. The Talmud is crucial to Jewish civilizations and religious life, and it was until recently considered as a sacred book of divine inspiration to be studied by all pious Jews. Moreover, the actual text of the Bible has given rise to frequent allegorical or theosophical speculation.

The Christian Bible

The Old Testament (or more precisely, the 'Covenant'), considered by Christians as the Bible, was joined by the New Testament, the standard texts of the Christian faith. The Greek version of the Bible, known as the *Septuagint*, was edited during the Hellenic period, and is longer than the Hebrew version, as it contains not only the standard 22 books of the latter, but also a further six books known as the 'Deuterocanonical'. The Latin translation, or *Vulgate*, which is attributed to Saint Jerome (AD 405) has become the official version, although it is still rejected by both Jews and Protestants. Translated into German by Ulfilas, then into Slavonic by Cyril and Methodus in the 9th century, the Christian Bible's popularity spread through Europe, rendering it the only 'Book'. However, in the 13th century, the Church banned laypersons from reading the Bible, their argument being that the proliferation of heresy would seem to indicate that the heretics were able to find the material and support for their arguments within its pages. The Reformation in the 16th century, which placed a much greater emphasis on the reading of the Scriptures than on Church Tradition, brought back the widespread usage of the Bible.

'**Emptiness, emptiness**, says the speaker, all is empty . . . Fear God and obey his commands; there is no more to man than this.' (*Ecclesiastes*, 12, 13)

'I give you **this commandment**: you must give freely to your borther, to the poor and distressed. (*Deuteronomy* 15, 1)

The Lord is my light and my salvation; whom should I fear? The Lord is the refuge of my life; Of whom should I go in dread?' (*Psalm* 27, 1)

Böhme (or Boehme), Jakob

1575 Altseidenberg — Gorlitz 1624

A great Christian gnostic

Although Böhme suffered persecution during his own lifetime, this self-educated visionary left works which have inspired philosophers and mystics throughout the centuries

Jakob Böhme was born into a Lutheran peasant family, and at the age of 14 he was apprenticed to a shoemaker. He then spent three years travelling all over Germany, becoming familiar with the works of mystics, alchemists, and astrologers. In 1594 he settled in Gorlitz where he opened a shoemaking business. He married a butcher's daughter and lived in relative comfort. In 1600 the sun's reflection on a pewter plate seemed to him like the spark of divine fire he believed burned within him. Böhme had prepared the way for this event, which was followed by a period of severe depression, by an in-depth reading of the Bible. Further visions allowed him to contemplate on 'the centre of nature and the light of divine

---

From the exterior to the interior

'All the exterior visible world, with all its creatures is a corollary of the inner spiritual world.'

Böhme's mission

'Through my own strength, I am as blind as the next man, and can do nothing, but through the Spirit of God my inner spirit penetrates everything.'

---

essence'. After his discoveries, he felt compelled to distribute his book *Aurora* among his friends. The book caused a scandal, and Böhme was thrown into prison. He was released on the condition that he never wrote again. Five years later he was writing once more, and during a 20 year period compiled some 20 tracts. *The Way to Christ* (1624), the only one published in his lifetime, resulted in a bitter controversy. Böhme moved to Dresden and stayed there until illness forced him to return to Gorlitz where he later died.

His works

His works were not published until the end of the 17th century, under the direction of his disciple Franckenberg who was also his first biographer. His most influential tracts were *Aurora or the Root of Philosophy* (1612), *On the Three Principles of Divine Being*, and above all *Mysterium Magnum*, a breathtaking allegorical and philosophical exegesis of the book of Genesis.

The theory

What was revealed to Böhme was the 'divine mystery', the secret of creation which comes from divine essence, the bottomless pit (*Urgrund*) from which the inseparable forces of good and evil, light and dark came. These forces are locked in an eternal combat in the cosmic drama which can be defined as divine life drifting away from itself in order to return to itself. This drama occurs not only in the celestial world but also in nature and in the hearts of men. Böhme's ideas spread through Germany, Holland, and England, then to France. Their influence was considerable not only on Angelus Silesius and Pietism but also on German idealist philosophy; in the 20th century they inspired Berdiaev.

Bonaventura

1221 Bagnorea (Tuscany) — Lyons 1274

Great theologian and mystic

A follower of Francis of Assisi, 'Doctor seraphicus' played an important part in the development of the Franciscan order and made a lasting impression on spiritual life.

More commonly known as Bonaventura, a name which, according to tradition, was given to him by St Francis himself, Giovanni di Fidanza, a man of noble birth, joined the Franciscans around the year 1238. They sent him to study at the Sorbonne, where he became friends with Thomas Aquinas and was the best disciple of the great English-born Franciscan theologian, Alexander of Thales, whom he succeeded in 1248.

Despite his youth, Bonaventura was elected general of the Franciscan order in 1257 and he had the difficult task of reconciling the two extreme groups within his order, the *Spirituales*, who adhered to the asceticism of St. Francis, and the *Relaxati*, who were more liberal in attitude.

If Bonaventura did re-establish peace, it was by bringing the order into line with traditional monastic practices, which Francis had always rejected, shaping it into an

---

God speaks to the soul

'I became a visible man so that on seeing me you might love me, the one whom in my divinity you could not see and did not love. I gave myself to you, give yourself to me.'
(Bonaventura)

---

intellectual order which produced some great philosophers. Bonaventura was universally venerated and, despite his humility, was unable to refuse the cardinalate. As cardinal he had to attend the great council of Lyons (1274), during the course of which he died. He was canonized in 1485 and proclaimed Church Father in 1587.

His works

His writings were undertaken entirely with a view to the spiritual direction of the Franciscans. In defining the condition of man, the image of the divine Word, in his *Soliloquium* (Soliloquy), Bonaventura expounds the *Itinerarium mentis in Deum* (The Soul's journey to God) and the *De reductione artium ad theologiam* (The reduction of art to theology) and depicts the founder of the order as an unsurpassable model in his *Life of St Francis*. He also wrote *Meditations on the Life of Jesus Christ*.

The theory

An eminent academic, Bonaventura intended to use the resources of theological and philosophical thought for the mystical journey that St Francis had lived spontaneously, tracing 'the soul's journey to God'. The human soul is made for the purpose of knowing God, to live and rejoice in Him. On its own it possesses an imperfect but nevertheless certain knowledge of Him, which is faith. It will therefore rise up to Him by contemplating vestiges of itself in the material world, and then its own image, before arriving at the pure beatific contemplation which will be its fulfilment. Since Bonaventura himself was a profound mystic, his teaching had much persuasive power.

Buddha

c. 566 BC Kapilavastu — Kusinagari c. 486 BC

The 'Enlightened One' shows others the path

This is the meaning of the term 'Buddha', which was applied to Sakyamuni who, in the 5th century, preached a philosophy and way of life still existing today.

Although it has been much embellished by legend, we know the essential details of the life of the man who was to become the Buddha. He was born in Nepal, where his father reigned over the Sakya tribe of the Gautama clan. His first name was Siddhartha ('goal reached') but he was commonly known as Gautama or Sakyamuni, the 'wise man of the Sakya'. In his youth, he led the life of a young prince; at 16 he married Yasodhana, with whom he had a son, Rahula. But he was tormented by the mysteries of an existence which seemed entirely given over to illness, old age and death, and decided to go off to search for the truth. In 537 BC at the age of 29, he secretly left his palace in order to live as an itinerant holy man.

Having followed the teachings of two yoga masters without getting the results he desired, he decided to carry on his search alone at Uruvila, accompanied by five other wandering religious men. For six years he submitted his body to rigorous ascetical practices to the point of endangering his life. When close to death, and yet no closer to his goal he renounced the mortification of the flesh. This scandalized his companions, who abandoned him. Left alone, Sakyamuni sat in the lotus position under a sacred fig tree at Bodh-Gaya, meditating on the mystery of death and rebirth in the illusionary world of appearances. After a night in 531 BC during which the memory of all his former existences came to his spirit, and the secrets of life and death were revealed to him, he became certain that having rid himself of passions and spiritual blindness, he was freed from the cycle of birth and rebirth once and for all. Sakyamuni had reached a state of perfect Enlightenment (*bodhi* in Sanskrit) thereby becoming a buddha.

The teaching of the Doctrine

Buddha overcame his doubts that the truth could possibly be transmitted to others and rejoined his five former companions in the Deer Park at Sarnath, near Benares. It was here that he gave his sermon the 'First Turning of the Wheel of Dharma' (Universal Law) in which the Four Noble Truths were outlined for the first time, and in which he declared the death of the self and the impersonality of all phenomena. Thus the Buddha began his public ministry which was to take him all over the Ganges valley. He preached his doctrine to all, regardless of sex, class or caste, disregarding his enemies and gathering followers as he went. For these followers, he created a new order of itinerant monks. Worn out

Towards Nirvana

'Of what I know, I have told you only a little ... And why have I not told you the rest? Because it would not help lead you to nirvana.'

Personal Experience

'Do not let yourself be guided by the authority of the sacred texts, nor by simple logic, nor by appearance or opinion, nor even by the teachings of your master; when you know in yourself that something is bad, then give it up, and accept the good and follow it.'

Graeco-Buddhist art, Afghanistan, 4th century BC (Musée Guimet, Paris)

with age and exhaustion, Sakyamuni stopped in the Upavarta wood near Kusinagari. He lay down between two trees and progressed through a series of ecstatic states before 'going out like a flame without fuel' into perfect nirvana.

For Buddhists the earthly life of Buddha only takes on its true meaning when seen in the Karmic context of his former existences. At birth, Sakyamuni was a future buddha or bodhisattva and had only reached that level through a slow upward progression through multiple existences.

Moreover, buddha is a generic term; many buddhas have existed before the historical Buddha, and others who will come to the aid of humanity and restart the Wheel are yet to come.

The theory

Sakyamuni left no written works. All we know of his doctrine comes from much later texts, which are records of a long oral tradition.

The *Tripitaka*, the first canon in Pali language seems to have been instituted by the 3rd Council of Pataliputra (245 BC). Since then, Buddhism has given birth to a vast body of literature which constantly revitalizes the amplifies the original Doctrine.

In the beginning, the Doctrine was seen as a remedy or solution to the problems of suffering, and was founded on a particular diagnosis of the human condition. It can be summed up in the Four Truths. The First Noble Truth is 'Suffering': existence is suffering and pain, birth, illness, old age and death, contact with unpleasant things, being separated from things one loves, not getting what one wants, all of these are painful for nothing is permanent and all beings are subjected to an eternal transmigration according to their *karma*.

In The Second Noble Truth, the 'Cause of Suffering', the Buddha states that existence is the product of desire which brings with it ignorance. Desire also works through 'conditioned production' in 12 stages from blindness, which produces the Karmic patterns which in turn cause a thirst for sensation and by extension for life which leads to rebirth, fresh suffering, and another death. The Third Truth, the 'Extinction of Suffering' states that pain can only be overcome through the absolute denial of self in order to reach nirvana. The Fourth Truth, that of the Path descends the eightfold path that is the way to the elimination of suffering and is made up of right view, right thought, right speech, right action, right livelihood, right effort, right mindfulness, and right concentration. These can be reduced to three fundamental elements: morality (*sila*), concentration (*samadhi*) obtained through frequent meditation which allows the lucid spirit to transcend the passions and reach the 3rd stage, comprehensive wisdom (*prajna*), or the state of perfect serenity, which in turn leads to nirvana.

Although the Buddha's teachings and theories have remained unchanged for over 2500 years, they have given birth to many different schools all over Asia, demonstrating the adaptability of his ideas to even the most diverse mentalities.

> **Buddha's Last Words**
> 'The doctrine and discipline which I have imparted to you, will be your leader when I am gone. Try hard to reach the goal.'

> 'Teaching is like a raft which is made for crossing but to which one must become attached.'

Buddhism

A way to freedom

While neither a religion nor a philosophy, Buddhism aims to guide each individual towards an understanding of profound reality.

After the death of the Buddha, his companions gathered at Rajagúha (477 BC) and began to codify his teachings. These included *sutra*, Buddha's words, the *abhidharma*, or the detailed elaboration of the doctrine, and the *vinaya* or monastic rule. At the second Council of Vaiçali (c. 370 BC) a new trend began to emerge in opposition to the Elders (*Thera*). Its intention was to make sainthood (*ashant*) more accessible and it was to grow in importance and popularity in the years which followed. The accession of Ashok, the first Buddhist emperor, gave rise to an important missionary movement resulting in the diffusion of the doctrine throughout Celon, north-west India and central Asia, reaching Persia in 240 BC.

The expansion of Buddhism

By the 1st century AD, Buddhism had already begun to take hold in China, where at first it was generally confused with Taoism. It went on to give birth to numerous Chinese schools of thought, the most active of which are the 'Land of Purity' (4th century) the Ch'an (beginning of the 6th century) and the T'ien t'ai (6th century). Chinese Buddhism had its golden age between the 4th and 9th centuries but was bitterly opposed in 845 under the Ch'ang dynasty. On the other hand it was protected under the Sung dynasty (10th–13th centuries), and even positively nurtured under the Mongol Yuan dynasty (13th–14th centuries). Its popularity waned with the restoration of the nationalist Ming dynasty (14th–17th centuries) and under the last Manchu dynasty. Nevertheless it had permanently influenced Chinese thought and art, to the extent that the great sinologist P. Demiéville felt able to write: 'China has assimilated Buddhism so well that we can see that it has become part of the collective unconscious.'

From China, the doctrine moved into Korea in the 4th century and from there to Japan (6th century) where over the centuries it split into several different schools, all of which are Chinese in origin. The esoteric sects Tendai and Shingon (beginning of 9th century), Amidism (11th–13th centuries), Zen, and finally the school of Nichires are prominent among the branches still active today. If in China Buddhism had to compete with Taoism and Confucianism, in Japan it only encountered opposition from Shintoism, but the two were able to reconcile their differences. Buddhism not only boosted Japanese art and literature, but moulded and continues to mould Japanese daily life and mentality.

In the 7th and 8th centuries, Buddhism started to spread to Tibet, imported by successive waves of religious leaders. Little by little, a distinctive school began to emerge, known as the Vajrayana. In south-

---

Doctrine
'Those who are blinded by attraction and repulsion cannot comprehend such a Doctrine which goes against the grain, is subtle, profound and difficult to define.'
(*Majjhimanikaja*)

The End of Fear
'If you think of Buddha, of the Law (*Dharma*) and the community (*sangha*), fear, trembling and terror will cease to exist.'

east Asia, the doctrine was preached by Singhalese monks and took root in Burma (5th–6th centuries), Thailand (11th–13th centuries), Cambodia (13th–14th centuries) and Laos (14th century). From the 2nd to the 3rd centuries, Buddhism was widely practised in Indonesia, but was superceded by Islam in the 12th century.

While Buddhism was becoming known in Asia, in India it had already reached the height of its popularity in the 4th and 5th centuries, and began to wane from the 7th century in the face of a Hindu revival. However Hinduism was not impervious to Buddhism: its influence can still be seen today. The Muslim invasions which brought about the destruction of Buddhist monasteries and universities also wiped out the cult from its country of origin.

In each of the different countries to which it spread from India, Buddhism gave birth to many varied schools, each one adapted to the particular mentality of its adoptive country. These schools more or less assimilated the indigenous religions like Taoism in China and the Bon religion in Tibet. However, the divisions were principally caused by the progressive separation of its two branches which had been in opposition from the earliest days of its inception. These two branches are known as the *Lesser Vehicle* or *hinayana*, which took root in south Asia and the *Greater Vehicle* or *mayahana* which spread northwards from Tibet to Japan.

The Doctrine of the Elders

The hinayana is often confused with the Doctrine or School of the Elders (*Theravada*) which declares itself to be the only true representation of the Buddha's original teachings; the Theravada is particularly insistent on the illusory nature of the self which is only a provisional combination of the five *skanda*: *rupa*, or form as separate entity, gives birth to the senses (*vedana*) which when activated result in perceptions (*samjna*) which determine conceptions (*samskara*). Finally, the last of the *skanda*, *vijnana* or conscience, appears. Vijnana instead of perceiving reality as it actually is, projects its own image like a screen between itself and the subject. The process of liberation which culminates in the end of suffer-

ing is necessarily very long and complex. involves the use of subtle psychic trainin methods and much introspection (*vipa sana*), as well as an extremely strict mor discipline. These three together allow th state of arhat to be reached which 'havin exhausted all that is impure, done what had to do and laid down its burden', lea to complete, definitive extinction, or *parin vana*.

Today Buddhism has the third larg following in the world after Christiani and Islam. It is the majority cult in S Lanka, Burma, Thailand, and Japan. China after years of persecution which we unable to eradicate it, Buddhism seems be enjoying a quiet comeback, as in Tib despite the departure of most of the Lam in 1959. But now in the 20th centur Buddhist groups have begun to emerge the USA and Europe, aided by the fact th as a religion, it is in no way elitist an respects all beliefs; there is no need 'convert', all that is required is a stror belief in the universal justice of a particul analysis of the human condition.

Buddhism and Hinduism

The Buddha himself stated 'I saw the Pa taken in the past by the Elders and it is t path on which I walk. At the outset, l teaching was presented as the restoration the old order, then Buddhism became distinct school, excluded from orthod Hinduism. Although Hinduism remain the official state religion, Buddhi attracted many followers throughout Asi

---

From the Dhammapada

The base of all things which rules over cosmic order and predominates all things is the spirit.

The Mission of Monks

'Go, oh monks! and travel for the good and happiness of others, travel out of compassion for the world, for peace and the happiness of the gods and man . . . Teach the Doctrine . . and advocate a saintly and pure life. There are those who are naturally without passion who are fading away for want of hearing the Doctrine; these people will understand it.'

Bulgakov, Sergei

1871 Livny, Province of Orel — Paris 1944

The great theologian of modern orthodoxy

As the author of several profound and controversial works, Sergei Bulgakov has been the driving force behind a spiritual renewal that continues to flourish today.

Sergei Nickolaivich Bulgakov entered the seminary but left to apply himself to social and economic questions, turning to Marxism to find his answers. But when he became acquainted with the theories of Solov'ev, he oriented himself more and more towards theology, joined forces with Berdiaev and was ordained a priest at the beginning of the religious persecutions. Expelled from Russia in 1923, he spent some time in Prague and then moved to Paris where he founded the Orthodox Theological Institute in 1925. This was also the year in which Bulgakov began compiling a spiritual book which caused a scandal, resulting in some people going so far as to accuse his sophiological doctrine of being heretical. With Berdiaev's support, he countered these accusations, invoking the right to suggest themes of reflection to believers and non-believers alike.

His works

His principal works are *From Marxism to Capitalism* (1903), a journal in which the author outlines the progressive steps of his reconciliation with religion; *Unending Light* (1917); then two lengthy trilogies written in Paris: *The Ardent Bush* and *The Friend of the Bride*, on Saint John the Baptist, and *Jacob's Ladder* on the angels; and the second, *Divine Wisdom and Theanthropy*, published between 1930 and 1940. These books make up the nucleus of his work, while his interpretation of the Book of Revelation is his spiritual legacy.

The theory

If the theme of *Sophia*, Divine Wisdom, is common to both Solov'ev and Bulgakov, the former, using non-traditional sources, identifies *Sophia* with the 'eternal female reality', while the latter brings it back into the heart of orthodoxy as the unfurling of divine nature, making it one of the essential points of a doctrine which is capable of solving all the questions left unanswered by classical theology. Bulgakov believed that God intends to participate in the world he had created. It was to this end that he became a real person, the Word incarnate, while divine Wisdom has its source in humankind, who through Christ's intervention can become the filial image of God. In this heady philosophy of the Creation and the Trinity, some saw a re-emergence of Gnosticism, evident both in the Cabala and the works of Böhme.

> **History and Christianity**
> 'All human history after Christ, with its strange and fragmented dialectic is essentially Christian, linked to Christ's Church as it is to its inner finality.'

Cabala

Esoteric Jewish teaching

Transmitted and enriched by an unbroken line of religious leaders, the Cabala reached its zenith in the 13th century with the Zohar.

The word *cabala* means tradition and pertains to the theosophical current which has run through Judaism until the present day. The first evidence for this current came with the mystical contemplation, firstly of the vision of God's throne, surrounded by angels and cherubs, then on the *Merkaba* and the divine chariot as it appeared to the prophet Ezekiel.

In the *Sefer Yesirah* (Book of the Creation), written between the 2nd and 4th centuries, the doctrine of the *Sefirot* is already set down. The *Sefirot* was considered as the essential ten digits which, combined with the 22 letters of the Hebrew alphabet provided the key to the created universe. The *Sefirot* was later used to describe how, through a series of emanations from God, the creation of the world took place. From this time on, the Cabala allowed the divine mysteries hidden in the Bible to be penetrated. With the *Sefer ha-Bahir* which, in its present form, dates from the 12th century, there were new developments in the Cabala: the introduction of the female element or 'Presence' (*Shekina*), appointed to the government of the extra-divine world and the community of Israel.

But the Cabala's apogee came in the 13th century, with the southern French and Spanish schools, particularly the Gerona cenacle in Catalonia. The authors distinguished the creative demiurge's principal unmanifested aspect, the cause of causes, unknowable to humankind. The Cabala is not only a theoretical teaching, but also a spiritual experience based on the different names for God which should lead to prophetic illumination.

The 'Zohar'

The *Sefer ha-Zohar* (Book of Splendour) was developed in Spain c.1260–1280. It was said to be the work of a 2nd-century doctor, Simeon bar-Yohhai, but in fact the main compiler was Moses of Léon who was the author of numerous other Hebrew texts. According to the *Zohar*, nothing exists unless it participates in divinity, which is the hidden substratum in Creation. The mystic's vocation is to find the elements of the hidden language in which the thoughts of God are revealed. Although it was at first speculative and reserved for an elite, the Cabala later inspired the messianic movements in Judaism, including Hasidism. From 1500 to 1800, it was considered to be a source of doctrine and revelation, and was attributed as much authority as the Talmud or the Bible. The Cabala also influenced Christian Humanists, like the Italian, Pico della Mirandola (1463–94) and the German, Reuchlin (1455–1522), and in the 17th and 18th centuries, the Theosophists.

Divine Creation
'All the divine powers make up a series of planes and are like a tree.' (*Sefer ha-Bahir*)

The Unknowable
'God spoke, this speech is a force which was separated from the secret of *En-Sof* (The Cause of unknowable causes) at the start of creative thought.' (*Zohar*)

Calvin, John

1509 Noyon — Geneva 1564

The 'second patriarch of the Reformation'

More radical in his beliefs than Luther, Calvin aimed at the purification of the Church and the creation of a new society.

Calvin's father was the attorney of the Noyon Chapter and intended his son to enter the Church. This allowed Calvin to study at the Montaigu college in Paris and then to read law at Orléans and Bourges. On his return to Paris he continued to study, turning his attention to literature, and became acquainted with certain humanist circles, which led to the publication of his intellectual commentary on Seneca's *On Clemency* in 1534.

His sudden conversion of the Reformation probably dates from 1533. In November of that year Nicholas Cop, rector of the university, delivered an address that favoured Lutheran ideals. The Parliament ordered his arrest as well as that of Calvin, who was supposed to have had a hand in the composition of the address. Calvin fled to Angoulême then took refuge in Nerac where Marguerite of Navarre, the sister of François 1, lived. Marguerite was known as the protectress of the Reformationists.

Calvin finally went to Basel where he also tried to help those Reformationists affected by the persecutions of 1534. Here he published the first Latin version of his *Institutions of the Christian Religion*.

From 1536 to 1538 Calvin was in Geneva, urged to prolong his stay by William Farel who had just introduced the principles of the Reformation to the Genevan people. Both were expelled from the town by their adversaries in 1538. Calvin accepted Martin Bucer's invitation to go to Strasbourg, a new Reformation centre, to look after the French refugees. He was recalled to Geneva by Farel in 1541, and firmly deciding to make this town into an exemplary Christian city, he became the undisputed leader of Geneva through his brilliant abilities as theologican and teacher.

The reformed Church

In accordance with his *Ecclesiastical Ordinances*, the four-fold ministry of the new Church was created, comprising of pastors, in charge of preaching, teachers responsible for the education of the congregations, deacons who took care of the old and infirm, and elders who were grouped into a 'consistory' and acted as arbiters of behaviour.

This strict organization led to opposition which Calvin summarily supressed. He exposed the half-hearted as well as those who purported to receive direct enlightenment from God. This led him to condemn the doctor, Michel Servet who had taken refuge in Geneva from the Catholic persecutions of 1533. Servet was burned at the stake. In 1559 the University of Geneva was founded, with Theodore de Beze as its first rector.

Calvin, who was not of a robust constitution and who had aged prematurely, was often ill in his latter years, but he was never to be diverted from his beliefs and work. Missionaries from Geneva took his teachings to the Netherlands, the Germanic countries, England, Scotland,

A New Wisdom

'The sum total of our wisdom, which deserves to be called true, and certain wisdom, can practically be split into two parts, that is to say, the knowledge of God and of ourselves.'

Poland, and even Hungary. By the time of Calvin's death, Calvinism was already more widespread in Europe than Lutheranism. Although of a shy and retiring disposition, Calvin had accomplished his mission as a leader of men in the name of the 'Glory of God', suppressing his gentler nature to the extent that he was accused of being uncompromising and hard in the pursuit of his ideals.

His works

Apart from *Institutes of the Christian Religion* (1536) and *Ordinances* which lays down the basic tenets of the Reformed Church, Calvin published a *Catechism* (1536) and a *Short Treatise on Saint Cène* in 1541 on the real presence of God in the Eucharist. We are also indebted to him for commentaries on the Holy Scriptures and several polemical tracts including *On Relics* (1543) and *On Scandals* (1550–1).

The theory

Calvin may not show the exhilaration and the generosity of Luther, but it would be impossible to accuse him of being any less original, for he took his inspiration from his own doctrines. Luther was an individualist and a mystic, while Calvin, who had had legal training, aspired first and foremost to create the new Christian city. Geneva was to become a state destined 'to nourish and support the exterior service of God', and to turn out charitable and virtuous men.

The Ecclesiastical organization implemented by Calvin consists of layers of assemblies incorporating both preachers and laypersons, which begin at the local level of parish councils, ascend to regional synods and culminate in the national synod/assembly. This system is a precursor of modern western democracy.

Calvin was also more sombre than Luther, taking a radically pessimistic view of human nature. He believed that man had originally been free and could obtain eternal life through union with God. But in disobeying Him, man became a rebel and a victim of the seducer, and can do nothing to liberate himself. Only God's mercy, given freely by Him, can set him free from eternal servitude.

This affirmation of God's sovereignty finally brought Calvin to formulate his theory of absolute predestination which only appeared later on in his work and to which few modern-day Calvinists actually subscribe.

Picking up the theory of double predestination first set out by Augustine, whereby the chosen are shown God's mercy while the rest must suffer His terrible wrath for their sins, Calvin carries it one step further, and the theory becomes 'supralapsary' that is to say, decreed by God before the Creation and the Fall.

Perhaps more relevant to us is the form of social humanism which Calvin instituted in Geneva which remains one of the foremost traits of Calvinism today. The members of the people of God form a united front and lend mutual assistance. Calvin also implemented one of the first social welfare systems for the sick, the infirm and the aged, as well as regulating employment in order to ensure that each individual was adequately provided for.

Evil and Mercy

'Desire is of man's making. To desire evil is corrupt, to desire good is blessed.'

Teaching from God

'I protest that I have toiled according to the gift God gave me in order to teach this word purely, both in my sermons and in my writing.'

Cathars

Enamoured of an uncompromising purity

The Cathars were considered heretics by the Church they condemned and which led a crusade against them.

From the Greek *katharos* meaning 'clean', Cathars expresses the requirements of the Cathars or Albigensians, a heretic sect whose teachings spread throughout the Toulouse region and in Languedoc from the end of the 11th century. The inspiration for this movement came from Manichaean Gnosticism. The movement saw itself as a return to the purity of the first Christians, in reaction to the Church which, they considered, had perverted the message of the Gospel. It was also an affirmation of the highly sophisticated culture of Languedoc as compared to the still barbaric north of France. At the end of the 11th century conflict had become inevitable and events were soon to become politicized when Raymond VI, Count of Toulouse openly came out in support of the Cathers. In 1208 the Papal Legate, Peter of Castelnau, was assassinated, and Pope Innocent III who until then had advocated a peaceful solution to the heresy, launched what was to become known as the Albigensian Crusade. The crusading army, made up principally of northern Barons and led by Simon de Montfort, waged a merciless war on the heretics. In 1229 the Treaty of Paris finalized the annexation of Languedoc to France, while the Cathars were persecuted by the Inquisition. Their last stronghold, Montségur, fell to the crusaders in 1244, and what remained of its defenders were burnt at the stake.

The theory

Today we can learn about the teachings and philosophy of the Cathars not only through the records of the Inquisition, but also due to the recent publication of a *Ritual*, and most importantly of *The Book of Two Principles*, which was compiled in Italy between 1250 and 1280. The doctrine of the Cathars was dualist in nature and was drawn from a strict interpretation of the Bible. It confirms the existence of two opposing principles, Spirit (the Good) and Matter (Evil) created by the one God who is the source of all Good. Man was dragged down by Satan into perishable matter, which is the lowest expression of creation, and over which he rules. In order to save man, God sent down Christ into this impure world. Having taught the way of salvation, Jesus ascended to heaven, leaving man's soul in the care of the Holy Spirit.

Incarnation is therefore a Fall and the only way to liberate the spirit is to detach it from the flesh. This can be achieved through extremely severe asceticism, comprised of the mortification of the flesh, fasting to the extent of eating nothing at all and abstention from marriage and procreation. Such measures could only be followed by the *perfect* who, having received the *consolamentum* or baptism by the Spirit (through which they became angels on earth) devoted themselves to a holy way of life. Simple believers or *bonshommes* continued to lead normal lives, but were given the consolamentum in time of mortal danger.

The principle of Evil

'God is not all powerful, He is totally simple, He does not desire evil and cannot perpetrate it . . .

That is why He wants us to know of the existence of another principle, the principle of Evil, which moves perniciously against the true God and His creation, and seems to rouse God against His creation, and His creation against God.' (*The Book of Two Principles*)

Ch'an

Method of 'Enlightenment'

Ch'an, a meditation practice, originated in India and was spread in China by its greatest leaders. In Japan it was to become Zen.

Ch'an comes from *ch'an-na*, the Chinese way of pronouncing the Sanskrit *dhyana* meaning 'meditation', the same concept that became the Japanese Zen. The origins of Ch'an, sitting meditation in the posture of the Buddha when he reached enlightenment, can be traced to the secret Sakyamuni passed on to Mahakasyapa, who was to head the community after the Buddha's death. That day, the Buddha gathered his disciples around him on the peak of the Vautours, near Rajagriha. Instead of addressing them, he showed them a flower which he held between his fingers. Nobody understood this gesture except Mahakasyapa, who smiled. Sakyamuni declared 'This treasury of the true Dharma I possess, I pass on to the great Kasyapa'. The Dharma is therefore 'the direct line of the Tradition which came from the Buddha's spirit after his Enlightenment'.

Ch'an, as a distinct school, seems to have been introduced in 520 or 527 by Bodhidharma, who arrived in Canton from south Ceylon. In Canton, tradition has it that he was welcomed by Emperor Wu, the fervent protector of Buddhism. However, his abrupt manner aroused the displeasure of the sovereign and he was forced to leave. He travelled north, and settled on Mount Song, near Lo-yang. He is said to have meditated 'face to the wall' in a cave for nine years. This strange behaviour brought him disciples to whom he taught: a special transmission from spirit to spirit, outwith the Scriptures; no dependence as far as

words were concerned; to aim directly for the mind; to discover one's own true nature in order to reach buddhahood. These four principles, which differentiate Ch'an from all other Buddhist schools, formed the basis of a school proper.

The patriarchs

With one of his disciples, Huei-ko, Bodhidharma is said to have had this famous dialogue: 'Calm my spirit, I beg of you!' — 'Bring it to me!' — 'When I look, I can't find it!' — 'Therefore I must already have calmed it!' Huei-ko then achieved Englightenment and Bodhidharma passed on the secret teaching which made him the second Chinese patriarch. The third patriarch, Seng-ts'an (died 606), is best remembered for his *Hsing-ming* (Poem on Faith in the Spirit), the first great Ch'an writing. While Ch'an developed under the fourth patriarch, Tao-hsin (579–651), and the fifth patriarch, Hung-jen (601–675), it blossomed fully under the exceptional leadership of the sixth patriarch Hui-neng (638–713). Of a humble background, Hui-neng was only a novice when Hung-jen asked all the disciples to compose a poem in order to choose which of them was to be his successor. The theme of the poem was to be their personal understanding of the Doctrine. Shen-hsiu, the most knowledgable of them wrote:

'This body is the tree of the *Bodhi*
The mind is like a shining mirror
Make sure to dust it
So that it will not be dulled with dust.'
But during the night, Hui-neng replied:
'There has never been a *Bodhi* tree
Nor a bright mirror
Since the beginning the Mind has been
Absolute absence.
How could dust gather on it?'

Hung-jen secretly transmitted the knowledge to Hui-neng but, fearing the jealousy of the other monks, ordered him to leave immediately. The sixth patriarch spent many years meditating in the mountains of the south before he began to teach. His preaching immediately brought him many followers and the influence of the school swiftly spread.

Soto and Rinzai

There were no more patriarchs because, after the death of Hui-neng who had trained five great disciples, Ch'an split into several branches of which two flourish in Japan today.

The Soto school (Ts'ao-tung) was founded by Hsing-su (died 740) and expanded by his successor, Shih-t'ou, who wrote *The Interpenetration of Essence and Phenomena*; however, its Chinese name is made up of the names of two of its greatest 9th century masters, Ts'ao-shan (840–901) and Tung-shan (807–869), author of the *Samadhi of the Mirror of Treasure*.

The Rinzai school bears the name of its most famous teacher, Lin-chi (died 867), in its Japanese form. Some very diverse personalities were part of the Rinzai school like Matsu (709–788), famed for his 'strange words and wild behaviour', and Pai-ch'ang (720–814), who goes down in history as the founder of the first large monastic community to practise Ch'an only, and who gave it the rule of 'One day without work, one day without food' which is still observed today. One of Pai-ch'ang's disciples was Huang-po, who was later Lin-chi's master. But, despite their originality, their spontaneity, non-conformism and diverse methods, all of these leaders remained faithful to Hui-neng's teaching contained in the *Sutra of the Platform*, a posthumous collection of his sermons. Under Hui-neng, Ch'an reached maturity.

Taoism and Ch'an affected each other, and in its Sinized form, the latter became the principal Mahayana school. It survived the persecution of 845 much better than the the other schools. Profiting from imperial as well as popular favour, it experienced an important revival in the 10th and 11th centuries with the publication of several anthologies, including the '*Collection of the Green Cliff* (Pi-yen Lu, 1125) and *Pass without Door* (Wu-men kuan, 1229), records of the exemplary statements of the great past masters. Although its popularity gradually waned over the centuries, Ch'an still survived in China. In the 12th century it was introduced in Japan by the monk Yosai (1141–1215) who began the Rinzai school in 1191. On his return from China in 1227, Dogen established the Soto school.

> **Tung-Chan**
> 'Don't look for the path far away, the path exists under our feet.'

> **Shen-Ching K'uen**
> 'In Zen, experience is everything. All that is not founded on experience is outwith Zen.'

> **Hui-Neng**
> 'When you no longer think of good or evil, what is your original face? If you turn your light towards the interior, you will discover the precious secret within yourself.'

Chuang Tzu

c. 350–275 BC

A Chinese master of wisdom

Chuang Tzu was also one of China's greatest writers, whose works have moulded the lives of countless Taoists. He has only recently become known in the West.

We know as little about Chuang as we do about Lao Tzu, whom he described as an Elder, except that his historical existence is unquestionable. A native of Meng (Honan), for some time Chuang Tzu held the position of 'intendant of the park of lacquer trees' in a little principality in central China. In his works he presents himself as a husband and father, 'dressed in darned cotton, his shoes in tatters', but he was proud of his independence to the extent that when King Wen of Chu, who had heard of his talents, invited him to court, Chuang Tzu laughed, declaring that he much preferred to remain a piglet wallowing in his sty rather than become a cow fattened for sacrifice. He then withdrew to Mount Nan-Hua (Chan-tong), where he died.

His works

Divided into three books and 33 chapters, the *Chuang Tzu* has engendered hundreds of commentaries from ancient times to the present day. It made an impression not only on Taoism, but also on Chinese Confucianism and Buddhism, and with its evocative, concise and subtle style, it has influenced all subsequent Chinese literature.

The theory

The originality of Taoist thought on humanity and the universe is better expressed and more accessible in the *Chuang Tzu* than in the rather difficult *Tao-te-ching*. In it, the author exalts the freedom of the wise man who 'embraces the 10 000 beings in one unique whole' and 'doing nothing . . .', serving nothing, suffers nothing.' Merging with Tao and reaching a state of ecstasy, he can travel all over the universe and 'frolic at the origin of all things'. For the wise man, truth and falsehood, light and darkness, and life and death finally blend harmoniously together in unity regained. Thus Chuang Tzu mocks the moral prescriptions characteristic of Confucian thought. In a long series of fables packed with wisdom and humour, he paints a lively and sympathetic portrait of the sage who, merely by contemplating nature, can discover its secrets. In one of these anecdotes he tells of how he dreamed he was a butterfly and how, when he woke up, he wasn't sure whether he was a man who dreamed he was a butterfly, or a butterfly who dreamed it was a man!

> **The sage**
> 'When he had escaped his own existence, a dawn illuminated him. Illuminated by the dawn, he possessed a harmonizing vision; after having the harmonizing vision, he had neither past nor present; when he had neither past nor present, he entered the sphere where neither life nor death exists.'

Church Fathers

The primitive Church's great theologians

Following on from the Apostles, these Greek and Roman authors developed Christian doctrine and defended it against heresy.

From the very first centuries of the Christian era, the title Church Fathers was applied to the Greek and Roman ecclesiastical writers who were famous for the orthodoxy of their theories and their personal saintliness. In the early Church, the bishops, as descendants of the Apostles, were also known as Fathers; later the word came to mean the doctors of the Church whose teachings were passed on from master to disciple, forming a living tradition that has its roots in the relationship between Jesus and the Apostles.

The concept of 'Church Father' as it appeared in the works of Saint Augustine was defined and clarified in Vincent of Lerins's *Commonitorium* (434), which highlights the fact that the Fathers' testimony can only be valid when it is unanimous, for it represents the unanimity of the Church itself, inspired by the Holy Spirit and therefore infallible. The criteria listed by Vincent of Lerins were used by subsequent authors, and became famous particularly through the efforts of John Damascenes in his *Doctrine of the Fathers* in the 8th century. The Fathers' writings became standard reference books for all theologians; extracts from the vast corpus of works were gathered together into separate books, the most famous of which is Pierre Lombard's 12th century *Livre de sentences* (Book of Sentences).

Patristic study, or the study of the Fathers, continues to the present day; fresh interest has recently been shown in their works as a return to the source of Christianity.

The golden age of the Church Fathers

It took place in the second half of the 4th century. The greatest Church Fathers came from the generations immediately following Constantine's declaration of Christianity as the Roman Empire's official religion. At that time, thanks to the Fathers, a fusion between the inheritance of pagan antiquity and fully matured Christian thought was worked out. The majority of the Fathers of that era were academics or professors before becoming monks or priests, and ending their lives as bishops. Among the Greeks this applied to the three 'Cappadocians': Basil of Caesarea (c. 330–390), Gregory of Nyssa (c. 335–394), and Gregory of Nazianze (c. 329–390); Cyril of Jerusalem (c. 315–386), John Chrysostom (c. 340–407), and Cyril of Alexandria (c. 370–444); and among the Latin Fathers, Hilary of Poitiers (c. 315–367), Ambrosia of Milan (c. 335–395), Saint Jerome (347–420), and Saint Augustine (354–430), who were almost all contemporaries.

This generation was preceeded by a group of Fathers termed 'Apologists' who, in a period of severe persecution, used their

---

The sentences of the church fathers

'Just as death had maintained its power over men, through men, so the Incarnation of the Word of God reintroduced the ruin of death and the resurrection of the body.' (Athanasius of Alexandria)

'Our spiritual nature exists according to the image of God, it resembles what is beyond it; being incapable of knowing itself, it reflects the inaccessible character of God.' (Gregory of Nyssa)

writings as a medium to fight paganism. This group includes Cyprian, Bishop of Carthage, who was martyred (c. 210–258) and Athanasius, patriarch of Alexandria (c. 295–373). In the centuries which followed, fewer writers were recognized as Fathers: in the West, there were Popes Leo the Great (end of 4th century–461) and Gregory the Great (c. 535–604), and Isodore of Seville (c. 570–636); and in the East, John Damascenes (675 (?)–741), the last Father. The patristic era therefore ends in the 7th century with the beginning of the Middle Ages.

The theory

When Christianity broke away from Judaism, questions arose as to whether it was actually a new religion with a different God from that of Israel — as Marcion and the Gnostics believed in the 2nd century — or whether it was a continuation of the old. Thanks to the 2nd and 3rd century Fathers, a solution to this problem was proferred and was later generally accepted. The Fathers put forward that Jesus was indeed the Messiah whose coming was announced by the Prophets and the New Testament and was also the renewal, the perfect realization and the abolition of the contract drawn up between Yahweh and his chosen people at the time of Abraham and Moses. From that time on, a new history of humankind had developed, that of its progressive education and finally of its salvation, which was punctuated by the events mentioned in the Bible, but duly reinterpreted according to the divine plan, revealed at last by the Gospels' message.

Not only did the Fathers inherit the traditions of Judaism, they were also influenced by all ancient culture. Exegis sometimes relied on the works of the classical poets; preaching used rhetoric, controversy used dialectic and theology replaced philosophy. Christian thought, which was close to Neoplatonism, considered Plato as one of its precursors.

The Fathers' other task was to define the relationship between Christ and God. Originally, Jesus was not believed to truly become the Son of God until after he had fulfilled his mission on earth, and even then, only by a form of adoption. But from the time of the 2nd century, another metaphysical and cosmological theory supplanted the original ideas. Jesus was identified with the divine Word and the Son recognized as eternal, equal to the Father and consubstantial with Him, joining with Him and the Holy Spirit to form a single, but three-person God. This theory was defended by the 4th century Fathers, and gave rise to interminable theological discussions which culminated in Arianism, a doctrine preached by the strictly monotheistic priest Arius in Alexandria (c. 320). Even more serious was the question of the relationship between the Son of God and Jesus the man. This gave birth to the Nestorian heresy (from Nestorius, patriarch of Constantinople in the 5th century), which attributed two distinct natures to Christ. The dispute was only settled by the council of Constantinople in 553, which adopted the theories of Cyril of Alexandria, and proclaimed the unity of Christ's nature, Jesus crucified forming one with the person of the Trinity. The Church Fathers fought against what they considered to be deviations from the true doctrine, and unfailingly upheld a strict orthodox line. They made a philosophy of Christianity, thus bridging the gap between Hellenic thought and biblical tradition which they reinterpreted according to Jesus's revolutionary message, thereby creating a new spiritual world in which, although we may not know it, we still live today.

Saint Augustine

'. . . and those servants have no reason to regret even from this life of time, for in it they are schooled for eternity. They enjoy their earthly blessings in the manner of pilgrims . . . while these earthly misfortunes serve for testing and correction. (The City of God 1, 29)

'We see then that the two cities were created by two kinds of love: the earthly city was created by self-love reaching the point of contempt for God, the Heavenly City by the love of God carried as far as contempt of self.' (The City of God 14, 28)

Clement of Alexandria

c. 150 Athens (?) — Antioch (?) c.215

The first great Christian apologist

Clement of Alexandria thought to discover a new philosophy in the Christian faith which would solve the problems set by the ancient thinkers. He believed himself to be the spiritual guide for pagans.

Titus Flavius Clemens, born into a pagan family probably in Athens, spent the first part of his life looking for a teacher who could quench his thirst for the truth. This quest led him to Italy, Syria, Palestine, and finally to Alexandria where he studied under Pantenos, a Christian philosopher who was both rationalist and mystic. Pantenos was rector of Didaskaleon school which Clement, who taught with him and later succeeded, was to make famous because of the many converts he attracted from the town's intellectual circles. In 202 or 215, Clement was in Jerusalem. The Bishop of Jerusalem sent him as a missionary to the Church at Antioch where, it would seem, he died.

His works

His work as a whole is didactic and makes up a complete guidebook for spiritual training. It includes the *Exhortation to the Greeks*

'God became man so that we in our turn may become God.'

intended to 'convert', *The Tutor*, intended to 'shape morals' and the *Miscellanies*, which taught the 'gnosis' or mystical knowledge. The *Miscellanies* end with the *Hypotyposes*, his interpretation of one part of the Bible, but of which we possess only a later résumé. Clement's works profoundly influenced his brilliant successor, Origen.

The theory

Clement's desire was to incite the interest of the upper eschelons of society and the intelligentsia.

The Greek philosophers of Clement's time were, in the main, spiritual directors who guided the souls of their disciples towards the acquisition of wisdom. However, for him, these people could only partially obtain Reason, for Reason is personified in Christ who is the Instructor of the human race. Therefore, one must not only follow Christ, but also imitate Him. The true wise man then, is the Christian and more precisely, the 'gnostic' who has attained true spiritual knowledge and understanding of the Holy Scriptures. The knowledge is esoteric, forming a 'gnosis' or the secret teaching which was transmitted orally by Christ to the Apostles from whom it was passed down over the years through a series of great spiritual leaders. The secret teaching deals with heaven; the initiated are assured that full knowledge and understanding of the teachings will come after death, whereupon they will experience eternal peace. Such a blend of Christianity with esoteric Greek philosophy could not fail to arouse the suspicions of the Church authorities, with the result that Origen was one of the few who carried on the tradition started by Clement.

Comte and Positivism

1798 Montpellier — Paris 1857

A mystic scientist

One of the greatest thinkers of the 19th century, Auguste Comte conceived a system whereby progress was made through mutual love, and intended to make this system his religion.

That he was the founder of Positivism is perhaps less important here than the fact that Auguste Comte truly believed that his life's purpose was to be a religious leader. Three major events prepared him for this. At 19 he became secretary to Saint Simon (1760–1825), the philosopher and social economist, but left this position in 1822. In 1826 a period of extreme delirium, probably caused by overwork and grave personal problems, led Comte to try to kill himself on several occasions and he had to be in hospital for nearly a year. Finally in 1844 when it seemed that he had nothing to live for, Comte fell in love with a young woman named Clotilde de Vaux, becoming her closest confidante, though their relationship remained platonic. Clotilde was

'Love as our principle, and Order as our base: Progress as our goal.'

The Great Being
'The continuing goal of human life is to preserve and perfect the Great Being who must be loved, known and served at the same time.'

consumptive and died in Comte's arms in 1846. He continued to worship her even after her death.

His works

His work is an imposing intellectual construction, which is particularly well demonstrated by his *Course on Positive Philosophy* (1830–42) and includes 2 volumes which specifically deal with religious problems: his *System of Positive Polity* (1851–4) and the *Positivist Catechism* (1852).

'The religion of humanity'

At the dawn of a new era, Comte intended to institute the religion of the future. Once enlightened by Positivism, humanity should make up a fraternal and harmonious whole in every aspect. In Catholicism without Christianity, spiritual power would pass out of the hands of the priests and into those of the wise men who would be led by a high priest of humanity (Comte himself). But in this utopia, the human mind would not be able to detach itself from the religious symbols of childhood, therefore there would be a Positivist Trinity made up of the 'Great Milieu' — space, the 'Great Fetish' – the earth, and the 'Great Being' – humanity; there would also be nine sacraments, and even an 'Immaculate Conception' represented by Clotilde.

After Comte's death, his disciple Pierre Lafitte (1823–1903) defined the aims of a Positivist society, including worship. Nevertheless, at the end of the 19th century Comte's ideas gained more support abroad than in France and were put into practice (especially with regard to education) in England and in Sweden, but above all in the Latin American countries of Mexico, Chile, and most importantly Brazil.

Confucius and Confucianism

c. 551 BC Shanping, Shantung — 479 BC Shanping

The great Chinese educator

Often contested and sometimes rejected, the 'Master K'ung's' teaching has nevertheless had a permanent effect on Chinese mentality.

Confucius is the Latinization of K'ung Fu Tze or 'The Honourable Master K'ung', whose life it is difficult to separate from legend and to whom has been attributed an immense body of work, which in fact can only be partially his own. He was born when the decadence of the Chou dynasty had reached its apogee, while rival states fought amongst themselves and the people lived in abject poverty. K'ung Tze's father died when he was three but, despite the fact that his family was poor, he managed to get a thorough education. He was married at 19, had two children, and soon afterwards was widowed. He entered the state of Lu's administration as a junior clerk, but at the age of 22 he began to teach and also to further his own education.

About 525, K'ung Tze went to Lu, the seat of the imperial court. He is said to have met Lao-Tzu there. After failing to be awarded the position he wanted, he returned to his own region where he attempted fruitlessly to put his reforms into practice. It was his reforms that attracted a growing number of disciples to him. With their help, he began to draw together a collection of the ancient canonical texts. But it was not until he was 50, when he received the governorship of the town of Chung-Tu that he was really given the chance to put his administrative talents to the test. It is said that he worked such wonders that the Duke of Lu appointed him

Minister of Crime. In this capacity, K'ung Tze established political order and implemented a more just legal system. In spite of his success, because he did not receive the duke's unconditional support, he eventually left government office. He then departed on a long journey, only returning some 14 years later to finish off the training of his disciples. His last years were dedicated to this end.

His works

According to tradition, Confucius finalized the text of the *Five Classics*, which are fundamental to Chinese culture. They are: the *I Ching* or Classic of Changes; the *Shu Ching* or Classic of History; the Shi Ching or Classic of Odes; the *Li Ching* or Classic of Rights; and the *Chu'un Ch'iu* or Spring and Autumn Annals, which are extracts from the History of Lu which Confucius was said to have compiled. The doctrine of Confucianism is outlined in the *Four Books* drawn up by the disciples: the *Ta Hsueh* or the great learning which traces the way to perfection through knowledge, the heart's purity and conforming to universal order; the *Chung Yung* or Doctrine of the Mean, which gives the 'tao of sincerity', the union of order and harmony, as the human ideal; the *Meng Tzu*, the work of K'ung Tze's disciple Meng Tzu (Mencius, 372–289 BC); and finally *Lun yu*, or 'Analects', the only work which is in the master's own words and conveys his teaching adjusted and

---

Confucius on himself

'At fifteen I applied myself to study; at 30 I walked on the path with a firm tread; at 40, I no longer doubted; at 50 I knew the laws of Heaven; at 60 I followed my own intelligence; at 70 my heart's desire became one with cosmic order. I transmit, I do not invent.'

modified to the individual development potential of each disciple.

The theory

To combat the confusion of his fellow compatriots in an era of extreme violence and misery, K'ung Tze advocated a return to more fundamental values, to a time when heavenly order prevailed and everything was in its correct place. He gave this time as being at the start of the Chou dynasty, five centuries before his birth. It is therefore necessary to study and fully understand the *Five Classics*, which date from that time and which reflect the ancient wisdom. Confucius also says that it is necessary to 'correct the appellations', that is to say, to give a corrupt vocabulary back its true meaning.

Order can only be restored to society as described by the 'Decree of Heaven', through the medium of the true gentleman (chun tze). Up until that time one could only be *chun tze* by right of birth, but Confucius said' birth is nothing where there is no virtue'. This true gentleman is characterized by *Jen*, a notion created by Confucius: Jen is the nobility of Heaven, it is the dignity of man . . . and every man has it within him. . . . If I want to find it, it is there immediately in me'. Through Jen, man discovers his inner nature in relation to infinity and other people. If a man is Jen by natural aptitude, this virtue must be developed by 'total education', which is the only method of transforming the ordinary individual into a 'true man'. But this education cannot come from outside, it is self-knowledge and self-discipline.

After Jen, man will remain faithful to the principles of his own nature (*chong*); he will apply these principles to others as to himself (*chu*); he will practise righteousness and

honesty (i), and will be attentive and generous; he will have the virtue of filial piety (hsiao), or obedience, which is the basis of social order, whereby the son is answerable to the father, the wife to the husband, the young to their elders, subjects to their king and the king to Heaven. He must also respect the rights of propriety and conventions (*li*). For Confucius this respect for ritual, which was later to become much more formal was spontaneous because it is through rite and ritual that man reaches a level of harmony with the tao. *The Great Learning* also aims to 'polish the tarnished', to 'renew men', for once men are renewed, so is society and the whole world will rediscover its former 'supreme excellence'. Whatever may since have been the fluctuating fortunes of Confucianism when it became the Law of the Empire and a contributing factor to the stagnation of the country, the actual teachings and philosophy of Confucius stay very much alive, relevant, and, in short, universal as the following quotation from Mencius demonstrates: 'the 10 000 beings (their totality) are present and complete in me. There can be no greater joy than to turn inwards and discover that one's words are in accord with one's inner self. There is nothing closer to *Jen* than to treat others as you would treat yourself.'

The sage

'The Sage does not worry about men not knowing him; he worries about knowing men.'

Tao

'That which leads nature is called Tao. Real education lies in practising Tao.'

David and the Psalms

First half of the 11th century, Bethlehem — Jerusalem 965 BC

The 'Psalmist'

During David's reign, a united Israel experienced glory and prosperity. He was also a religious leader and the author of songs of praise still in use today.

In his youth David, son of Jesse, was anointed by the prophet Samuel, distinguishing him as elected by the Eternal Father to replace Saul. Saul was the first king of the Jews, but had fallen from Divine Grace because of his sins. Admitted to Saul's court, David killed Goliath, the giant, with his catapult and subjugated the Philistines. He was both favoured by the king, whose daughter he married, and persecuted as his rival. On Saul's death (1012), David was elected king of the tribe of Judah, then from 1005 onwards, he governed all Israel. He chose Jerusalem as his capital and Holy City, and had the Ark of the Covenant deposited there. Although David may have reigned for over 30 years in the kingdom that he had united and pacified, his passion for Bethsheba undid him for he had her husband put to death and from then on he had to bear the

---

From psalm 42

'Judge me oh God and plead my case against an ungodly nation . . . For Thou art the God of my strength; . . . Oh send out Thy light and Thy truth: Let them lead me; Let them bring me unto Thy Holy hill, Unto Thy tabernacles.'

---

revulsion of his sons for his criminal act. Before he died, David anointed Solomon, his second son by Bethsheba. In popular memory, David remains the image of the ideal king, for despite his faults he always aspired to be the instrument of Divine Providence. Revered by Islam, for Christians he is the forefather and prefiguration of the Messiah. Tradition depicts him as the author of the Psalms which he is said to have composed on his harp while dancing in front of the Ark.

The Psalms

The Greek word *psalma* translates the Hebrew *mizmor* meaning praise. The Psalms are in fact songs of praise which were sung in synagogues long before they became the Psalms chanted in churches and monasteries as well as used in the Protestant faith, where they form a central part of worship. There are 150 Psalms in the Book of Psalms which follows the Book of Law and Prophets in the Bible. The oldest of these date back to David's own time and are similar in form and content to the hymns used in worship in both Mesopotamia and Egypt.

Many Psalms glorify the all-powerful but compassionate nature of Divinity, while celebrating the Holy City and the chosen people; they often end with 'alleluia' (Praise Yahweh). The so-called Psalms of Penitence (for example the 'Miserere', psalm 51) reflect the supplication of the pitiful soul to God. Finally, others evoke the fluctuating fortunes of Israel and the numerous occasions when divine intervention has changed its history; some of these recount the capture of Babylon and therefore date from the 5th century BC.

Desert Fathers

Precursors for monks and their model

The spirituality which came out of the desert from the 4th century onwards was the source of monastic life; it inspired countless mystics, both in the West and the East.

For the first three centuries of the Christian era, martyrdom was the highest peak to which a soul in search of perfection could aspire. When the persecutions ended and it became the religion of the Empire, Christianity seemed to lose some of its impetus. It was then that a number of Christians turned their backs on the world in order to lead lives that were totally dedicated to renunciation, contemplation and the mortification of the flesh. By the end of the 3rd century, some of them, were already established in the deserts of Egypt, particularly those of Scete and Nitree near Syria, and of Palestine, near Gaza, in Judea and around Mount Sinai.

These anchorites ('those who live apart') were most often to be found in hermitages, beset by anxieties that are incumbent on absolute solitude and facing the forces of Evil sent to try them. The first and most famous anchorite was Saint Anthony who was over 100 years old when he died. His

---

The desert in the Old Testament
'I will woo her, I will go with her into the wilderness and comfort her.' (Hosea 2, 16)

---

asceticism became gradually more severe until he was surviving on bread, salt, and dates alone. Little by little, visitors began to flock to him in search of spiritual or physical healing; some went to him to be comforted and enlightened, others remained, forming a community in which each member lived alone, but everyone grouped around Anthony the 'Father of the Monks' for communal prayer. This was roughly the first version of what was to become monastic office. In order to fend off the dangers of solitude, Saint Pachomius (died 348) founded a new form of monasticism known as cenobitism (from the Greek *koinos bios* meaning 'communal life') which had a rule intended to regulate the monks' life of prayer and work. The first monastery was founded in 323 in Upper Egypt; by the time of Pachomius's death, there were 11, 9 for men and 2 for women.

Prayer of invocation

In the decade between 330 and 340, Macarius the Egyptian (c. 301– c. 392) founded the Scete desert community which has survived to the present day. Macarius instituted the use of 'monological' prayer, the constant repetition of a very brief invocation of the Lord, which should engender hesychasm. This desert spirituality, according to which man is indispensable to God, just as God is indispensable to man, was enlarged upon by a series of important figures like Evagrius of Pontus (4th century), Dorothy of Gaza (6th century), Isaac the Syrian and John Climacus from Mount Sinai; it is at the root of hermetic and cenobitic Byzantine monastic life and mysticism in the Eastern Church.

Dionysius the Areopagite

5th–6th centuries

The father of Medieval mystic theology

Dionysius was a mysterious author of genius and a guide for many contemplatives whose personal experiences were often reflected and explained in his works.

Dionysius declares himself to be one of Saint Paul's disciples who converted after hearing the Apostle preach at the Areopage in Athens; he was later confused with the so-called First Bishop of Paris who was martyred at the end of the 3rd century. Dionysius's works appear to have been written between 482 and 530. Many theories have been put forward as to the true identity of the person now called the 'pseudo-Dionysius'. The most likely theory describes him as a Syrian monk, a student of Proclus, of the Neoplatonic school before converting to Christianity. In fact, the Sophist Apollophanes accuses Dionysius of having used 'the Greeks against the Greeks in an impious manner'. The identity that Dionysius attributed to himself was no doubt more than a subterfuge in order to link himself more closely to the apostolic tradition. This does not however detract from his value either as a great author or as the leader of both Eastern and Western

mystics, who inspired parts of Dante's *Paradise* and who continued to influence religious thought until Saint John of the Cross in the 16th century.

His works

His works consist of two groups of tracts: *The Celestial Hierarchy* and *Ecclesiatical Hierarchy*, which systematically examine the two categories of being worthy of receiving Revelation; *Divine Names* and *Mystic Theology* which were the most complete theological works produced before those of Thomas Aquinas.

The theory

For Dionysius the whole universe, both visible and invisible, is governed by a sacred order which dictates the exact position in that universe of all those given over to deification (on the one hand, the angels, and on the other, the members of the Church) according to their degree of perfection. The whole is animated by a movement of ebb and flow, from God, to God, by a downward then upward moving process: for humankind, incarnation, then conversion and deification. Our knowledge of God comes firstly from the study of names dedicated to Him, but must go beyond that study, for any definition of God would be to limit the transcending unlimited. Theology, the science of God, can only be negative or 'apophatic'. God cannot be reached through knowledge, only through total ignorance. The mystic, like Moses going up Mount Sinai, must go beyond all light into the dark cloud which hides Him from the world, but which is the true source of light.

> **The love of God** is a motivating force, the manifestation of Him and conversion to Him, the eternal circle which comes from Good and returns to Good.

Djalal ad-Din Rumi

1207 Balk — Konya 1273

The founder of the Whirling Dervishes

He was also the greatest mystic poet and is to this day a 'leader of awakening'.

Born at Balk in Khorassan (Afghanistan), Djalal ad-Din Rumi was the son of the great theologian Baha ad-Din Walad. He was struck by his son's saintly nature even in his infancy and nicknamed him *Mevlana*, 'Our Master'. To escape the Mongol threat, the family fled Balk in 1219 (Balk was destroyed the following year) and went on a long pilgrimage. On their travels they met the poet Attar at Nishapur who, on seeing the child, exclaimed, 'What a flame, what fire he will bring to the world!' At Damascus, the illustrious Ibn' Arabi seeing Djalal following his father is said to have cried, 'Praise God, here is an ocean walking behind a lake'. On the journey, Djalal met and married a young girl from Samarkand

> 'My life is in three words: I was raw, I have been cooked, I am burnt'
> 'I was snow, you melted me. The sun drank me. Mist of spirit, I go up to the sun.'

> **Mathnawi**
> 'In the night of my heart
> Along a narrow road
> I dug and light
> sprang forth
> An infinite land
> of day.'

with whom he had two sons, Ala ad-Din and Sultan Walad, also a poet who later organized the brotherhood of Dervishes founded by his father.

The family finally settled in Konya (Turkey) where Baha ad-Din Walad began teaching again until his death 2 years later in 1230. Although he was still very young, his son succeeded him but later left for Alep and Damascus, where he studied under Ibn'Arabi. But Rumi was looking for a way to achieve union with God.

It was then that he met a strange wandering dervish known as Shams ad-Din Muhammad ibn'Ali of Tabriz in whom he recognized his true master. In 1244 Shams settled in Konya and Rumi gave up his teaching in order to live in seclusion with him. One day, Shams disappeared but was found in Damascus. He came back, only to disappear once more in 1247, supposedly assassinated by disciples who were jealous of Rumi. The latter had identified with Shams to the extent that he signed Shams's name to his collection of *Divan-e Shams e-Tabrizi* (Mystic Odes) and devoted himself exclusively to meditation and dance, founding the Maulawiyyah whirling Dervishes (from his surname). It was also at this time that he compiled his major work, the *Mathnawi*. When Rumi died, the whole town of Konya went into mourning. Admirers still visit his magnificent mausoleum today.

His works

Apart from the *Mystic Odes*, he wrote numerous quatrains (*Ruba'yat*) and the *Mathnawi*, an immense poem 45 000 lines long. This is a veritable odyssey of the soul which must die to its 'self' in order to have eternal life in God. In the West, *Mathnawi* was much admired by Goethe and Hegel. The *Fihi-ma Fihi* (Book of the Interior) is a record in prose of Rumi's ideas and was

Djalal ad-Din Rumi *Earliest portrait Turkish miniature (Municipal Museum of Istanbul)*

compiled by Sultan Walad. It allows us to better understand Rumi's philosophy and Sufism in general.

The theory

After having studied all the great spiritual leaders of his time, and reached a state of complete mystical understanding, Rumi confirmed his mission as a 'maker of souls' by perfecting a method by which union with God could be achieved. To him, terrestrial music evoked that of the celestial spheres, the initial creative vibrations.

The sacred dance of the Dervishes, the *sama*, which can be seen as their liturgical office, is a manifestation of the heady dance of the planets, the triumphant joy which animates the cosmos. Both his preaching and his work sing passionately of love, firstly divine love, but also love of all human beings, and all living things. A firm pantheist, Rumi saw God's presence everywhere, which led him to deny the existence of Evil — which for him was but the shadow outlining the sun. Although he was staunch Muslim, this did not prevent him from considering all other religions as equal and even during the aftermath of the Crusades, incorporating Christian parables into his works.

We know Rumi's teachings today not only because his poems are read and sung on pilgrimages but also because of the Maulawiyyah brotherhood which spread throughout the Ottoman Empire after his death, and which is still active today in many Muslim countries.

The retreat imposed on Dervish novices is much longer than in other *tariqa*. They must remain in a monastery for 1001 days, or nearly three years of which 'the first is devoted to the service of others, the second to the service of God and the third to watch over one's own heart'. The new disciple leads a life of extreme austerity in the community; to mortify him he is given difficult or distasteful tasks. But once initiated, he may participate in the ceremony of *sama* or cosmic dance, 'dressed in white, the symbol of the shroud, wearing a tall black felt hat, representing the tombstone and wrapped in a long black coat which represents the tomb itself'. Before the dance actually begins, the dancer divests himself of this coat 'as if he were freeing himself from his flesh in preparation for a second birth'. In the dance, the sheikh, in the centre of the circle is the sun, the reflection of God, while the disciples symbolize the planets. This is how the supreme union or *ney* is brought about.

Thanks to the recent work of Western Orientalists, Djalal ad-Din Rumi is now recognized as one of the greatest mystics of all time. Not only does his vast work contain the very essence of Sufism, which with him reached its apogee, but through his wholehearted devotion to 'nostalgia for the divine' to the celebration of a love which was 'earthly in appearance' but 'which is in fact the hypostatis of divine love', it takes on a more widespread meaning.

'Many paths lead to God, I have chosen that of dance and music.'

'In musical rhythms a secret is hidden; if I revealed it, it would overturn the world.'

Dominic of Guzman

c. 1170 Calaruega — Bologna 1221

The Founder of the Order of Friars Preachers

When he founded an order dedicated to preaching, Dominic, a contemporary of Francis of Assisi gave the Church new theological and mystical impetus.

Son of an old Castillian family, Domingo de Guzman studied at the University of Palencia. The Bishop of Osma singled him out for his skills as a preacher and took him to France. While travelling through Languedoc, the two priests were struck by the growing Cathar heresy and decided to fight it, using the spoken word and the example of poverty as their weapons. After two years, Dominic was left alone and he travelled all over the region, preaching against the heresy. Despite the general hostility, he obtained several conversions and in 1206 at Prouille, near Toulouse, he established his first convent.

When the Albigensian Crusade was launched in 1208, Dominic played no active part in it, but tried to carry on preaching: his overwhelming desire to train well-educated preachers of impeccable

---

The Motto given by Dominic to his order:
'Talk only to God, or of God.'

Dominic according to Lacordaire
'In his inner life, every breath was an act of love towards God or mankind.'

---

morals led him to found the Order of Preachers in 1215 at Toulouse. Two years later he sent the 16 first Dominicans to start up communities in Madrid, Paris, Bologna, and Rome. Honoured by the pope, he was head of the first Chapter of his order in Bologna, where he died. He was canonized 13 years after his death. One century later there were roughly 15 000 Dominicans, divided into over 500 monasteries and convents from northern Europe to Morocco and from Ireland to Russia.

The Friars Preachers

Like the Franciscans, the Dominicians introduced a new type of monasticism. As beggar priests they were more in touch with the needs of contemporary society than the older, contemplative orders. But, while the Franciscans were an example of perfect apostolic poverty and spread the Gospel to the people, the Dominicans were first and foremost an intellectual order, devoted to theological study; each monastery had its teacher, and each province its centre of education, the most important being Paris, Oxford, Cologne, Montpellier, and Bologna. It is noteworthy that the most prominent members of the Order are known for their intellectual capacities, like the German, Albert the Great (1206–80) whose extensive knowledge earned him fame, and above all his friend, the Italian, Thomas Aquinas. If the Dominician Order fed the ranks of the Inquisition, and Savonarole (1452–98) belonged to it, we must not overlook the fact that it was this same Order which produced Fra Angelico (1387–1453) and the great 14th century mystics and religious leaders, Meister Eckhart, Suso, Tauler, and Catherine of Siena (1347–80).

Eckhart, Johannes (called Meister Eckhart)

c. 1260 Hochheim, Thuringia — 1327(?)

The genius of Rhenish mysticism

Eckhart was a great preacher whose succinct and trenchant ideas overwhelmed his followers but worried the authorities. The universal significance of his theory has only recently been rediscovered.

Having entered the Dominican Order at Erfurt as an adolescent, Johannes Eckhart was sent to the Cologne *Studium generale* to continue his studies. Even before 1298 he was prior of Erfurt and vicar-general of Thuringia. He taught theology in Paris for some time and on his return c. 1300–03, was appointed provincial of the new Dominican province of Saxe, then in 1307, vicar-general of Bohemia. In 1311 he was again sent to teach in Paris, later becoming rector of the Strasbourg *Studium*, where he preached with great success and went on to become rector at Cologne. But between 1325 and 1326 the Archbishop of Cologne, who was opposed to the Dominicans, condemned certain themes in Eckhart's works. Eckhart appealed to Pope John XXII and in 1327 joined him at Avignon. He died shortly afterwards, either in Avignon or on the journey home.

His works

His work consists of commentaries, tracts, and Latin sermons. It is a daring synthesis of Thomist intellectualism and Neoplatonic mysticism. In fact, Eckhart uses metaphysics to further his mystical theory, the same theory that is found throughout his major German works: *Spiritual Instructions*, the *Book of Consolation*, and about 60 popular German *Sermons*.

The theory

Erudite in his Latin writings, Eckhart was nevertheless an impassioned and sometimes virulant preacher. He never hesitated to manipulate paradox or to use striking and sometimes disconcerting turns of phrase in order to shake his congregation out of their apathy. He advocated the need to get out of the self in order to penetrate eternity and became One with it. Only then can God's plan, which is to make of each one of us his 'Only Child', be carried out. The soul must then perform the ultimate sacrifice, the 'most intimate death' and even lose God, in order to become truly divine.

If, in Eckhart's life, these ideas led him to be accused of pantheism, it is particularly these ideas that make him so interesting today, with the result that he has a much stronger following now than he ever had in his lifetime. Comparisons have been made between Eckhart's mode of enlightenment through the discovery of the inner void, and that of many Eastern religious leaders particularly in Zen Buddhism. Despite the suspicions this theory aroused, it was carried on after Eckhart's death by two of his disciples, Suso and Tauler.

God and the creature

'Where the creature ends, God begins. All that God urgently demands is that you come out of yourself in so far as you are the creation, and to let God be God in you.'

Egyptian Book of the Dead

A guide to the afterlife

Placed with the body in the tomb, the Book of the Dead was intended to help the deceased overcome the obstacles that faced him, and to achieve his own deification.

A collection of incantations and magical formulae which were often magnificently illustrated, the *Book of the Dead* was laid in Egyptian tombs, either placed on top of the sacrophagus, or slipped directly into the mummy's bandages. These apparently incoherent texts date from no earlier than the 17th century BC, but were inspired by the *Coffin Texts* (2300–1700 BC) which can be found written on the walls of tombs. The *Coffin Texts* were preceeded by the *Pyramid Texts*, which were painted around the coffin chamber in pyramids, and were only used in royal burials. The *Book of the Dead* therefore represents a process of democratization as the rites formerly reserved for kings and queens became available to the middle classes.

'Going out by day'

With the exception of a few passages at the beginning, corresponding to the funeral ceremony, the book was to be recited by the dead person. It permitted him to 'go out by day'. In fact, during the night, the deceased followed the course of the sun in the other world which was invisible to the living. And just as the sun is reborn with every dawn, by using the appropriate phrases from the book, the dead underwent a second birth and were completely restored to life. They

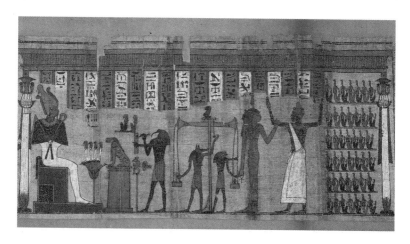

Anubis weighing the deceased's heart, watched over by Osiris, god of the Dead, on his throne Detail from a Book of the Dead, *Egyptian painting on papyrus, dating from the New Empire (Louvre Museum, Paris)*

then descended into the underworld where Osiris, god of the Dead, presided over their judgment, during which the heart had to be entreated not to testify against them. However, the deceased only had to go through this ordeal once they had been duly purified, regenerated, transfigured, and even deified.

If in this instance, incantatory magic plays a fundamental role, it is because the Egyptians believed firmly in the sovereign power of the World. The *Book of the Dead* also manifests a certain kind of spirituality, for in essence it is not Osiris who judges but the dead themselves; Osiris only confirms the judgment already made by the bearer of the heart. Absolute faith in life after death, through a process of self-deification, is also striking in this text. The *Book of the Dead* is proof of the advanced degree of initiation reached by the Egyptians, which was far superior to that of any other contemporary society. It can therefore be seen as the first in a long line of spiritual teachings. Read-ing it today, it is as though we were present at the spasmodic unwinding of a roll of images, where a bizarre phantasmagoria accompanies the invocations to the gods, and the teachings received from them in return.

Invocation to the sun god

'Make your paths passable for me, widen your roads in front of me, so that I can travel the earth as you do the sky. May your light be upon me . . . while I approach the god (Osiris, god of the Dead).'

'Going Out By Day'

'He who knows this book on earth, or he who has it with him in his coffin, may go out by day in any form he wants, and return to [his] place without being turned away.'

Empedocles

c. 490–430 BC

A complex and enigmatic personality

Empedocles is at the outer edge of Greek classicism as the last of their great inspired religious leaders.

It is the personality of Empedocles rather than his teachings that has always intrigued both philosophers and historians. Their conceptions of him have often been extremely contradictory, some seeing him as a charlatan and others a genius. His way of introducing himself, stating that he had 'come amongst you, forever delivered from death, as an immortal god that all worship' is certainly quite shocking until one is aware that he uses the words of an Orphic (see **Orphism**) initiate who has reached a state of pure contemplation and has therefore escaped the cycle of birth and rebirth, and ascended to the realm of the gods. As a healer, philanthropist and sage combined, Empedocles is representative of the visionary and inspired men who followed in the footsteps of Pythagoras, whom he seems to have greatly admired. However, Empedocles was functioning in an amoral materialistic world where the teachings of the Sophists were fast becoming popular. Hence the conflicts with authority also gave rise to the many legends surrounding his character and deeds. One particular legend has the philosopher throwing himself into Mount Etna which promptly spits out one of his bronze sandals.

About his life we know only that he was the son of a wealthy and distinguished family from Agrigentum, one of the largest towns in the Greek world. There he played a role in politics, sharing his scientific knowledge with his fellow compatriots. Then he travelled in Italy and the Peloponese where he remained in exile until his death.

His works

As we only possess fragments of his two magnificent and powerful poems, any interpretation is extremely difficult. *On Nature* deals with the origins of the universe, of living creatures and of humankind, and in *Purifications* Empedocles deciphers destiny of the human race and by allusion, his own.

The theory

In order to explain how unity gave birth to multiplicity, Empedocles describes God as a sphere outside of which is strife. Strife attacks the One, dispersing it, but Love tends to unify it in its centre. Living things spring from this constant battle of forces, during which the four elements are sometimes brought together, sometimes separated. Organ by organ the philosopher describes the evolution of these living things, attributing monstrous characteristics to them before they develop into more harmonious and usuable forms. He also describes the lost souls which are condemned to wander through inumerable lives taking on diverse shapes, before being purified and once again able to enter the blessed dwelling place.

From life to life

'I am vagabond exiled from the divine abode . . . I have been boy and girl, bush and bird, a mute fish in the sea.' (*Purifications*)

Epicurus

341 BC Samos — Athens 270 BC

A maligned sage

Epicurus, who was an example of extreme sobriety, was one of the greatest leaders in antiquity.

Epicurus was born on the Island of Samos of Athenian colonial parents. He went to school on the island and at the age of 12 decided that he would devote his life to philosophy.

As an adolescent, he studied at Teos under Nausiphanes, a disciple of Democritus. Between the ages of 18 and 20 he did his military service in Athens, but was not able to return to Samos as the Athenians had been expelled. He lived in poverty as an exile until he founded a school at Mytilenus, and then a second at Lampsacus where he remained for five years. In 306 BC Epicurus opened the school at Athens which was to become known as the 'Garden' and which he ran until his death. Although frequently unwell, he was a warm and accessible leader, living frugally, surrounded by the admiration of his disciples. All the same, he was denigrated by his enemies, the Stoics who outrageously perverted his doctrine. Only as a result of recent studies, has he been reinstated as one of the most powerful thinkers of ancient Greece.

His works

There would have been about 300 volumes, but we only possess fragments passed down to us by Diogenes Laërtius who compiled them in the 3rd century BC.

The most important of these fragments are three letters, written by Epicurus to his disciples, which give abreviated versions of his theories on physics, astronomy, meteorology, and ethics. Important parts of a long tract *On Nature* were discovered in 1750 at Herculaneum.

The theory

When Epicurus was teaching, Greece was in the throes of a serious moral and political crisis. Greek cities had lost not only their independence but also their humanitarian ideals. In this troubled time, Epicurus assumed the responsibility of leading people back on to the path of wisdom. Although his doctrines applied to everyone, including women and slaves, he was none the less aiming at a particular élite. Epicurian doctrine relies on a world view inspired by Democratic Atomism, and a perception of the soul as corporeal and therefore mortal. The aim is to deliver humanity from all fear, especially fear of death and of the gods, for if the gods do not interfere in human life, they should only be models of perfection. Having overcome these sources of anxiety the educated human being can bear inevitable pain with serenity, and give himself over to pleasure, which is defined as the fullness of being and inner peace.

Letter from Epicurus to Menoeceus, his disciple
'One cannot have a happy life without wisdom, honesty, and justice, but these three are inseparable from pleasure.'

A fragment of Epicurus's writings
'While we are alive, death not exist, and when death comes, we are no longer here.'

Esoterism and Initiation

Knowledge transmitted only to the initiated

Although in Eastern religions esoterism complements general education, in the West, because it was banned by the Church, it became a secret doctrine.

Esoteric teachings (from the Greek *esotero* meaning 'inner') or 'acroamatic' teachings ('given orally') were transmitted by Greek philosophers only to the best educated of their disciples. They complemented state or exoteric education, were passed on orally and were never written down. This applied to the 'sacred science' in all traditional civilizations which could not be 'made profane', that is given to the profane—like the teachings of the Druids in the Celtic tribes, and in Greece, the mysteries of Pythagorean doctrine. Parts of Plato's and Aristotle's teachings were also esoteric.

In its principal and universal meaning, the term esoterism can be applied to all limited teaching which is only passed on after certain precautionary actions, for example Gnosticism (see **Gnosis** and **Gnosticism**), the Cabala, or the Upanishad in India which, even when written, were formulated in such a way that they were inaccessible to the uninitiated. Buddha's doctrines were perhaps destined for general consumption, but certain of his theories, in particular the tantrics, can only be passed from master to initiated disciple (see **Vajarayana**). This also applies to the more advanced yoga techniques. In Islam, esoterism is represented by the Shi'ites, the Isma'ilis and the Sufis. In other words, every religion exists on two levels, one for everybody and another reserved for the chosen few, quite simply because those who are not prepared to receive the esoteric

teachings would be quite incapable of understanding them. Therefore it is not a question of discrimination or élitism but of didactic necessity. Moreover, the two levels of teachings have different goals: exoterism or religion itself, aims at the salvation of the individual, while esoterism teaches that the individual status must be transcended in order to achieve final liberation.

Initiation

The need for a spiritual leader capable of transmitting the esoteric part of the doctrine and of taking the disciple out of himself arises here. This is the role of the guru in Hinduism and the lama in Vajrayana. Most frequently, the transmission of information can only be made during a retreat in which the spiritual guide or leader and the disciple live together. Well-known examples of this are the ashram in India and the Sufi tariqa. This is also applicable to certain Christian monasteries in which a spiritual director plays a comparable role, particularly in the case of the Hesychasts, or the Starsi of Russia.

Although the progressive phases do not have quite the same significance, in some ways the manner in which priests are ordained contains certain elements of initiation rites. Thus there is a laying on of hands by the Elders and the transmission of the Holy Spirit. However, these are only barely recognizable traces of traditional initiation rites.

> 'The esoterism in all traditions, apart from being a metaphysical and cosmological doctrine, includes an entire hierarchy of traditional sciences which are the applications of the doctrine in different domains, and of which some furnish the support and technical methods for spiritual realization.' (Jean Reyor)

Initiation is firstly a process of personal purification and secondly a direct transferral of spiritual energy from master to disciple. The disciple must be initiated before he can receive the esoteric teaching, and therefore in Tibetan Tantric Buddhism, each time the disciple reaches a more advanced level of teaching and practice, his progress is masked by a new set of rites. This is comparable to Hellenic mystical practices.

Initiation stems from the Latin *initium* meaning 'beginning' which gave the verb *initio* and the expression 'to initiate into the mysteries'. It means therefore a 'new beginning', the initiate emerging from the rites as a totally different being. This passage from the profane to the sacred is considered to be a 'second birth', a regeneration of the being, through which the individual rediscovers his original spiritual state which was hitherto disguised by material conditions. Without this new awareness esoteric teachings would be of no use whatever.

From esoterism to the occult

If the above explanation defines esoterism as it is in the traditions still active today, it has taken a somewhat different meaning in the modern era, especially from the 18th century onwards, in the context of Western Christian society where the Church, considering itself to be the only true source of Doctrine, completely rejected all esoteric teaching. Esoterism, although driven underground by the Church, managed to survive over the centuries. It claims to be the only inheritor of a tradition that dates from long before the Christian era and which only decreased in popularity with the expansion of Christianity. Esoterism presents itself as the way to metaphysical, transcendent and intuitive knowledge, the path leading to *philosophia perennis* which was once unique and universal. And finally, it is the only doctrine capable of leading man from darkness to light, to let him overcome the Fall to rediscover his original contemplation and through communication of secret knowledge during the rites of initiation, which is passed down from master to master.

It is not surprising that it is difficult to trace the development of this doctrine in history, for it had to be kept a close secret. The various works which refer to it are extremely obscure; moreover as they were trying to communicate the abstract and the irrational they often have recourse to the use of a symbolism which can only make sense to the initiated. It was only with the Rosicrucian movement and especially the Freemasons in the 18th century that this trend could come out into the open. The occultism and theosophy prevalent at the end of the 19th century are also considered representative of esoterism. More recently, René Guénon devoted his life and works to a detailed exposé of esoteric doctrine, which brought about a renewal of interest in it.

René Guénon

'Any teaching on the inexpressible can obviously only suggest it with the help of borrowed images which aid contemplation.' 'The being is in no way *absorbed* when it obtains deliverance . . . on the contrary it expands beyond all limits for it has actually reached its fullest potential.'

Essenes

Mysterious Jewish sect

A large part of the Essenian beliefs was revealed with the discovery of the Dead Sea Scrolls.

Until the 1950s, all we knew of the Essenes, who date from about the same time as Christianity (1st century BC–1st century AD), came from certain passages in the works of the Jewish historian Josephus Flavius and especially from Philo of Alexandria. The Essenes were a close brotherhood, living in the desert in exceptionally simple conditions under the guidance of 'A Teacher of Righteousness' whose role was to transmit 'the wonderful and true mysteries' hidden in the Bible to initiates. Full membership of the sect depended on a postulate of one year, and a novitiate of two years, followed by the decision of a 12 man council assisted by three representatives of the Levitican priesthood.

The texts

The texts were discovered in 1947 in a cave at Qumran on the western shore of the Dead Sea. Further excavation uncovered the ruins of the buildings which had housed the community. Although 600 manuscripts were discovered, only 11 of them were even relatively intact. Several different types of text were discovered, some alluding to the Bible, others of an apocryphal and apocalyptic nature, which were held in great esteem by the early Church before they were banned. Perhaps most interesting was the discovery of works particular to the sect: biblical *Commentaries*, *Hymns*, and especially the *Scroll of the War of Sons of Light against the Sons of Darkness*, which was intended to encourage the Essenes in their struggle against the unholy. Although the *Manual of Discipline* is valuable for its portrayal of the sects' spiritual practices it also builds a picture of warrior monks, similar in nature to the Assideans or Hasidim (see **Hasidism**). The *Damascus Document* discovered in 1897 at Old Cairo, is set out in the same way, but is a later manual edited when the sect was in exile at Damascus.

The theory

The Essenes believed that they alone knew the truth about the 'order of time', God's plan for the world which humankind caused to fail but which must eventually triumph. They believed that in order to greet God's arrival like 'angels' they should lead an extremely monastic existence, renouncing the material world and also where possible, marriage. This isolation from the real world lead to bloody conflicts between the 'elect' and the 'unholy' during which the 'Teacher of Righteousness' fell. In 63 BC the Essenes were exiled to Damascus, where the sect seems to have died out. Even if it is certain that Essenism played some part in the early development of Christianity and Christian monachism, modern day research is still unable to establish the actual extent of the sect's influence.

The Teacher of Righteousness

Through the 'Teacher of Righteousness', 'father of the men of God', the Essenian community was 'consolidated in truth by eternal plantation.' (*Rule of the Sons of Light*)

From the Dead Sea Scrolls

'When I am the prey of terror and fear, I shall bless Him . . . when I am in distress, I shall praise Him. And when He saves me, I shall shout out with joy.' (*extract*)

Evagrius of Pontus

345 Ibora, Asia Minor — Egyptian desert 399

Theoretician of Asceticism

He was the first Christian philosopher to withdraw to the desert and was considered the leader of Byzantine monachism.

Born on the banks of the Black Sea, in his youth Evagrius was ordained a reader by Basil of Caesarea, then deacon by Gregory of Nazianzus in Constantinople, where he was admired for his skill as a preacher. However, he was compelled by his demanding vocation to withdraw to a hermitage in 382, then to Egypt and the Desert of the Cells. There he became a disciple of the Macarii who advocated 'monological' prayer which is the constant repetition of a brief prayer centred around the invocation 'Lord'. After this, Evagrius lived alone in the desert. He only emerged from his deep state of contemplation in order to write his books. Several councils condemned him for his audacious additions to Origen's theories and a number of his works were destroyed. Nevertheless, Evagrius strongly influenced Oriental mysticism of which he became the principal theoretician.

His works

Several of Evagrius's tracts on asceticism have served as a guide to monastic life: *Antirrheticus* (Against the Temptation of the Demon), which not only defines the seven cardinal sins for the first time, but also tells how to overcome them; *The Monk or On Active Life*; and above all the *Chapters on Prayer* in which, in brief phrases, Evagrius outlines the various stages of the spiritual journey.

The theory

According to Evagrius, mystical teaching must 'contain both practice and theory'. Practice aims at the purification of the soul to teach it to be passive and silent before God. Practice leads to theory, or 'gnosis', which itself is divided in two branches: the 'physical' or contemplation of nature as God's creation, and the 'theological' or active participation in the angelic knowledge of the Light. As the soul advances towards heaven, it becomes progressively more pure and refined; the world it discovers at each new level is correspondingly more subtle. But it is only at the end of his period as an ascetic that an individual can rediscover his original coherent state, whose loss has caused his unhappiness and Fall.

As an ascetic, Evagrius remained strongly influenced by the Neoplatonic school as is shown by his conception of the divine. He preached a theory of disembodiment before intelligence which was not without danger and which aroused a predictable reaction. In the later Hesychastic sect, the tendency was to favour a 'prayer of the heart' over the prayer of the intellect. Despite this Evagrius is recognized as the creator of a mystical vocabulary widely used in the Middle Ages.

'**Prayer** is the ascent of the intellect towards God; it is a conversation between God and the intellect.'

Fox and the Quakers

1624 Fenny Drayton, Leicester — London 1691

Directly inspired by inner light

The Quakers form the Society of Friends, a popular movement without clergy, ritual or sacrament. They are well known for their religious tolerance and charitable works.

Born Anglican, George Fox was religious from childhood but being too poor to study theology, he was employed looking after sheep and at 19 he decided to take to the road in search of personal spiritual truth. He seems to have been guided by the works of Böhme and in 1646 a sudden revelation transformed him into an impassioned preacher, who burned with inner light. He accused both the Puritans and the Anglicans of holding back the advance of Christianity and was arrested 36 times in the 40 years of his mission, spending a total of 6 years in prison. This did not prevent him from travelling throughout England, Scotland, Ireland, North America, and Holland, and making converts. The converts formed the Society of Friends, nicknamed *Quakers* after the way in which they behaved at their meetings where each individual showed his inner illumination by shudders and cries of enthusiasm, and impromptu speeches.

From 1650 to 1689 more than 3000 of Fox's disciples were imprisoned, some being tortured and others dying in prison. Nevertheless, by the time of Fox's death,

there were still 50 000 'Friends'. Many of them emigrated to North America, where the Quaker William Penn (1644–1718) founded Pennsylvania in 1682, with its capital Philadelphia, the city of 'fraternal love'. He gave the new state a remarkable constitution which was the inspiration for the constitution of the United States. Today, there are nearly 200 000 Quakers of which 108 000 live in the United States and only 18 000 in great Britain.

The Quakers

The Quakers reject all dogma, creed, sacrament, and hierarchy. They believe firmly that within each individual is a 'seed' or a 'divine light' which must be uncovered through meditation. The same Spirit which inspired the Bible is at the disposal of all those who know how to hear it. Supreme authority in both administrative and religious matters is associated with the 'meetings' where the spirit is present; decisions must be unanimous. The Quakers, like all the followers of radical reform questioned the existing social and religious order, which in part explains the persecution they had to suffer. But they have always distinguished themselves through their humanitarian efforts. They fought the institution of slavery, helped the victims of the two world wars, and today campaign for third world countries, human rights, and the position of women.

> **'Create your own salvation** in fear and trembling.' *(maxim attributed to Fox)*

59

Francis of Assisi

1182 Assisi — Portiuncula 1226

'Poverello'

Today Francis of Assisi is adored worldwide for his simplicity, joy, and deep love of nature.

Son of Pietro di Bernardone, a rich cloth merchant, and of Pica, a Provençal, Francis lived in luxury until he was taken prisoner after participating in an attack on Perousa. This experience, followed by a long illness brought about his conversion. Impetuous and enthusiastic by nature, Francis, on leaving the crucifix of the Church of Saint Damian admonished 'Francis, go and repair my home which is falling into disrepair'. The future saint took the words literally and began to repair the church. The structural repairs depleted the family coffers, and his father had him thrown in prison. Francis promptly turned his back on his inheritance and even gave away his clothing, then went to look after the lepers at Gubbio. He returned to Assisi and lived as a hermit, begging with the poor.

The Friars Minor

On 24 February 1209, in the little church of Portiuncula his new mission was revealed to him: he was to preach the word of Jesus. He was soon joined by several companions whom he called 'Friars Minor', the 'smallest', the 'humblest' of all. It was for them that he compiled the now lost *Rule* which was based on the Gospels and was approved by Innocent III in 1210. The little community of laymen and itinerant clerics and beggars left to preach a message of peace, penitence, and the Eucharist in

central Italy. It increased in size thanks to the foundation of the Poor Clares by Saint Clare in 1212.

The 'brotherhood' began to spread all over Italy and even beyond the Alps. During the absence of its founder member (Francis had gone to bring the good news to the Saracens) the order expanded at such an uncontrollable rate that it entered a period of grave crisis, further exacerbated by the policy of absolute poverty imposed on the order by Francis. On his return in 1220, Francis had to submit himself to the will of Pope Honorus III who accorded him a year's trial period at the end of which he was to hand a detailed report on the Rule of the movement. Francis handed over the running of the community to a vicar and devoted himself to his task, compiling two different texts in 1221 and 1223. The second *Rule*, approved by the Pope, is still in use today. Towards 1221 Francis created the tertiary order of Penitants for laypersons of both sexes which caught on very quickly and played an important moral and social role.

Ill and tormented, Francis wanted only to devote himself to contemplation, and withdrew into solitude. On 14 September 1224 he received on his body the marks of the crucifixion which he was to keep until his death in 1226. Two years later Gregory IX had him canonized and laid the first stone of the basilica to which Francis's remains were transferred.

His works

Apart from his two *Rules*, we have Francis's *Testament*, a short account of his nostalgia for the bygone days at the start of the order of Friars Minor, some short Latin poems, and the *Canticle of the Sun* a celebration of God in all His creations. But it is above all the *Little Flowers* (edited at the start of the 14th century), a collection of the Saint's

'Lord make me an instrument of Thy peace.'

achievements and miracles that made him very popular.

The theory

Francis's teaching can be resumed completely in the love and imitation of Christ. For him, the Gospels were messages to be obeyed. The Franciscan way of life was based on these precepts and is ideally illustrated by the life of Saint Francis himself whose union with Christ was both intimate and fervent.

Each subsequent century has served to intensify the love felt for this gentle, humble and charitable Saint. In his lifetime, Francis carried with him an aura of almost other worldly peace and joy which he communicated to others, and this along with the principle of poverty, was to unmistakably shape his order.

The Franciscans

Even before the death of Saint Francis, his ideal was compromised. Francis himself felt some bitterness about this: the golden age of the order which had lasted from 1209 to 1217 was already over. Although the order was incessantly requested to open new establishments from Scandinavia to Syria and from Portugal to Poland, this success brought with it certain dangers. The papacy recognized in the dynamic new order a potent instrument of general reform. In 1230 a Papal bull attacked the principle of absolute poverty. In addition, the order which had started off with such simple aims, now numbered many intellectuals and philosophers in its ranks. Under the governorship of Bonaventure the influence of these men became overwhelming.

The first companions of 'Povorello' and their disciples were saddened to see the order dying. In fact it was soon to split into two factions: the Celestines who served the rule strictly while the others admitted a more relaxed form of the original rule; and the spirituals who were accused first of insubordination and then heresy. In 1517 after 150 years of controversy and dispute, Leo X separated the 'Observants' (of the rule) from the 'Conventuals', who were less strict as far as poverty was concerned. It was still believed that in one way or another, Francis's original ideals were being betrayed. This led to the strictest of the Observants forming a further group, the Recollects, and a new order, the Capucines. Despite their internal differences, the Franciscans have played a fundamental role in spiritual life throughout Europe.

The Rule
'May the brothers not have any possessions . . . Therein lies the excellence of very high poverty . . . Attach yourselves to it totally, beloved brothers, and in the name of Jesus Christ, never desire to own anything else under the sun.'
(Rule 4)

Canticle of the Sun
'Praise be to you my Lord, with all your creatures, especially the Sun my brother who gives us day, and You illuminate us through him. And he is beautiful and shines with great splendour; he brings us the meaning of You, Most High.'

Francis of Sales

1567 Chateau of Sales, near Thorens — Lyon 1622

The spiritual director of society

Francis was a model pastor and popular preacher. His works deeply influenced the whole of the 17th century. His theories and teachings are perhaps not out of date today.

As the son of a well-to-do noble family from Sarvoie, Francis was intended to become councellor at the Chambéry senate. To this end he studied law at Padua returning as a doctor of law. But his urgent vocation compelled him to go against his father's wishes and he was ordained priest in 1593. The Bishop of Geneva who was also his uncle, and who had ordained him, then sent him as a missionary among the Calvinists, where he obtained unhoped for conversions. He was sent to Paris and preached to the court. Henry V wanted him to stay but he went home to Savoie, becoming bishop in 1602. He devoted himself to his diocese distributing his belongings amongst the poor and also acting as spiritual guide to believers in the outside world. It was also at this time that he began to compile the works which brought him such a wide audience. He gave one of his Penitents, Madame de Chantal the task of founding the Order of the Visitation in 1610 to whi even the infirm were admitted. By the ti of his return to Paris in 1619 he was alrea considered to be one of the greatest ligious leaders of his time. There he ma the acquaintance of Vincent de Paul a was also closely linked with Louis XI whose Port Royal reforms he encourag He was canonized in 1665 and in 1877 v proclaimed a doctor to the Church, the fi and only French speaker to be awarded t honour.

His works

His *Introduction to Devotional Life* (16 which was extremely popular is made u letters of guidance addressed to one of penitents and is completed by the *Trac the Love of God*.

The theory

Francis of Sales has often been reproac for his charm and leniency which were o expressions of his profoundly charita nature. As Bishop of Geneva, Fran aimed to adapt himself to his congregat and to show respect for them in order convince them. As a spiritual director wanted to be a discreet instrument of div grace revealing to each individual's p sonal need for God. When preaching to l persons, he once separated daily life fr love for God. After Calvin and bef Jansenism, Francis of Sales left a lasti impression on the 17th century, but teachings cannot be consigned entirely the past. Through his passionate love nature and his knowledge of the hum soul's needs and limitations he can still considered as a teacher today.

Love and obedience

'Everything must be done by love and not by force. You must love obedience (to God) more than you fear disobedience.'

Gandhi, Mohandas Karamchand
1867 Porbandar — Delhi 1948

The Mahatma ('Great Soul')

Gandhi was not only India's liberator but also one of the great 20th century religious leaders whose influence is felt over the whole world.

Born into the merchant caste, Gandhi was married at the age of 12 and had four children. In 1888 he left for England where he became a lawyer (1891). From 1893 to 1914 he lived in South Africa where, with the large Indian immigrant community in mind, he began to formulate the ideals that were to shape his life. His ideas were based on love for India, and her political and moral regeneration in accordance with *satyagraha* (holding firmly to the truth leading to a refusal to conform to unjust laws) and *ahimsa* (non-violence). Non-violence, which is the refusal to fight evil with evil, brings about passive resistance to every kind of injustice. The principle of non-violence was to attract many converts throughout the world. In India these principles led to Ghandi becoming the leader of the Nationalist party in 1916. He was categorically opposed to British imperialism, advocating 'civil disobedience' which was related to non-violence and obliged the British to negotiate. Although the struggle he had undertaken resulted in the independence of India, Gandhi's last years were darkened by the divisions between Hindu and Muslim, and the ensuing massacres. He was assassinated by Hindu fundamentalists.

His prowess as a national leader and social reformer has sometimes diverted our attention from the fact that he was also a great spiritual leader. Behind Gandhi's actions was the quest for moral progress which remains the overriding message of the Mahatma's teachings.

His works

Besides the innumerable articles and official and popular speeches, there are two major works: *Experience of Truth* (1931), a spiritual autobiography, and *Letters to the Ashram*, written in 1930 during his imprisonment. These letters are addressed to the disciples who lived in the commune, and expound the fundamental points of the Mahatma's ascetic way of life.

The theory

The search for truth is actually the search for God himself ('God is truth' and reciprocally 'Truth is God'), and for love and inner life. It can only be successful through strictly observing vows of *brahmacharya* (purity and self-control), non-denigration, and non-possession. Gandhi did not simply advocate his way of life but set an example by purifying his own life, renouncing material goods and dedicating himself to the serivce of others, and like Gandhi, each individual was held responsible for his own needs, which were to be kept to a bare minimum.

'**Ahimsa** is our supreme duty.'

Gandhi's hope
'I am waiting for complete purification of men's hearts.'

Ghazali, al-

1058 Tus, north-east Persia — Tus IIII

Nicknamed the 'Proof of Islam'

This great theologian ushered in a new era in Islamic spirituality, through the synthesis of orthodoxy and mysticism.

Abu Hamid Muhammad al-Ghazali studied at Nishapur under the great Sunni (see **Islam**) theologian and lawyer Djuwayni. In 1091 al-Ghazali was appointed rector of the Nisamiyyahh College at Baghdad, where his reputation as a great teacher grew. He left the capital suddenly going on a long pilgrimage to Islami holy places, and then spent ten years in retreat before coming back to teach at Nishapur. He left teaching finally in order to live in his home town surrounded by Sunni disciples.

Al-Ghazali gave the reasons for his withdrawal in *The Deliverer from Error*. It would seem to have been caused by a crisis of faith and conscience concerning all that he had learned and taught in his life. He felt that the only way to resolve this crisis was through inner contemplation, through the 'life of the heart' to which he dedicated the rest of his life. While safeguarding the purity of his faith al-Ghazali managed to incorporate elements of Greek philosophy and Christian asceticism into Islam. Traces of his influence can be found in the theories of Western thinkers, in particular Thomas Aquinas.

His works

Apart from *Al Munqidh mia ala-dalal* (The Deliverer from Error) his spiritual auto-biography, which has been compared both to Saint Augustine's *Confessions* and Descartes's *Discours de la méthode*, al-Ghazali wrote a substantial amount of tracts on Muslim law, philosophy and theology. The most famous of these are the *Tahafut al-falasifa* (Destruction of the Philosophers) in which he attacks the Islamic Neoplatonists, Avicenna and al-Farabi; and the *Ihya'ulum al-din* (Revival of the Religious Sciences) in which the author bitterly criticizes dogmatic theology which he sees as ruined by controversy. He goes on to outline the conditions for a true religious science which is founded on obligatory purification and is capable of drawing one closer to God.

The theory

Having reached a state of total scepticism al-Ghazali looks back over centuries of Islamic thought. He condemns the bad habits of theologians and philosophers past and present, whom he believed to have struck at the unity of Islam, and laid the foundations of a religious revival which he believed would be acceptable to all the branches of his religion. This reform assumed the re-admission of the mystical Sufi sect (to which al-Ghazali belonged) into the bosom of Orthodoxy. The reform gave a new direction to Muslim thought and had a definite influence on Sohrawardi and probably Ibn'Arabi.

Al-Ghazali's conversion

'At last, feeling the weakness and exhaustion of my soul, I took refuge in God, like someone at the end of his courage and strength. He who answers the unfortunate who call on Him, answered me. He made it easy for my heart to sacrifice honour, riches and family.'

Gnosis and Gnosticism

The revelation of divine mysteries

As mystical knowledge, the gnosis claims to provide certain salvation to initiates.

By radically transforming the human soul, the gnosis (from the Greek meaning 'knowledge') as absolute knowledge is capable of allowing the soul access to Eternal Light even on earth. Most religions have some form of gnosis including modern day freemasonry and occultism though in a less extreme sense. Historically, the gnosis may be linked to the origins of Christianity: its presence can be detected as far back as the Jewish mystical speculations which were to give both to the Cabala, and also in the Essene sect. Islam too has its gnosis, represented by Shi'ite and Sufi thought. In Judaism and Islam as well as in Christianity these doctrines were linked to profound mysticism and as such have aroused the mistrust of the more orthodox trends.

Good and Evil

Regardless of the religion to which it is linked, the gnosis corresponds to a certain state of mind or even psychological temperament. The gnostic sees the soul as imprisoned in the body and the universe as dominated by two opposing forces. As spirit is opposed to matter, so is light to dark, Good to Evil, life to death and knowledge to ignorance. Ignorance is the ultimate cause of human suffering.

Gnosticism

The universal phenomenon of the gnosis must be distinguished from the various gnostic groups, a collection of essentially Christian sects which were considered as heretical perversions by the early Church. Dating from the Epistles of Saint Paul, allusions are made to these sects; they were particularly popular from the 1st century to the 4th century, but as their written works were systematically destroyed, it is only through the violent attacks made on them in the writing of the Church Fathers that we have been able to build a picture of the typical sect. New light was shed on the teachings by the discovery of an important cache of Gnostic texts at Nag Hammadi in 1945. The written fragments discovered contained numerous Gospels and apocryphal texts, particularly the *Gospel of Thomas* a precious compilation of Jesus's words, indisputably Judaeo-Christian in origin, and the *Acts of Thomas* where the great myth of the redemption appears in poetic form.

It is thought that the earliest Gnostic leader was Simon Magus, a Samarian who appears in the Acts of the Apostles. His disciple, Menandrus, seems to have been the master of Saturninus, who taught at Antioch at the start of the 2nd century and also of Basilidus, who at Alexandria taught an extremely complex version of the redemption characteristic of Gnosticism. According to Basilidus there were three superimposed worlds. In the first the supreme divinity, or one God resides, the God who defies description: 'He was nothing neither matter, nor essence, nor non-essence, nor simple nor complex nor intelligible nor unintelligible nor sensitive, nor insensitive. . . .' (Basilidus) The same God who is 'named only by silence, worshipped

> **Gospel of Thomas**
> 'When you can make two into one,
> and the outside like the inside
> and what is above like what is below,
> male and female becoming one . . .
> then you may enter the Kingdom.'

only by silence'. Nevertheless, all the seeds of the future are in God.

The second world, or intermediate world is composed of 365 heavens each ruled over by an '*archon*' and inhabited by '*eons*'. The third world is the one in which we live. The archon of the first heaven in the second world who created the subluminary world is none other than Yahweh. Several saviour-sons undertake to redeem the whole world, the last of these, our world's Saviour, is incarnated in Jesus.

At the same time as Basilidus, in Egypt Carpocrates pushed the certainty of re-incarnation to its most extreme conclusion which is the need to carry out the most immoral acts necessary to every soul before being saved. Valentinus, who was both a remarkable metaphysicist and an accomplished Christian moralist, was born in Upper Egypt, where he not only studied the works of the Neoplatonists but also those of the ancient Egyptian religions. He went on to found a school at Rome which affected the whole empire. Marcion, who also came from Rome and was excommunicated there in 144, put forward a version of the New Testament from which every trace of Judaism has been erased.

Gospel of Truth

(probably written by Valentinus)

'What does he want (the gnostic) to think? This: I am like the dark shadows and the ghosts of the night.

When the light comes, he understands that the fears which beset him were nothing. This is how they were ignorant about the Father, He whom they did not see . . . being filled with troubling dreams. But they threw ignorance and sleep away from them.'

Amongst the other sects we know of the Ophites who worshipped the Serpent of Genesis and were opposed to the wicked demiurge. Although Gnosticism effectively reached its apogee in the 2nd century, it nevertheless continued to spread during the 3rd century; thus Mani was a member of a Babylonian Gnostic sect, before going on to found Manichaeism.

The Christian Empire pushed all Gnostic schools beyond its frontiers but their popularity was already on the wane and, at least in the West, they soon disappeared.

The theory

Theories may differ from leader to leader and from school to school, but they share a common principle, believing that the material world can only be the work of an evil god, the demiurge, who is Yahweh, the God of the Old Testament. He stands between the true transcendent God and the souls He created, which the demiurge has had encased in flesh.

Only the 'pneumatics' in whom the *pneuma* ('breath of God' or 'spirit') is revitalized can free themselves because they are aware of their condition. It was specifically for them that God sent Christ the Saviour to reveal the gnosis and guide them back to the source of Light.

Gnosticism was finally rejected by both pagan philosophers and the Church. A major contributing factor for this rejection was the immoral excesses to which it sometimes led, but there was also a great deal of irresponsible behaviour as the demiurge alone was seen as capable of evil. And of course, the Church could not possibly admit the existence of two distinct divinities, one of which, the evil one, was strongly identified with Yahweh.

Gospels

They brought the 'Good News'

The Gospels are the news of the redemption through Jesus, Son of God, who had come to deliver the human race from sin. Christian faith and teaching depend principally upon them.

Gospel is the popular translation of the Latin *evangelium* which is a virtual transliteration of the Greek *euangelion* meaning the 'good news' spread by the Apostles. Although the order of the Gospels is given as Matthew, Mark, Luke, and John in the New Testament, modern historians tend to consider Mark, who was probably the 'John known as Mark' of Acts, to be chronologically first. The Gospel of Mark was written in Greek in Rome towards AD 70 and addressed to non-Palestinian Christians. Matthew, a Jewish convert who lived in a mixed community of Christians and Jews, used it as a model when he wrote his Gospel (AD 80–90), as did Luke who was previously pagan and a disciple of Paul. Both Matthew and Luke however, drew on other sources. These three Gospels have so many points in common that they have become known as 'synoptic' because they can be read as a coherent whole. The last Gospel was written by John in his old age, between AD 96 and 98. Forty to seventy years would have elapsed between AD 30, the probable year of the crucifixion and the writing of the Gospels. This gap is explained by the fact that Christ's teachings were primarily transmitted by word of mouth: the need to record Jesus's message would only become pressing when the last of his close witnesses could no longer

spread the Word. It is obvious that the text of the Gospels gives us a version of the events as perceived by the first Christian community as they are above all an expression of firm faith in Christ.

Because of this, normal historic perspective is inversed, for it is only hindsight, the certainty of salvation to which the Resurrection and the Ascension gave birth, which permits the fundamental meaning of past events to be revealed. Understandably, the Apostles remained blind to the true nature of the events they were experiencing as the first Gospel, the Gospel according to Mark, underlines.

The Synoptic problem

Whatever the similarities between the three Synoptic Gospels, each retains its own character which is a reflection of the personality of its author and also of the public for which it was intended. Thus only Mark, who wrote at Rome probably for Peter's followers uses the formula 'Evangelist of God's Kingdom' and states in his first few words that Jesus is the Son of God. Consequently his narrative deals mainly with the public career of Jesus. Jesus does not immediately reveal his true identity. It is only in answer to the question 'And you, who do you think I am?' when Peter replies 'Christ of God' that Jesus admits who he is. A short time afterwards, he shows himself transfigured to his disciples, swearing them to silence for 'the Son of Man must be put to death and rise again on the third day.'

Matthew wrote his gospel in Aramaic while he was in Jerusalem, and it was later translated into Greek. He completes his predecessor's narrative, giving an account of the traditions concerning the Messiah's childhood and early public career. In his writing, Matthew principally targeted the Jews, hence his desire to show that Jesus had fulfilled the Messianic prophecies and that he had not come to abolish the Law, but to perfect it in the light of the coming of God's kingdom.

On the other hand, Luke, writing for converted pagans, and more literary than both Mark and Matthew has a more historical flair. Studied objectively, he is also a theologian attempting to define God's all-embracing plan. For Luke, the Gospel's universal nature is already a fait accompli; poverty has triumphed over affluence, humility over pride and the doctrine of the Salvation appears bathed in the miraculous light of the Holy Spirit.

The fourth Gospel

The Gospel according to John is so different in tone that some have seen it as a later meditation on the tradition recorded by the other three. This theory has since been disproved although, very few critics acknowledge that the fourth Gospel could have been completely the work of 'he whom Jesus loved'. Undoubtedly certain memories of the son of Zebedee who, with Mary and the holy women, witnessed the Crucifixion are set down, but they seem to have been used as only a starting point for the more elaborate version of the Gospel that exists today. Our version is thought to have been compiled by theologians and John's preaching disciples who represent the 'Hellenic branch of Palestinian Judaism' estab-lished at Ephesia or Antioch. This would explain the philosophical Greek phrases in the Prologue: 'In the beginning was the Word . . .'

The Apocrypha

Nevertheless, it cannot be denied that the four gospels are complementary. It is precisely through their diverse points of view and interpretations of the period that a fuller picture of Jesus and the essence of his teachings come to light. Outwith the Gospel Canon, we have other documents, known as the Apocrypha. Some were written before or at roughly the same time as the Gospel Canon (for example, the Gospels of Peter, Hebrews, Egyptians, and the Ebionites) and are now considered as archaic texts produced by the Judaeo-Christian milieu. This also applies to the Gospel of Thomas which is part of the large Gnostic library discovered at Nag Hamma-di in Upper Egypt in 1945, which dates from the 2nd century. A simple collection of 114 *logia* (words) of Jesus, this text provides evidence for a tradition which predates the Gospel Canon. When the research on these texts is finally completed, the findings will give us a fuller understanding of the early Judaeo-Christian community and by extension the origins of Christianity and even Jesus's own teachings.

Gregory of Nazianzus

c. 329 Anzianzus, Cappadocia — Anzianzus c. 390

A theologian of inner life

Although he was involved in the controversies of his day, Gregory of Nazianzus was above all a mystic, whose depth and sensitivity are still perceptible today.

Together with the brothers, Basil of Caesarea and Gregory of Nyssa, Gregory of Nazianzus made up the famous triad of 'Cappadocians' who instituted the theological tradition of the Eastern Church. While he was still very young, Gregory left on a voyage that took him to Caesarea, Alexandria, and Athens, where he met up with Basil and stayed for several years. Gregory was baptized at Nazianzus in 367. He would have liked to have withdrawn from the world but his father, the Bishop of Nazianzus, convinced him to take only orders. A short time later he was ordained bishop by Basil, and in 374 he succeeded his father. But he had accepted his bishopric against his will and withdrew to Selucia of Isauria where he wrote his major works. He was recalled to Constantinople in 379 to fight the Aryan heresy. The following year he was appointed bishop of the capital, but when his candidature was contested, he seized the opportunity to retire to a small town near Nazianzus, far from political and religious intrigue.

His works

Gregory of Nazianzus is the author of numerous *Theological Orations* including the famous orations 27 to 31 on the Trinity and the Holy Spirit which he delivered at Constantinople in 380. He also wrote *Homilies* and *Letters*, but also *Poems* (more than 600 lines) which are mainly autobiographical and as sincere as they are moving. The longest and best known of these, *On My Life* contains echoes of his suffering, his outrage, and his disillusionment.

The theory

Gregory of Nazianzus is distinguished from the other two Cappadocians by his more introverted personality. He was more subtle and sensitive than the other two which made him favour meditation over action. His hesitant style and need to justify himself, and his love of nature, which he thought was the visible image of the invisible, lend his works an almost romantic tone, rendering them extremely modern. In his definite affirmation of the divinity of the Holy Spirit and the absolute equality of the three Persons, it was Gregory more than Basil who helped elaborate the dogma of the Trinity, but Gregory is better known and better loved for the intensity of his mystical experience. In his eyes, only the intimacy of the purified soul with the Divine Light counts.

Deification

'Let us become gods because of Christ, as he became man because of us.'

'Be the tiny reflection of a great light.'

'Nothing appears more enviable to me than the secret communion of the soul with itself and with God.'

Gregory of Nyssa

c. 335 Caesarea, Cappadocia — Nyssa c. 394

Most famous for his theology on redemption

Gregory carried on the tradition of Greek philosophy, but at the same time was highly original. Medieval mystics often found inspiration in his ideas which even today have their followers.

Gregory was the brother of Basil of Caesarea and of Macrina who was both mother and spiritual teacher to him. Despite family pressure, he preferred marriage and the career of professional rhetorician to entering the Church. At the behest of Basil, he was later to adopt an austere way of life and was appointed Bishop of Nyssa in Cappadocia in 372. He channelled his energies into the fight against the Aryan heresy and subsequently was a victim of their slanderous accusations. He was deposed and sent into exile in 376. However, in 378 he re-entered his diocese and was received with great public acclaim. By 385 Gregory was a widower and thus able to fulfil his original desire in becoming a monk. After the death of Basil, who had been a hard taskmaster, Gregory began to formulate and promulgate the theory of salvation that was to leave a lasting impression on the Eastern Church.

His works

His works include several dogmatic tracts and *Letters*. Two further works testify to the depth of his thinking, for not only had he been brought up on the Bible, but he was also versant in the theories of Plato, Plotinus, and Origen: *On the Making of Man* (379) and *Dialogue on the Soul and the Resurrection* (380), which Gregory presents as a moving conversation between himself and his dying sister, Macrina.

The theory

With his powerful, incisive intellect, Gregory of Nyssa was able to synthesize later Greek philosophy with Christian thought. Created in God's image, like Him, man is definable and incomprehensible, but at the same time he must progress spiritually. This spiritual progression ends with the radical transformation of the soul, which in turn leads to a more complete participation in divine life. Man was separated from God by original sin, and can only be reunited with Him through the mediation of Christ. This spiritual path is in three stages, whose parallels can be found in philosophy: the ethical, which aims to purify; the physical, which teaches the soul to struggle with and overcome the sensory world; and the metaphysical, which leads to divine transcendence. This affirmation of man's capacity for spiritual renewal constitutes Gregory's major contribution to Christian theology.

Divine Shadows

'True knowledge of him whom (the Spirit) seeks and this true vision, consists in recognizing that He is invisible, categorically separated from everything by this innate incomprehensibility, as if by a dark shadow.'

Gregory the Great

c. 535 Rome — Rome 604

A great teacher of contemplative life

A monk who became Pope Gregory I, Gregory the Great, was not only the founder of the medieval Church but also a role model for the clergy and monks for many centuries afterwards.

Gregory was born into a family of Roman senators and for several years he occupied the public position of prefect of the city of Rome. However, he was moved by the miserable plight of the populace and attracted to a more spiritual life; to this end he established a monastery in his own home and founded six others in his Sicilian estates. In 579 Gregory, now a deacon was sent to Constantinople as a papal representative. On his return to Rome, he picked up the thread of his monastic life, but on the death of Pope Pelagius he was elected to the papacy on 3 September 590 by a unanimous decision of both clergy and people. Although he tried to avoid this burden and was always somewhat nostalgic for the suffering of humanity, as Pope in a troubled and unsettled era, he took his duties and responsibilities very seriously. He deserved his title of 'Great' not only for his reorgani-

zation of the Church on the administrative level, but also on the liturgical level, although it is not certain that he was the instigator of the chant that bears his name. His spiritual works left their mark on the Middle Ages.

His works

His works consist of 854 extant *Letters* which enable us to learn about Gregory's intense activity; *Homilies* on the Gospels and Ezekiel, which are 'models of pastoral eloquence and liturgical preaching'; the *Liber regulae pastoralis* (Pastoral Rule) on the training of priests and the 'governing of souls'; the *Dialogues* on the lives and miracles of the Italian saints with particular emphasis on Benedict of Nursia (the fourth book of *Dialogues*, was an inspiration to many poets, including Dante); and finally the *Moralia on Job*, a magnificent masterpiece and rich source book for subsequent theologians.

The theory

Gregory was above all a comtemplative leader of spiritual and mystical life who was anxious to provide his followers with a sound theological grounding and a workable rule. He recommended both a life of chanting and meditation, and one of preaching and chantable works. He also wanted to bring the works of the Greek Fathers, Clement of Alexandria and Gregory of Nyssa, as well as Augustine, within reach of an ignorant clergy. His own works, which had general appeal, spread quickly throughout Europe with lasting effect.

> 'It was less a question of his illuminating the Church, than of his building it.' (P. Battifol)

Gregory Palamas

1296 Constaninople — Salonica 1359

The 'Saviour of the Church'

Gregory Palamas, guardian of the theology of the 'Light', expressed the philosophy of orthodox mystical spirituality clearly.

Gregory was born to a noble family which had emigrated from Anatolia before the Turkish invasions. He was brought up in the imperial court of Andronicus II, the most pious of the Byzantine emperors, where he studied ancient philosophy. When he decided in 1316 to become a monk, he persuaded the rest of his family to join him, thus we find him accompanied by his two brothers at Mount Athos, where he spent 20 years. At first he lived in monasteries, even becoming director of one establishment, but he gradually spent more and more time in various hermitages.

Gregory defended the Hesychasts and his fame is largely due to the bitter arguments he had with Barlaam, a Calabrian monk who was staunchly opposed to the movement and of the opinion that this practice bordered on the heretical. Barlaam and his followers were condemned by three Councils in 1341 and 1351. When he

was appointed Archbishop of Thessalonica in 1347, Palamas ministered to his flock with such pastoral zeal that they soon learned to love and respect him. In 1353, on a sea voyage to Constantinople, he was captured by the Turks and held prisoner for one year during which time he was able to talk with Muslims and express his wish for a better mutual understanding. Gregory Palamas was canonized in 1368 and remains one of the most important figures in the Orthodox Church.

His works

Among Palamas's theological writings, two works are particularly well known today: *Triads in defence of the Holy Hesychasts*, a theological synthesis of monastic spirituality, and *Theophanes*, a spiritual work devoted to the visible light of God as manifested during the Transfiguration, which he compiled towards the end of his life.

The theory

In explaining the experience of the Hesychasts, Palamas shows that this experience provokes a genuine change in the Spirit, which when assimilated with the simultaneously human and divine intelligence of Christ, manages to group divine plenitude through participation in it. In fact, if God is essentially unknowable, he reveals himself to us in love as energy through the Son and in the Holy Spirit. This trinity of energy is both one and many; in Creation, God divides himself without being multiplied. Man is defied by identifying himself with Christ and is elevated 'to the eternal summits' where he begins to 'contemplate supra-cosmic reality, without separating himself or being separated from matter . . . which leads to God, and through Him, the whole of Creation'.

The body and the Spirit

'In Spiritual men, the uncreated grace of the Spirit, transmitted to the human body via the soul, also gives knowledge of godly things to the body.'

'God transcending all things, being incomprehensible and undecipherable, consents to become participatory and invisibly visible.'

Guénon, René

1886 Blois — Cairo 1951

He restored the metaphysical 'Tradition'

According to Guénon, the West set itself upon the present path of destruction specifically because it had turned its back on Tradition.

Guénon went to Paris in 1904 in order to study mathematics. In his youth he was attracted to many occultist circles as well as the Freemasons, each of which purported to be the sole holder of esoteric 'knowledge'. He was later to disassociate himself from these groups and in 1909 found the magazine *La Gnose* (Gnosis) in which he published his first article. As his disillusionment with the West grew, so he became more aware of Eastern doctrines, turning first to India and then in 1912, the year of his marriage, he adopted Islam joining the Tariqa Shadhiliya. He devoted himself to the writing of his books and numerous articles in which he attacked not only the prevalent materialism of his era, but also all the pseudo-spiritualist movements. When his wife died in 1930 he left for Egypt where he lived as a Muslim under the name of Abd el Wahed Yahia and married the daughter of a sheikh who bore him three children. Guénon continued writing until his death.

His works

Some 20 volumes are known, several of which were only published after his death. The majority of them draw together the active elements of lost Tradition: *Introduction générale à l'étude des doctrines hindoues* (1921) (General Introduction to the Study of Hindu Doctrines), *Orient et Occident* (1924) (East and West), *L'Homme et son devenir selon le Vedanta* (1925) (Man and his Destiny according to the Vedanta). *Le Symbolisme de la Croix* (1931) (The Symbolism of the Cross), *La Crise du monde moderne* (1927) (Crisis of the Modern World), then, as a dramatic warning *Le règne de la quantité et les signes des temps* (1945) (The Reign of Quantity and the Signs of the Times). From 1946 onwards, articles which had originally been published in a number of different reviews were published as compilations. These articles complement his books and clarify certain parts of his theory.

The theory

Guénon made it his mission in life to transmit the one true Tradition which is common to all doctrines. In assembling the elements of Tradition he unfailingly rejects all those parts that he considered to be dangerous deviations, for example, those that he analyses in *La Théosophisme* (1921) and *L'Erreur Spirite* (1923) (The Spiritualistic Error). Starting from such a pure metaphysical standpoint, he was able to efficiently and virulently denounce contemporary society which had turned its back on spirituality to plunge into materialism. Guénon gained a vast following largely due to the irresistible severity and prophetic nature of his works.

The men-machines

'Not only have they (men) limited their intellectual aims . . . to the invention and construction of machines, but they have ended up becoming machines themselves.'

Gurdjieff, Georgei Ivanovich

1877 Alexandropol, Leninakan — Paris 1949

A mysterious teacher

An enigmatic figure in whose life myth intertwined with fact, and whose personality and teachings have never ceased to intrigue.

Born in Russian Armenia of a Greek father, Gurdjieff studied for both the priesthood and medicine. Having achieved brilliant results in Greek and in Russian schools, he went on long journeys in central Asia with a small group of likeminded 'seekers of truth'. Their travels were to be decisive in the formation of his theories. On his return to Russia, he met the Russian physicist and philosopher P. D. Ouspensky (1878–1947) who was later to write a book on the education Gurdjieff gave him. Gurdjieff had founded his 'Institute for the Harmonious Development of Man' to the north of the Caucasus but the 1917 Revolution forced him to flee to Istanbul then to France. In 1922 at the Prieuré d'Avon near Fontainebleau, he was able to establish the Institute on a firmer basis, his fame bringing him disciples from the French and the English intelligentsia. In 1933 he moved to Paris where he had numerous pupils.

His works

Three of Gurdjieff's works were published after his death: *Beelzebub's Tales to His Grandson* which was intended to 'clear away the conceptual schemes and beliefs rooted in one's psyche'; *Meetings with Remarkable Men*, a collection of more or less autobiographical reminiscences for the re-education 'of man by himself'; *Life is Only Real When I Am* which was aimed at encouraging 'the blossoming of a true representation of the real world'.

The theory

Gurdjieff's works tell us very little about the radical re-education he put into practice. For a more complete outlook we must refer to Ouspensky's *In Search of the Miraculous* (1945). According to Gurdjieff, modern people live in a sleep-like state, a hypnotized trance, like a machine activated by movements foreign to it.

It is therefore necessary to show the disciple his weaknesses but also his strengths through certain exercises which must be carried out daily and are exhausting and sometimes dangerous. This is the price he must pay to achieve the harmonious development of his faculties. From the little that is known about this secret teaching, it would appear that it took the form of traditional practices adapted to modern people.

The true man

'Only the one who knew how to get the necessary information to keep the lamb and the wolf safe in his charge is worthy of being called a man and can count on something being prepared for him above (in Heaven).'

Hadith

The spoken word of the Prophet

As records of what Muhammad said, the Hadith completes the Koran and constitutes the sunnah, the Islamic 'rules of conduct'.

The Hadith or 'tradition' which report Muhammad's words and deeds were collected during his lifetime by his first disciples. There are reportedly, hundreds of thousands of Hadith which were transmitted orally for many years before being written down and classified firstly according to who reported them, then according to subject matter. The most reliable six collections date from the second half of the 9th century (more than 200 years after the Prophet's death). The most famous of these were the work of Abu Abdullah Muhammad al-Bukhari and are known as the *Sahih* ('Solid' or 'Authentic'). Some passages are even recited in the mosque.

Born on 19 July 810 in Bukhara (Turkestan) although of Persian extraction, al-

Bukhari first went to Mecca on a pilgrimage at aged 16 then stayed on to compile the Hadith. He carried out his research all over the Muslim Empire from Egypt to Iraq before returning to his native city after an absence of 16 years. Al-Bukhari died at Khateng near Samarkand on 31 August 870. He gathered together 7275 Hadith—about 2700 not counting repetitions—grouped into 97 chapters. Each Hadith is made up of two parts, the actual words of the Prophet or the anecdotes centred around him, and the list of names of those who transmitted it orally before it was put down on paper, intended to guarantee its authenticity.

The content of the Hadith

Totally diverse subjects are dealt with in the Hadith: the many facets of Muhammad's personality; theological and moral teaching which completes that given in the Koran; and also the Prophet's decisions concerning the organization of the first Muslim communities. As a whole it makes up the base of the sunnah or 'rules of conduct' which engendered a new type of society and civilization. These collections gave birth to the canon of law in the Sunni sect (see **Islam**). For all Muslims, the Hadith is very important as it is recognized that in certain cases, tradition may rescind the Koran.

Although many of the elements cannot be traced to Muhammad himself, their value is not diminished for they reflect the intensity of the disputes within Islam in the first two centuries of its existence. Their proliferation and frequent contradictions demonstrate how difficult it was to solve the problems left by the Koran.

Equality of men

'All men are as equal as the teeth of a carder's comb: there is no difference between Black and White, between Arab and non-Arab, apart from their degree of faith in God.'

Predestination

'There is not one among you whose place has not already been prepared in Hell or in Paradise.'

Hallaj, al-

c. 857 Tur, Persia — Baghdad 922

The great Sufi martyr

Sent to the gallows for having celebrated Divine Love in terms that were considered blasphemous, Hallaj remains the most adored figure in Islamic mysticism.

Abul-Mugith al-Husayn ibn Mansur ibn-Mahamma al-Baydawi, known as al-Hallaj, the 'cotton carder' either because it was his father's profession or as an allegory, 'carder of souls', was born in the south of Persia and experienced very early on the desire to devote himself to God. At 20 he became a Sufi and was married, moving to Baghdad where he lived among other Sufis. In 895 al-Hallaj went on a pilgrimage to Mecca and spent a whole year there in retreat. Believing that he had a vocation as a preacher he wandered through Persia and Khorasan before making a second pilgrimage to Mecca, this time with 400 disciples. He next set out for India, going as far as the border of Turkestan and China, seeking primarily Hindu and Turkish converts.

The death which is life
'Kill me, my trusty companions,
For in my murder lies my life;
My death, means to live, my life means to die.'

The void in the heart
'When God takes a heart, He empties it of all that is not Him.'

Back at Baghdad he began to preach with growing exhaltation which impressed the populace and shook even literary circles. He performed several miracles and went as far as to demand that this scandalous person he had become, who claimed to be joined with God, be put to death. Soon the startled Sunnis denounced him, and a legal – religious opposition party came into being, which accused al-Hallaj of blasphemy for having declared 'I am Creative Truth'. He was exposed on a pillory before being sent to prison for eight years, until the time of his second trial, at which he was sentenced to death. On 26 March 922, he was flogged, mutilated, hanged, and not cut down until the second day. His body was burned and the ashes strewn in the River Tigris.

His works

His work is contained in the *Diwan*, published by his disciples after his death. al-Hallaj's works and personality are known today mainly through the efforts of the great Islamicist, Louis Massignon.

The theory

His teachings can be summed up in one word: Love, Divine Love, burning love becoming madness, blasphemy. For al-Hallaj the only aim of spiritual life was the transsubstantial union with God – the human personality being wiped out in order to make way for the presence of God. This preaching, which overwhelmed his listeners could only arouse the indignation of the doctors of law for whom al-Hallaj, with his excesses, cut himself off from the Muslim main stream, but these very excesses and his martyrdom, were to make him a unique role model.

Hasidism

Jewish pietist and ascetical movement

Hasidism has resurfaced three times in history. It revolves around its teachers who have made a lasting impression on Jewish mysticism.

In Hebrew the *hasidim* are the 'pious men' who 'act through love'. Their continuing action at the heart of Judaism has manifested itself in no uncertain terms under diverse historical conditions.

In the 11th century BC the Hasidim or 'Assideans', mighty men who were voluntarily devoted to the Law, supported the Maccabeans in their revolution against the Hellenistic Antiochus IV Epiphanes. But as soon as victory ensured freedom of worship, they withdrew from a struggle that had become political.

In the 13th century in the Rhineland, the Hasidim 'holy men of Germany' created an ascetical and mystical movement which swiftly became popular. It was based on the *Sefer Hasidim* (Book of the Holy) which both outlines a veritable philosophy of history and serves as a guide book to inner piety, renouncing love of God and love of one's fellow compatriots. The most remarkable representative of this second wave of Hasidism was Rabbi Yehuda the Hasid. He was active round the same time as Francis of Assisi, and his movement was doubtless influenced by the renewal of Christian monachism and mysticism.

Modern Hasidism

The most famous of the Hasidic movements developed in 18th century Eastern European countries where Jews were numerous and severely persecuted. To Talmudic Judaism, which was founded on study and erudition, Israel ben Ellezer (1700–60) known as Baal Shem Tov (Master of the Good Name), opposed inner reflection, the love of God the Saviour and charity. The relationship which grew between these charismatic leaders, the 'Just' or 'miracle-working rabbis' and their disciples was such that it sapped the traditional powers and status of the orthodox rabbis who denounced Hasidism as heretical in nature. Born in Podolia in 1720, Hasidism spread throughout Poland and Russia, and is still active in the 20th century. Among the various modern representatives of the movement are Martin Buber (1878–1965) an Israeli philosopher of Austrian extraction who defined Hasidism as 'A Cabala become an ethic', and Isaac B. Singer (born 1904, Nobel Prize for Literature 1978).

There is a large Hasidic community in Jerusalem today, leading a massive movement for a return to a more Jewish way of life through observing traditional rituals.

Baal Shem Tov
'The world is full of marvels, of splendid and frightening mysteries and man places his little hand over his eyes to veil the trembling light.'

Rabbi Baruch (19th century)
'I hide, said God, but no one wants to find me.'

Hermetism

The revelation of Hermes Trismegistos

This philosophical and magical doctrine of salvation is outlined in a series of tracts which date from the first centuries of the Christian era.

The term Hermetism is often misused today. It comes from the name of Hermes Trismegistros, keeper and revealer of the supreme knowledge. He is presented as an extraordinary amalgam of the Hermes of Greek mythology, the Lord of Science and the Word, and the God Thoth; he was also scribe, magician, and an exemplary figure upon whom Egyptian priests and initiates modelled themselves. At the end of the Hellenic period, Hermes Trismegistros, that is to say 'Thrice Greatest', was seen as the instigator of an important series of works which appeared in Alexandria, where Eastern, and especially Greek, thought was represented by the Neoplatonic school. The influence of late Egyptian popular religion, astrology, and alchemy is evident in these texts which date from the 2nd and 3rd centuries BC.

The Corpus Hermeticum, compiled at an earlier date, contains 17 short tracts in Greek, which present the revelation in the form of dialogues between the God and the initiate. The principal dialogues are *Poimandres*, where the initiator is none other than the Nous, or Supreme Intellect, and

Kore Kosmou ('Virgin of the World') which the creation of the world is seen a alchemical experiment. *Asclepius*, the L version of a Greek text called *Perfect Sp* was later added to this collection. Her ism is a curious blend of popular devc and mystical philosophy; it resem Gnosticism, but is distinct from it and had a lasting effect on Western mystic The *Corpus Hermeticum* enjoyed great pe larity in the Middle Ages, and was re covered by the Neoplatonic Huma during the Renaissance.

The theory

In Hermetism as a doctrine of salva through initiatory knowledge, man i usory, mortal, and a source of evil, or one hand, because his body belong matter, but on the other hand, he detached fragment of the Supreme Inte and Creative Word because of his soul. vation is dependent upon a recognitic his true nature, which is a result of soul's elevation beyond the limits of human into ecstasy. This is the prepara for the meeting with God, the orig source of all beatitude to which the a purified through several existences, eventually return. This view of hu nature is founded on the central conce Hermetism: 'What is above is like wh below; what is below is like what is ab The existence of a secret correspond between the visible and the invisible, w the 'royal art' or spiritual alchemy reveal, is therefore confirmed.

> **Immortality**
> 'So if you learn to know yourself as made of life and light . . . you will return to life.'

> 'The **vice of the soul** is ignorance.'

Hesychasm

Keystone of Eastern spirituality

Born with the first Christian hermits, the hesychast practice has since been a popular mode of spiritual expression employed by many movements including the Russian Starsi, and up to the present day, the monks of Mount Athos.

The term 'Hesychasm' comes from the Greek *hesychia* meaning 'tranquillity, rest', but also 'solitude, retreat'. In the Eastern Church it is used more specifically to describe the practice of repeated prayer, offered up to God by the contemplative spirit which has withdrawn from the world and is given over to reflection in solitude and silence. The origins of Hesychasm can be traced to the Desert Fathers who were also the true founders of monasticism. As hermits, they devoted their lives to a form of purified prayer which was stripped of all image and concept and reduced to a simple formula. The constant repetition of these prayers had the effect of emptying the soul which could then be filled with the presence of God. In the Desert Fathers' *Apophthegms* (sentences and anecdotes) and *Lives*, the word appears frequently: 'The hermit's day should be divided into prayer, psalmody, and *hesychia*, allowing him to construct an inner sanctuary day by day, in this haven without the intrusion of the outside world. Should he have to go through spiritual trials, he gives thanks, for he has faith in the One who tries him.'

From invocation to theology

In the 5th century with the appearance of Gregory of Nyssa's mystical theory of the Redemption which was later systematized by his contemporary, Evagrius of Pontus, Hesychasm became one of the fundamental practices in Eastern monachism. John Climacus, abbot of the Mount Sinai monastery and author of *Holy Ladder*, considered it to be one of the highest steps in the soul's ascension to God. In the 13th century, the usage of the 'Jesus Prayer', a simple invocation consisting of the suppliant's plea: 'Lord Jesus Christ, Son of God, have pity on me', became widespread. The prayer was supposed to be accompanied by a breathing technique instituted by Nicephorus the Solitary or Hesychast, an Italian monk at Mount Athos. In his tract *On Guarding the Heart*, Nicephorus teaches how to regulate the breathing in order to 'draw the spirit back into the heart' where the hidden treasure that is God's presence resides. Nicephorus won over many followers from the Byzantine Church élite, who faithfully and fervently put the technique into practice. It was systematized in

---

Vision of God and man's deification

'All of us have known the Son through the voice of the Father who gave this teaching from on high . . . and the Holy Spirit itself came down and remains with us . . . God allows himself to be seen face to face and not in enigmas, he attaches himself to the worthy and comes to live in them completely so that, for their part, they may live completely in him.'
(Gregory Palamas)

John Climacus (7th century)

'The Hesychast is someone who aspires to surround the Incorporeal in a house of flesh.'

*Flanked by the patriarch of Constantinople, metropolitans, and monks, the Emperor John VI
Cantacuzenus presides over the council at which he ratified the doctrine of Gregory Palamas
Greek manuscript 1370–75 (Bibliothèque nationale, Paris)*

the following century by Gregory of Sinai (1285–1346), a native of Asia Minor who settled first at Mount Sinai then at Mount Athos, but was forced to leave due to the Ottoman raids. He went on to Bulgaria, and his disciples, including Cyprian, carried Hesychasm to Russia.

Gregory Palamas (1296–1359) defended the prayer of the heart against vicious attacks by a faction of the Byzantine Church, creating a veritable theology for the Hesychasts. He further extends his theory in *Life in Jesus Christ*, on the spiritual nature of the sacraments and liturgy. The latter were considered as the actualization of the Christian mysteries by Nicholas Cabasilas (died 1371), who was a close friend of the pious Emperor John Cantacuzenus, and probably his companion when he withdrew into a monastery.

Mount Athos

After the fall of Constantinople, the hesychast practice did not die out in the East. Its headquarters remained Mount Athos, where the first monasteries were founded in the 10th century, becoming the principal centre of Orthodox monachism in the 14th century. Cenoebitism, or communal life, and Hermetism, whose followers were known both as hermits and as 'Hesychasts', were practised there. The Hesychasts believed themselves to be the only true monks, for the word monk comes from the Greek *monos* meaning 'alone'.

Mount Athos was again a centre of controversy when one of the monks, Nikodimos Hagioritis, published his *Philokalia* in 1782. When the text was translated into Russian, the ensuing renewed interest in Hesychasm was to change the face of Russian spirituality, particularily affecting the country's 19th century *starets* movement.

Presence of god in the Heart

Perhaps the main reason for the prestige of Hesychasm in the Eastern Church and its survival over the centuries is that it maintains that the true Christian is the monk, and the true monk an ascetic and contemplative hermit. *Hesychia* is therefore the ideal life for it not only quells the inner voice, but also the noise from the outside world. Before Christianity, Apollodorus of Athens had already declared, 'Mystical silence honours the gods by imitating their nature'. For the Hesychast, calling on Jesus first quietens the spirit, then sensitizes the presence of God in the heart. Prayer is not only the participation in Creation through helping all creatures, but it becomes igneous like the Holy Spirit and reaches up to heaven like a candle's flame. Solitary prayer must be coupled with participation in the collective liturgy, which is also the revelation of God's mysteries. Finally, Hesychasm is also the prayer of the whole body because of the use of breathing control, similar to the techniques taught in Asian spiritual movements. The Jesus Prayer can even be compared to Hindu or Buddhist *mantras*. This voluntary union of body and soul died out early in the West, but is still common practice in the East, principally at Mount Athos which is still the strongest bastion of Hesychasm.

Isaac the Syrian (7th century)
'The man with a (sympathetic) heart cannot think about or see creatures without his eyes filling with tears because of the immense compassion which seizes his heart.'

Nicephorus the Hesychast (13th century)
'Force it (the Intellect) to go down into your heart at the same time as the air you breathe . . . when it gets there, you will feel the joy which follows.'

Hinduism

A multi-millenary tradition

Hinduism, which includes schools of philosophy and mysticism is constantly evolving even today.

Hinduism was introduced into India by Aryan invaders e. 1500 BC, and is adhered to by 80% of the country's 600 million inhabitants. It has a corpus of sacred literature known as the *Veda*, which provides the standards for religious life (and indeed for the whole universe), and is based on a class or *varna* system in which the *brahmana* with their ceremonial and ritual duties dominate the *kshatriya* (warriors), the *vaisya* (farmers, artisans, and traders) and the *sudra* (workers). In the first three *varna*, the men were called 'twice-born', having received an initiation which was regarded as a second birth; the *sudra* were prohibited from participating in the rites. Over the centuries, the four *varna* have been further subdivided into a series of castes (jati). At the very bottom of the social scale are the 'untouch-

---

Hinduism and the West

Since the beginning of the 19th century Hinduism has fascinated the West and vice versa. When it came into contact with Christianity, Hinduism began to feel the need for religious regeneration. There followed a real philosophical and religious renaissance. At the end of the 19th century, Vivekananda, who had received a Western education, became the disciple of Ramakrishna and went on to spread his message in the United States and Europe. At the same time, the Theosophical society in Madras claimed to have revived ancient initiatory customs. More recently, Sri Aurobindo attempted to synthesize Indian and European thought.

---

ables' who perform the 'impure' tasks. It was this concept of untouchability that Gandhi fought against and won.

Although a large part of India's population adheres to religions other than Hinduism, it is worthwhile noting that Buddhism and Jainism both stemmed from it, and that Christianity and Islam were introduced by foreign invaders. In fact, it can be said that Hinduism was part of and still is part of every Indian's life no matter what his particular beliefs may be. Hinduism has naturally evolved in the 3000 years of its existence. Primitive Vedic religion incorporated certain elements of pre-Aryan beliefs and is internalized: little by little ritual sacrifice was replaced by asceticism and the search for knowledge.

The Darshanas

Without one particular founder, and with no organized Church, Hinduism accepts all manner of philosophical speculation and mystical experiences, as it recognized the validity of different 'points of view' (*darshanas*), perceived as so many different visions of the truth seen from diverse angles and therefore complimentary. The principal darshanas are Nyaya, or way of logic and analysis; Mimamsa, or study of ritual; Samkhya or enumeration; Yoga or technique of concentration; and finally the Vedanta ('end of the Veda'), an uninterrupted metaphysical exegesis, which over the centuries has become more important and now represents Hindu metaphysics par excellence.

Indeed, Hinduism, which calls itself the 'eternal religion' (*sanatana dharma*) is an ongoing explanation of God, the Universe, and man, and the interrelationships of these three. It is also a guide to the behaviour which is a result of these relationships. The very base of Hinduism is the *Dharma*, the Divine Law which upholds

Hindu worshippers at the temple

and governs every individual. The term *Dharma* therefore defines both cosmic ordinance and the rules of conduct appropriate for each individual and adapted to the conditions of his present incarnation. Cosmic life is cyclic, punctuated by the *kalpa* ('days of Brahma') and subdivided into four *yuga*. Partial destruction of the world follows the end of each *yuga*. At the end of the fourth (*kali yuga*), the universe is reabsorbed into the non-manifested Absolute or Supreme Reality. Each 'kalpa' is followed by the 'night of Brahma', during which a new kalpa is born.

The quest for deliverance

The Hindu's principal preoccupation is deliverance (*mukti* or *moksha*) from the conditioning that results from life, and most importantly from the interminable cycle of births and rebirths (*samsara*), to which the *karman* or act is submitted and its far-reaching consequences which cause another incarnation. We can only attain this deliverance through knowledge, for we are prisoners to the illusions created by our desire and our ignorance. In other words, we are prisoners of the *maya*, the mirage of appearances, the divine game through which God manifests himself but which is also the magnificent veil which hides Him. Deliverance then is our understanding of our true nature which was originally divine, and can be obtained in this life, as in the case of the 'living free' (*jivan-mukta*).

The traditional life of every 'true-born' individual, in particular of the Brahman, is governed by the Hindu conception of our

destiny which they believe is divided into four successive phases, called the *ashrama*.

Traditionally the Hindu male is initiated in childhood and sent to study with a guru to whom he owes absolute obedience. During this time, he must observe a vow of chastity (*brahmacharya*). At the end of this period which normally lasts 12 years, he founds a family and becomes a householder. Twenty five years later, with his children grown up, he may leave home an retreat into the forest in order to create and *ashram* where he will in turn communicate the teachings of his guru, and his own personal experience. The fourth stage is that of the renunciant (*sannyasin*). It is the most perfect of the four stages and alone can help put a definite end to any further reincarnation. Having renounced everything, even his citizenship, the sannyasin may take to the roads, and become an itinerant beggar, owning only his bowl for alms and a stick. He has understood that the world is only an illusion, and from this time forth he identifies himself completely with the *atman*, the eternal principle which gives him life and is identical to the *Brahman* or Absolute with whom he is fused. There are millions of sannyasins in India today.

Nowadays in India only the second and fourth stages have survived, that of the householder (*grihastha*) and that of sannyasin which is still considered as a model for others. The brahmacharya barely exists now, except in the form of scholastic communities where the pupils share the life of their teacher in a religious atmosphere. The fourth stage, that of leaving home in old age is rarely observed nowadays, although many men and women do leave to spend their last years in an ashram. The ashram remains an ideal for the majority of Hindus. They also observe an extremely strict moral code founded on righteousness, both inner and outer purity, faith in the Scriptures, veneration of the guru, the adoration of God and finally the *ahismsa* or, 'non-violence' which is also respect and compassion for all living things.

Although it is usually considered to be polytheistic in essence, Hinduism does in fact recognize the existence of one God, the *Brahma*, the impersonal and unknowable Absolute or *Paramatma*, the supreme 'self'. In the masculine form *Brahma* refers to God

> 'Liberated, the soul goes up towards the Supreme Light which is **Brahman** and identifies itself with him.' (*Shankara*)

> '**Dharma** is the king of kings. That is why there is nothing superior to the Dharma.' (*Brihadaranyaha Upanished*)

> **Ramakrishna**
> 'Have love for everyone, no one is other than you.'

the Creator who forms the Trinity (*Trimurti*) with Vishnu and Shiva. But while the former has almost no following, Vishnu, preserver of the created world with his many avatars—Krishna and Rama for example—and Shiva, god of procreation (*lingam* cult) but also of destruction, and renunciants are extremely popular and fervently worshipped. This very personal form of worship is known as *bhakti* and enables the worshipper to participate in the essence of God, making the final deliverance a certainty. In later Hinduism, Shakti, the feminine aspect of the Absolute, who is considered to be the external manifestation of his power, also has her own cult and followers. Therefore in Tantrism, feminine divinities as wives of the gods, are more powerful than the gods themselves.

The Guru

In Hinduism the guru or religious leader plays a primordial role: he initiates the young Hindu, transmitting knowledge orally. Later, it is at the feet of a guru in an ashram that the way to the deliverance can be learned, taught by a guru who has already travelled the path he now shows to others. The guru, who is completely detached from worldly things, and totally impartial, must be 'calm, self-controlled and compassionate', his 'only aim is to help others' and his only desire is to 'make the

Brahma known'. The relationship between disciple and guru is founded on mutual suitability and attraction, the disiciple chooses his own guru, and the guru chooses his disciple. For the disciple, the god himself is the incarnation of the divine Instructor. In the Bhakti, the god himself is the devotee's guru, like Krishna is the *Bhagavadgita*. Although any 'living-freed' ('*jivanmukta*) may become a guru, Hindu history lists some who are particularly illustrious like Shankara, Ramanuja or the more contemporary Ramakrishna. The role of their teaching is very important, for Hinduism is in constant evolution.

'**Deliverance**, in reality, is only obtained through knowledge: it alone can break the ties of the mind, it alone leads to beatitude.' (*Shankara*)

The Hindu Genesis

'In the beginning the darkness covered the darkness, all that could be seen were indistinct shapes. Shut up in emptiness, the One reached out to the Being and, through the power of that, was born.

'First to develop was desire, which was the first seed of thought. Searching their souls, the Wise men found the seat of being in the nonbeing.' (*Rig-Veda*, 10, 129)

Ibn'Arabi

1165 Murcia, Spain — Damascus 1240

The 'Sultan of the Gnostics'

He was also known as the 'greatest of sheikhs' and has never failed to fascinate the Muslim world he overturned.

Abu Bakr Muhammad Muhyi al-Din Ibn al-Arabi was born in Murcia into a very pious and cultured milieu. When he was seven, he and his family moved to Seville, the capital of the Almohades Empire which extended all over North Africa. At 16, having studied with Andalusian spiritual leaders, he 'entered on the path'. He was so cultured that at an early age he was awarded an important administrative post; it was also at this time that he met and married a young woman whom he considered to be the spiritual ideal. But a grave illness which brought with it powerful visions led him to give up his career and his possessions in order to practise asceticism in strict seclusion. Several long years of pilgrimage followed, during which Ibn'Arabi met the greatest mystics in Spain and the Mahgreb, where he spent some time before a vision compelled him to go to the East.

In 1201–02 he travelled to Cairo, Jerusalem, and finally to Mecca, where he was welcomed into the home of an eminent Persian sheikh and his sister. Ibn'Arabi fell in love with the sheikh's niece, Nizam, to whom he dedicated his masterpiece of spiritual poetry *The Interpreter of Longings*. From 1204 to 1233 he took up his travels

again, coming into contact with all the great Sufi masters of the Middle East. His works brought him fame and he was sought out by princes and accompanied by a group of disciples, but was challenged by the doctors of law who found his doctrine worrying. At last in 1224, Ibn'Arabi settled in Damascus where he remained until his death, setting out to train the minds of his followers and to compile his vast body of work. On his death he was honoured with the title of 'Vivificator of the Religion', and his body lies at Damascus in the mosque mausoleum built for him by Sultan Selim I in 1517. Since then Ibn'Arabi's thought has dominated Sufi spiritualism, but has always been contested, due to the fact that his ideas go beyond the framework of orthodox Islam.

His works

Ibn'Arabi was an extremely prolific author, composing more than 300 works of which half remains. His works range from poetry to commentaries on the Koran, the most famous of which are the *Kitab al-Futuhat al-Makkiyya* (Meccan Revelations), his monumental encyclopaedia in which he studies all aspects of spirituality in 156 chapters; *Kitab al-tadjalliyat al-illakiyya* (c. 1204) (The Book of Theophanies), in which he develops his philosophy of the Being, and *Kitab fusus al-hikam* (The Wisdom of the Prophets). The latter was compiled in 1229 and is a spiritual testament in which the messages of the prophets from Adam to Muhammad are exposed. The messages are described as so many reflections of the divine Revelation, which is absolute light and therefore colourless, but the receiver

---

Existence
'The existence of created things is the existence of God.'

The Universe
'The Universe is God's own shadow.'

86

acts like a prism, endowing it with many colours. By common consent this is Ibn'Arabi's most important, daring work which has met with resistance from the heart of Islam since it first appeared.

The theory

Ibn'Arabi's doctrine, known as 'unity of existence' is centred on the absolute unity of the Being. 'Existence is a single reality: if we look at it from one angle we consider it to be the existence of created things and if we look at it from another, we consider it to be the actual existence of God. Reality is therefore no more than one thing appearing in many forms'. It follows that in his profound and essential being, man himself is a divine possibility. The development of this archetype, which is capable of directly receiving God-given light, is therefore the aim of spiritual life. As man is the object of his own knowledge, God is the subject, the 'transcendant Witness'. If, in order to know God, man must first know himself in his spiritual essence, he can only come to know himself in God and through Him. This audacious statement can only be made in Ibn 'Arabi's words in a methodically paradoxical manner. The author prevents the reader's mind from taking up a definitive stance or viewpoint. Instead he continually pushes it towards what he qualifies as 'perplexity' and 'astonishment' in the face of something which goes beyond the rational.

His monism was denounced by the majority of orthodox theologians. They also condemned what they considered to be his dangerous pantheism, dangerous in that it came close to abolishing the necessary differences between Creator and creature, Lord and servant. Ibn 'Arabi's theories were a decisive step in the development of Islamic spirituality, in particular that of the Sufis who went on to organize themselves into brotherhoods (see **Tariqa**). His works which are so rich and so dense, technical, esoteric and paradoxical at the same time, are not only valued for their theoretical content but also because they are the expressions of a pious man's profound mystical voyage of discovery. These books have become standard reference works, not only for his modern-day disciples but also for his adversaries. They are of universal value.

The One Soul

'Adam, both God and creation . . . is the "One Soul" from which the whole human race was created.'

Muhammad

'The creative act began and ended with Muhammad; for on one hand, he was a "Prophet when Adam was still water and clay", and on the other, during his earthly life, he was the seal of all the prophets.'

The Islamic metaphysician

A passionate mystic and great visionary, Ibn'Arabi was intimately acquainted with divine mystery, which led him to found Islamic metaphysics on views inspired by extreme daring. These views provoked a strong reaction in Orthodox Islam, which is still active today. Nevertheless, Ibn'Arabi affected all Islamic spirituality through deepening it and giving it new outlets of expression.

I Ching

Manual of divination
which became a guide to wisdom

*Dating from ancient times, the
I Ching, or Book of Changes,
is at the root of Chinese philosophy
and wisdom.*

The ancient Chinese word *I* described the chameleon which changes colour in order to match its environment; *Ching* means 'holy book'. According to tradition, the first elements in the *I Ching* were determined by Fu Hi, the mythical and heroic emperor who invented a method of divination by yarrow sticks. This primitive system is said to have been perfected by King Wen of the Chu dynasty, and by his son, the Duke of Chu (11th century BC); it was apparently used for several centuries. In his extreme old age, Confucius began to study the book, and is believed to have added some important commentaries to it. Whatever the case may be, the *I Ching*, which is closer in essence to the works of Lao Tzu than to those of Confucius whom some believe it could have inspired, is still seen not only as a book of divination but also as the oldest exposé of the cosmic system so characteristic of Chinese thought.

The theory

The *I Ching* is presented as a way of deciphering the constantly changing universe; it is also capable of guiding human actions which are the infinitesimal reper-cussions of those changes. This path of changes is none other than *tao*, the One, creator of the many, represented in this world by *Tai Chi*, first principle of all things and symbolized by a circle cut into two interlocking halves: *yang*, which is light, good, and male; and *yin*, dark, evil, and female. The various different combinations of these elements explain the development of all beings. From *yang*, represented by a whole line, and *yin*, represented by a broken line, a series of eight trigrams is produced, which are images of Heaven and Earth, thunder, water, mountains, wind, fire, and lake. Combining these trigrams two by two results in the 64 hexagrams that make up the *I Ching*, and which are supposed to contain all the possibilities of change. As a method of divination, it presents these possibilities in embryonic form, which allows the future to be read as well as leading to a better understanding of the past. When consulted, the oracle indicates which is the correct attitude to adopt, or, if it is not too late, which plan of action should be put into force. However, divination can only work if the questioner has a pure heart that will be receptive to the cosmic influences hidden within the *I Ching*.

> **Universal interdependence**
> 'The problem of the *I Ching* is finally nothing more than universal interdependence . . . The idea of an unvarying structure underlying a changing super-structure is classic in Chinese philosophy.' (*Charles Hirsch*)

Ignatius Loyola

1491 Loyola Castle, Guipúzcoa — Rome 1556

Founder of the Society of Jesus

Director of conscience, he was also one of the great leaders of Christian asceticism; his Spiritual Exercises have guided countless believers.

Son of a noble and rich family, Ignatius led a life typical of young nobles of his time, until he received a wound during the siege of Pamplona that left him with a limp. He began to read the mystic writers and changed his lifestyle to one of severe self-mortification at Manresa. It was there that he began to compile his *Spiritual Exercises*. In 1523 he left on a pilgrimage to Jerusalem, and later studied at the universities of Alcala, Salamanca, and Paris. There, with several companions including Francis Xavier, Ignatius founded the Society of Jesus, which was confirmed by the Pope in 1540, and he wrote his *Constitution*. By the time of Ignatius's death there were already a thousand members in the new order. He was an extremely sensitive mystic—'the gift of tears' almost blinded him during prayer, and in his *Diary* he discovered the contemplation during which the divine essence 'in great clarity' was revealed to him.

The theory

His teachings are contained in the *Constitutions* (1541–56) but above all in the *Spiritual exercises (1548)*. While the author was certainly interested in Rhennish mysticism (see **Eckhart**) and was partially inspired by Ruysbroek, the *Exercises* are characterized by their methodical nature. Conceived firstly as margin notes on a personal experience, they came to form a detailed daily guide to Christian ascetism. According to the *Exercises*, the individual must examine his conscience, confess his sins and meditate in order to prepare his soul to meet the particular conditions demanded by God before He will reveal His Will. Once the revelation has been made, all the soul must do is bow to the Will of God. Those who seek this knowledge must first overcome their more earthly leanings through obedience and humility. And on his part, the director of consciences will adapt his methods to each person's individualities and to their particular level, never forgetting that even he is only an instrument in the hand of God. He deciphers God's wishes for each individual and then helps that person accomplish God's will. 'To cure what seemed to be identical illnesses,' wrote his contemporary Ribaderreira, '(Ignatius) used completely different, and even sometimes opposite, methods . . . However, the results showed that the remedy used for each one was the most appropriate.'

> **Like a dead body**
> 'Those who live in obedience must allow themselves to be led, moved about according to the will of Divine Providence, just like a dead body which is manipulated and moved in all directions.'

Illuminism

A spiritual vision of humankind and the world

For many centuries, illuminism remainded a discreet presence in the background of spirituality, until its explosive apogee in the 18th century.

The term illuminism is applied to a philosophical and religious current which stands independently of any official Church. Its forefathers include various theosophists, Plotinus and the Neoplatonic schools but also the Gnostics (see **Gnosis and Gnosticism**), Christian and Jewish Cabalists (see **Cabala**) and especially certain leading lights of the Renaissance, like Paracelsus (1493–1541) who was doctor, naturalist, and theologian, and Valentine Weigel (1533–88) who was the founder of a German mystic sect. His sect believed that truth can only be found in the hearts of men, and that man could only become aware of this after a profound personal regeneration, but in the main, the Illuminists turned for their inspiration to Jakob Böhme's *Mysterium Magnum* and the revelations received by Swedenborg (1688–1772).

At the end of the 17th century the movement, which in some ways closely resembled German pietism, appeared to be the reaction of sensitivity and spiritualism to the extreme material rationalism of the Renaissance. It became popular among a certain part of the cultivated European élite, which was already involved in esoteric and occult circles. Swedenborgian societies were created all over Europe. In Zürich the fame of Pastor Lavater (1741–1801), the author of *Vues sur l'éternité* (1768) (Views on Eternity) attracted many followers, including Madame de Staël. The Order of Elus-Coëns, founded by a Theosophist Portuguese Jew, Martinez Pasquals (died 1779) gave birth to Martinism which, basing itself on Freemasonry, attempted to draw together the initiated, regardless of creed. At the same time the works of Louis Claude de Saint Martin were being circulated; some of the more illustrious members of his wide readership were Goethe, Schiller, and von Baader. William Blake (1757–1827), the English poet and painter as well as P. S. Ballanche (1776–1847), author of *The Social Palingenesis* can both be linked to illuminism which influenced the Germans, then the French Romantics, and had a lasting effect on poetry in general.

The theory

While reaffirming the primacy of the spirit over the word and matter, which is the corrupted manifestation of pure invisible light, illuminism underlines the need for a total inner conversion which will give man back his original divine status. Only then will he be able to take on his true vocation in a world where because of the equivalence of microcosms and macrocosms, he is responsible and will return it to its original splendour, which has been eclipsed by man's fall into matter.

Lavater
'What is in me is bigger than the world; if God is not there, he is nowhere.'

Ballanche
'Regenerated man regenerates the earth.'

The Eternal, *1827, watercolour by William Blake, English painter, poet and visionary (1757–1827) (Whitworth Art Gallery, University of Manchester)*

Imitation of Christ

A revival of personal piety

The Imitation has been the most popular spiritual guide for all Christians from the 15th century onwards.

This small book emerged in 1425, and shortly afterwards, was printed in most European languages. The most famous French translations are by Pierre Corneille (1653), who paraphrased and versified it, Lemaistre de Sacy (1662), and Lamennais (1824). As the book was anonymous, much effort was made to uncover the author. Now, he is generally agreed to be Thomas Hemerken a Kempis (1379–1471), master of novices at the Mount Saint Agnes monastery in Zwolle (Netherlands). The *Imitation* is therefore closely connected to the Dutch spiritual movement known as the *Devotio moderna* due to its novelty.

Devotio Moderna

The founder of the movement was Gerard Groote (1340–84), who renounced all the ecclesiastical benefits to which he was entitled, gave away all his wordly goods,

'Do you want to understand and taste the words of Jesus Christ? Apply yourselves to making your whole lives conform to his.'
(*Imitation* 1, 1)

and founded the Order of Brothers and Sisters of Communal Life, who lived in small groups and did not take vows. After his death, a congregation of regular canons was created, who, although a large part of every day was devoted to contemplation, also carried out many charitable works. They even opened schools, where, amongst others, Erasmus was educated. Although the *Devotio Moderna* had been inspired by the mystical spirituality of Meister Eckhart and Ruysbroek, its particular aim was to develop personal piety through introspection and private prayer. As such, it heralded the reforming current prevalent in 16th and 17th century spirituality.

The theory

The *Imitation* is made up of four graduated parts: *Admonishments to Inner Life* invites the believer to detach himself from the world; *Admonishments to Spiritual Life* helps him to reach into his own heart; *On Inner Consolation* introduces him to divine Love; and finally *Devout Exhortation to Holy Communion* unites him to God through the Eucharist. In response to theological science and the dominant intellectualism of his time, the author reaffirms the need for humanity and charity, without which good works are worthless. He recommends contemplation and solitude, obedience to the spiritual leader, silence and discretion in personal devotion. Because of its simple yet colourful language and its methodical treatment of subject matter, the *Imitation* made a substantial contribution to the internalization of Christian asceticism.

Islam

Religion, social order, and civilization

Islam is based on the Word of God, transmitted to the people by Muhammad.

The word *islam* means 'submission to God's Law', as presented in the Koran. At the present time, Islam has almost one billion adherents, or roughly one sixth of the world's population, from the African shores of the Atlantic to Indonesia. Although Islamic practices can differ greatly from one country to another, the religion as a whole is characterized by its strict monotheism and by the use of a common liturgical language, the Arabic of the Koran, whose verses are ritually recited every day. It is also characterized by the observance of the fundamental tenets, or 'Five Pillars,' of Islam:

1. The affirmation of faith (*shahada*) – 'there is no god but God, and Muhammad is his Prophet'.
2. The five daily canonical prayers at dawn, midday, mid-afternoon, sunset, and during the night, which are preceded by ritual ablutions and involve prostration. Preferably these prayers should be said communally as they always are on Friday, the Lord's day, in mosques.
3. The fasting during the month of Ramadan from dawn until sunset, which Muslims must observe from the onset of puberty. The fast involves abstention from food, drink, sexual intercourse and, today, tobacco.
4. The giving of alms on a stipulated scale to the poor and to orphans.
5. The *Hajj* or Pilgrimage to Mecca accomplished once in a lifetime by those with the means to do so.

The precise and simple nature of these practices and especially the belief in one god have made Islam a worldwide religion, attractive to people from all walks of life. As it makes no distinction between the spiritual and the temporal, Islam has engendered a particular type of society, a sort of 'egalitarian civil theocracy' (L. Massignon), for the Divine Revelation takes the place of a constitution and by law Muslims are equal, and must help each other. Furthermore, in Islam there is neither priesthood nor ecclesiastical hiearachy. Finally, Islam is a civilization, moulded by many generations of philosophers and intellectuals whose lives revolved around the interpretation of the Koran, and by religion-inspired art, in which the representation of animated beings is prophibited. Islamic art and thought enjoyed an early golden age during the Middle Ages.

Islam in the world

The explanation for the presence of Islam in so many parts of the world, can be found in its history, beginning with the rapid expansionism which followed Muhammad's death. The armies, which were originally Arab and then Muslim as their ranks were swelled by the converted from conquered countries, surged through Egypt, the Magreb, North Africa, Spain, and even France. At the same time this powerful impulse carried the Muslims to the borders of India and Chinese Turkestan. Islam went on to conquer North India (9th–14th centuries), Indonesia (14th, 15th, and 16th centuries), while from the 11th to the 18th centuries it gradually penetrated Black West Africa then the rest of the continent.

> 'The Most High has created all things and well proportioned them, who has ordained their destinies and guided them.' (*Koran* 87, 3)

93

However, almost from its inception, the unity of Islam was threatened. As Muhammad had not approached a successor, two groups fought for power: on the one hand, the descendants of the Prophet, his daughter Fatima and her husband Ali (who was also Muhammad's adopted son) with their two children; and on the other, Muhammad's fathers-in-law, including Abu Bakr, who, by popular consensus was elected in 632 first caliph, that is to say lieutenant or vicar. On his death Omar, another of the Prophet's fathers-in-law, succeeded him until his assassination in 634. The third caliph, Uthman, was also assassinated, and Ali regained power until he was implicated in the murder of his predecessor and assassinated in 661. Ali's adversary Mu'awiyah, the governor of Syria, then founded the first hereditary dynasty, known as the Umayyads.

These bloody quarrels, which were at the root of the divisions within Islam, were further exacerbated by the ethnic diversity of the converted peoples: Sunnis and Shi'ites who are the 'partisans' (of Ali and the Prophet's family), and the Kharijites or

'seceders,' who blamed the two warring factions equally and stated that any pious Believer could carry out the duties of a caliph, but that the caliphate is in no way an absolute necessity. This democratic attitude, coupled with a moral and religious austerity which culminated in the excommunication of the opposition, has led to the Kharijites being nicknamed the 'Puritans' of Islam. Throughout history this party has regrouped rebels against the official powers that oppressed them. Today only small communities remain, dispersed in the Sunni countries, although they are still extremely possessive of their independence. At the start of the 2nd century of the hijrah, a fourth sect emerged, called the Mu'tazilites, the 'withdrawn' or 'separated,' which opened up the first school of speculative theology (*kalam*). As a rationalist movement at the very heart of Islam, the Mu'tazilites are behind the 19th and 20th-century Muslim reformism.

The Sunni sect

The Sunnis, who make up almost 90% of all Muslims and are present in North Africa, Libya, Egypt, Saudi Arabia, Syria, Iraq, Pakistan, Indonesia, and Black Africa, consider themselves to be the true guarantors of Orthodoxy. In effect, they rely on the *sunna*, the rule or custom, exactly as it was laid down in the words and deeds of the Prophet, which were later collected into the *Hadith*. Contrary to the Shi'ites, the Sunnis see Islam's golden age in the era of the first four caliphs, and challenge any messianic idea. They accept the Koran literally and reject esoteric or allegoric commentary on it.

Where the Shi'ites or Kharijites follow passionate ideals, the Sunnis represent realism and moderation according to the Koranic verse 'We have made of you a community of the just'. Mistrustful of theological speculation and even more so of the wanderings of mystics, the Sunnis give precedence to the *fiqh*, Muslim jurisprudence, considering it to be a 'way of life'.

The Exordium

Praise be to Allah, Lord of the Creation,
The Compassionate, the Merciful,
King of Judgment day.
You alone we worship, and to You alone
We pray for help.
Guide us to the straight path.
(Koran 1, 1–5)

Believe in God

'Believers, have faith in Allah and the apostle, in the Book He has revealed to this apostle, and in the Scriptures which were revealed before Him. Whoever does not believe in Allah, in his angels, in his Scripture, and his prophets, and in the Last Day, is in complete error.'
(Koran 4, 136)

Isma'ilis

Islamic extremists

Isma'ilism has always influenced Islamic religious and mystical thought.

Originally part of Shi'ism, Isma'ilism became a distinct sect when the partisans of Isma'il, who had been appointed sixth Imam by his father Ja'far (died 765) but who died before him in 751, seceded from the Shi'ite branch of Islam. Ja'far had already appointed his second son, Abdallah to succeed Isma'il, but he only survived his brother for a matter of days. In 765 the Shi'ites recognized Musa, who was also Ja'far's son, as their seventh imam, but Isma'il's partisans, under the leadership of his disciple Mubarak, stayed faithful to him and honoured his son Muhammad as their seventh and last imam. Since that time, the imams have been 'hidden, revealed only to a few initiated', and are represented by lieutenants, bearing the title *hujjah* (witness). The followers of Isma'il became known as 'Seveners' for they believed that Isma'il was the seventh imam, and that with him a cycle had been completed; they would bear this name until the advent of the last imam, who would make their

---

'**The reform** undertaken by the Isma'ilis aims, in the sphere of religion, at the triumph of spirit over the written word, truth over the Law, and in the sphere of intelligence, it aims at the liberation of the spirit from all that could impede or condition it.' (O. Yahia)

---

doctrine triumph over the others.

Isma'ilism was the cause of much dispute in Islam, and gave birth to the Fatimid State which reigned in North Africa from the 10th century to 1171. Today it is represented by the Druzes, the Alaouites, and the Nizaris whose sects are spread throughout Pakistan, India, Sudan, and Syria, with the Aga Khan as their chief. But Isma'ilism has also survived as an intellectual and religious movement.

The imam

The Isma'ilis, who are particularly inspired by Neoplatonic theory, are even more esoteric than the Shi'ite 'Twelvers', and they push the concept of the *imama* to its most extreme conclusion. For the Isma'ilis, only the imam, who is absolutely pure, infallible, and transcendent, can reveal divine secrets or serve as a guide on the path to resurrection and the final liberation. The first being created is universal Intellect which gives birth to all the other forms of intelligence including the angelic. The angelic Intellect comes directly from the universal and is proper to prophets and imams. But imams can transmit it to their disciples who then become universal beings in whom macrocosm and microcosm are joined. In Isma'ilism, interpretations of the Koran are in the main allegorical, and the practices imposed on every Muslim take on an inner and symbolic meaning.

Isma'ilian doctrine has attracted the attention of many Muslim mystics. It was also the inspiration for the *Thousand Nights and One Night*, which, seen from this point of view, appear as a series of initiatory narratives.

Jainism

The teachings of the Jinas or 'Victors'

With its long uninterrupted line of spiritual leaders, Jainism is an austere and demanding religion with 3 million followers in India.

Jainism comes from *Jina* (the 'Victor'), the title given to Vardhamana Mahavira; in the 6th to 5th centuries BC, he was responsible for the reforming and dissemination of a religion which was believed to date from much more ancient times. Vardhamana is given as the 24th and last *Tirthamkara*, but history only provides evidence as to the existence of his predecessor Parvsa, who lived two centuries before him.

The history of Vardhamana's career runs along curiously similar and parallel lines to that of his contemporary, the Buddha. He, like Buddha, was a prince who renounced the world and 'sky-clad', that is to say naked, spent 13 years in meditation and severe asceticism. Under a sala tree, he finally became all-knowing, then went on to

Mircea Eliade

'Released from "karmic matter" the soul speeds upwards "like an arrow" towards the summit of the Universe; there, in a kind of Empyrean, it meets and communicates with its fellow souls, forming a purely spiritual, almost divine community.'

preach for 30 years before his 'entry into nirvana' at the age of 72, in 468 or 477, only a few years before the Buddha's death.

His doctrine was then transmitted by the *Stahviras* ('Elders'). One of them, Bhadra-bahu (3rd century BC) compiled the Jain Canon, and was responsible for the split between the *Svetambara* (white-clad), and the *Digambara* (sky-clad), for whom complete nudity was a precondition for deliverance.

The theory

Jain doctrine is based on a cosmological system which is strictly classified and regulated by numbers. It denies the existence of God, but not of the gods, who are not immortal. Every being has a soul. Respect for every living thing is the first Jain commandment. *Karma* forces the soul into perpetual transmigration, until such time as it has detached itself from all matter, and is released from bondage. To this end, suicide by fasting is permitted. Only monks and nuns can hope to be released, but from the age of eight onwards, a child may enter the monastery. At his initiation the novice pronounces vows of poverty and chastity, then leads the life of a wandering beggar, equipped only with an alms bowl, a broom to sweep the path in front of him, and a piece of muslin with which he covers his mouth. The broom and the cloth are to prevent him from destroying even the tiniest of living creatures. Gandhi's policy of 'non-violence' was based on Jain doctrine.

Jansenism

An attempt at reforming religious life

Jansenism reopened the theological debate on God's grace which was soon turned sour by politics. The movement provoked a spiritual revival.

This movement has its roots in the controversy surrounding God's Grace that had begun with Saint Augustine, and was revived during the Reformation. In 1588 the Jesuit Molina (1536–1600) proposed that God passed down 'sufficient grace' for all, and that each individual is free to use it or not. The Dutchman Cornelius Jansen (called Jansenius), Bishop of Ypres (1585–1631) defended the opposite point of view in his *Augustinus* (published posthumously in 1640). He stated that since the original sin, one cannot do good without the help of 'efficient grace' which is not given to everyone.

Port Royal

In Paris, Jansen joined with Du Vergier de Hauranne, abbot of Saint-Cyran (1581–1643), who became director of the Port Royal nuns, whose way of life he reformed with the help of Mother Superior Angélique Arnauld (1591–1661). But the abbot was denounced by the Jesuits and thrown into the Bastille, where he died shortly afterwards. The austere rule in the two religious establishments of Port Royal de Paris and Port Royal des Champs attracted many followers from high society. The 'Petites Ecoles' (Little Schools) where Jean Racine was raised, were created for their children. After Saint-Cyran's death, Antoine Arnauld brother of Angélique, defended Jansenist doctrine against attacks by the Jesuits. In 1653 the Pope condemned five propositions taken from the pages of *Augustinus*. The Jansenists were then helped by Pascal, who had great success with his *Provinciales* in 1656–7. Pascal launched an attack on the lax ways of the casuists or Jesuits who were often the confessors of important figures and who did their best to soothe troubled consciences.

The debate became political. In 1660 several bishops and the religious order at Port Royal, refused to sign the form of disavowal which was being imposed on them. Arnauld fled to Holland. Louis XIV who was dominated by Jesuits and worried about the opposition of the imprescriptible rights of the conscience to the authority of the monarchy and the papacy, had Port Royal destroyed in 1710. On his insistence, the Pope distributed a bull *Uningenitus*, condemning any form of dissidence which became State Law in 1730. Although they were beaten, the Jansenists still played an important part in the struggle against arbitrary power which was to culminate in the Revolution of 1789.

Pascal

'Jesus will be in agony until the end of the world; we must not sleep during this time.'

Jesus Christ

c. 6–5 BC Bethlehem — Jerusalem c. 30 AD

The holy leader

How has the brief public ministry of an obscure Galilean managed to convince such a large part of the world's population for 2000 years? This was and still is the mystery of Jesus.

If, for Christians, Jesus is the Son of God, the second person of the Trinity who became a man in order to save all humankind, the devout of other religions, and even non-believers, admit him to be one of humanity's greatest religious leaders, and it is from this point of view that we will consider him here. It is some time since any doubt has been cast upon his actual historical existence; he is no longer seen as just a mythical figure, but at the same time, very little is known about his life. The Gospels in no way constitute a biography of him, but rather are a justification of faith in the Resurrection and the Messiah, whose coming had already been announced by the Prophets.

His public ministry

Of Jesus the Galilean we know only that his public career began after he had spent some time on the banks of the Jordan in a region inhabited by the Essenes, in the company of John the Baptist who announced the imminent coming of the Messiah, and who baptized Jesus. After his baptism, Jesus spent 40 days in the desert, in the manner of the ancient Prophets. Then, when he was about 30 years old, he began to preach in Galilee, accompanied by the 12 chosen Apostles. Rather than preach in the synagogues, Jesus preferred the open air, where the lowly, humble people gathered around him. He called them the 'fishers of men'. He declared that it was for them, neglected as they were by the official religion, that he had come, curing the sick and 'casting out demons'. We do not even know how long this itinerant ministry lasted because, although the Gospel according to John speaks of three Easters in a row, the three synoptic Gospels only mention one, which would shorten the length of Jesus's public ministry to one year.

Nevertheless, Jesus went to Jerusalem where discontent at his preaching and the miracles which accompanied it, began to crystallize. In Jerusalem his teachings aroused the hostility of the Sadducean and Pharisean priesthoods, for Jesus denounced the hypocritcal nature of their Law. During his last supper with the Apostles, he celebrated the Passover, then, accused of disturbing the peace and blasphemy, he was arrested and brought before Jewish and Roman tribunals. At the insistence of the Jews, he was condemned to the Roman punishment of crucifixion. This took place on the day of Passover (the synoptic Gospels) or the day before (John) in about 30 AD, when Jesus was 34

'Love the Lord your God with all your soul, with all your mind. That is the greatest commandment. It comes first. The second is like it: Love your neighbour as yourself.'
(*Matthew* 22, 37–39)

'I am that living bread which has come down from heaven; if anyone eats this bread he shall live forever. Moreover, the bread I give is my own flesh; I give it for the life of the world.'
(*John* 6, 51)

or 35 years old. After a period of understandable confusion, the Apostles, certain of whom saw Jesus after his death, announced the Resurrection. It is at this point that the history of Jesus, Christianity's history begins.

The teaching

One who declares 'I am the Way, the Truth and the Life', and 'I am the Resurrection' but also 'I have come to bring fire on the earth' must expect conflicting reactions in return, as is amply demonstrated by the Gospels and the Acts of the Apostles. Speaking to the Jews, Matthew stressed that Jesus had not come to abolish the Law of Moses, but rather to fulfil it, in making it more just 'for if your righteousness does not exceed the righteousness of the scribes and the Pharisees, you shall not enter the Kingdom of Heaven'. With these words, Matthew begins his description of the public career of Jesus. In his narrative, as soon as he was born Jesus was recognized by the three magi as the 'King of the Jews', the 'chief who will be the pastor of my people of Israel'. Matthew is anxious to show in his text that Jesus fulfilled every one of the prophecies concerning the Messiah; we also find this preoccupation in John's Gospel, when Jesus says to the Apostle Philip, 'Follow me!' and Philip replies 'We have met the man spoken of by Moses in the Law, and by the Prophets'.

These considerations fade into the background with Mark and Luke, who wrote for converted pagans. They had mainly been influenced by Paul, the Gentiles' Apostle, and therefore emphasized the universal nature of the mission of Jesus who had come to take away the sin of the world. John, chronologically the last of the Gospel writers and representative of the strong Hellenistic tendency of the Churches of Antioch and Ephesia, goes even further, exclaiming that Jesus is really the 'Saviour of the world', and the 'Lamb of God who will take away the sins of the world'. In fact we know that from its earliest days, there were two opposing factions within the Church: the Judaeo-Christian faction in the Jerusalem Church, which preached the coming of the Messiah to the people of Israel, and the missionaries, whose first and greatest representative was Paul, who undertook the spreading of the 'Good News' throughout the Graeco-Latin world. The latter faction won so categorically that in the Acts of the Apostles, which reflect Paul's views, those of the Judaeo-Christians are barely mentioned.

Budding Christianity was presented with another difficulty concerning the 'Kingdom of Heaven'. Was it still to come, or was it already here? Was it something exterior, or did it happen in the heart of each Christian? We already know how much the Apocalypse which describes the second coming of Christ prior to Judgment Day troubled the minds of Christians. The relative ambiguity of texts pertaining to Jesus's personality was only resolved through a long series of Councils spread out over the centuries which engendered innumerable heresies. Divergent interpretations of the New Testament are still produced today. But does the real wonder not lie in the fact that Jesus and his teachings have aroused, and continue to arouse, such diverse reactions, without losing any of their power and vitality?

'. . . for in fact, the kingdom of God is among you.' (Luke 17, 20)

'So the Word became flesh; he came to dwell among us.' (John 1, 14)

Joachim of Fiore

c. 1135 Celico, Calabria — San Martino c. 1202

An outstanding mystical reformer who became a prophet

Joachim of Fiore's writings announced the coming of a new age governed by the Holy Spirit and as such stirred up Christianity over several countries.

While he was on a pilgrimage to the Holy Land, Joachim of Fiore was struck down by a serious illness and suddenly miraculously cured. On his return to Calabria he renounced the world and entered the Cistercian monastery of Corazzo, of which he subsequently became abbot in 1178. He defended the strict observance of monastic rule and withdrew into solitude before founding the abbey of Saint John-of-the-Flower, the first member of an order that at its height numbered 32 religious establishments. Joachim of Fiore denounced the vices of a corrupt clergy; he led an austere existence dying with a reputation for saintliness. One century later Dante was to mention 'the Calabrian abbot Joachim, gifted with a prophetic spirit' in his *Paradise*.

Shortly after his death, Joachim's apocalyptic writings caused havoc, particularly in Francis of Assisi's newly founded order.

'God, who once gave the prophets the prophetic spirit, has given me the spirit of intelligence.'

Certain Franciscans saw in him the coming of the spiritual people whose task it would be to guide the world in the new era which was due to commence in 1260; one who believed this theory was Gerardo of San Donnino, the author of *Eternal Gospel* (1254) who was condemned by the Church. In the 14th century several schismatic movements based themselves on Joachim's writings, which also inspired Böhme in the 17th century and Berdiaev in the 20th century.

His works

Three of Joachim's tracts in Latin have been extremely popular over the centuries: *Concordance of the Old and New Testaments; Commentary on the Apocalypse;* and *Treatise on the Four Gospels*, his last and unfinished work.

The theory

His teaching is based on a reinterpretation of the Old and New Testaments which would illuminate the future of Christianity. Joachim tries to decipher God's will through a complex system of numerological and symbolic keys. For him, humanity's evolution is brought about in three distinct stages, each stage dominated by one of the three persons of the Trinity. Thus in the Jewish Bible which corresponds to the first stage of the Father, the second stage, that of Christ, is announced, and in the same way the New Testament predicts the imminent arrival of the third and final stage, that of the Holy Spirit. Then, under the guidance of a totally spiritualized Church, humanity will be lit up by divine Grace.

John Cassian

360 Dobruja, Romania — Marseilles 435

The first great organizer of Western monachism

Having learnt from Eastern anchorites, John Cassian adapted their teachings for the first Western monasteries.

Having gained a good education, John Cassian entered a monastery in Bethlehem, then, attracted by the monastic communities of Egypt, he left for Thebes in 385. In Constantinople he was ordained a deacon by John Chrysostom, and subsequently went to Rome to defend the work of the latter who had been exiled in 404. Ten years later Cassian, who was by this time a priest, founded two monasteries at Marseilles: Saint Victor for men and Saint Sauveur for women. It was at Marseilles, during the last 20 years of his life, that Cassian composed his work which, after its diffusion amongst the contemplative orders, was and still is praised and studied.

His works

His principal works are: *De Institutis coenobiorum* which defines external life, seen as a necessary initiation before the secret of contemplation can be penetrated, and the *Collations*, which is a report of the discussions Cassian had with Egyptian anchorites, and is addressed to the 'inner man' in order to facilitate access to purity of the heart, the source of man's future godliness.

The theory

Although, using his personal experience as a base, Cassian was anxious to adapt the traditions of the Desert Fathers, Origen, and Evagrius, to the Western Church, he also defined the ideal Christian life which he associated with the Apostles and the strict adherence to the precepts in the Gospels. For him, the search for God can only be accomplished far from the world; it presupposes renouncement. In return for this, the monk can immediately begin to live out eternity, to share in the angelic condition and, coming before the presence of God, be transformed by divine Grace. Cassian stresses the traps which threaten monks, particularly *accidia* (sloth), disgust, anxiety, and discouragement. But they must never forget that whereas the Devil tempts them from outside, God is present within them. John was called 'the most perfect of the masters of monastic perfection' precisely because of his perspicasity and his obsession with the details of monastic practices.

Contemplation

'No other virtue makes man more equal to the angels, than the initiation of their way of life.'

John Chrysostom

354 Antioch — Comana, Cappadocia 407

The most famous Eastern Church orator

Nicknamed Chrysostom 'Golden Mouth', he preached moral reform and insisted on the need for each individual to conform to the new Christian ideal.

John was the son of an officer in the Syrian army, and a pupil of the famous rhetorician Libanius before his baptism and subsequent entry into an ascetic community. He spent four years as the disciple of one of the hermits and then a further two years in solitude in a cave. Exhausted by immoderate austerity he finally understood the inanity of personal salvation by withdrawing from the world, and returned to Antioch to serve the Church. John was ordained a priest in 386 and fought the opponents of orthodoxy in his sermons and writings. His impassioned eloquence and the moral reform he advocated made him very popular, resulting in his appointment as Bishop of Constantinople. However, as he was also openly criticial of those in power, in the eyes of both civil and religious authorities he soon became undesirable and he was deposed and exiled in 403. He was re-

instated by popular acclaim. But after he launched another attack on his enemy, the Empress Endoxia, he was again exiled in 404, this time much further from the city. He died of exhaustion in a ditch at Comana. Shortly after his death his true value was realized and he was reinstated. Today John, who knew how to uphold the rights of the conscience against the abuse of power, is one of the most respected pastors in the Church's history.

His works

John was a prolific writer, producing numerous tracts, the most important of which are *On the Incomprehensibility of God; On the Priesthood; On Divine Providence; That No One is Damned, Except by Himself*, as well as his famous *Homilies* and more than 200 *Letters*, written in exile, which encourage the community he had seen forced to abandon.

The theory

As a contemporary of Basil of Caesarea, Gregory of Nazianzus and Augustine, John Chrysostom contributed to the edification of the Church which was only just emerging from the troubled period that followed the creation of the Christian Empire. He was firstly an ascetic and a mystic, and then selflessly devoted himself to his congregation and his role as a pastor. If, like Basil, John believed that the ideals of Christian life could only be fulfilled by monks, he also believed that where possible the laity should attempt to conform to those ideals, for the Incarnation shook human existence to its very foundations. Salvation can only be collective and true perfection lies in forgetting the self in serving others.

Christian Charity

'You, the pure, would it not be better to become less strong and reach others, rather than staying up in the heights watching with indifference while your brothers become lost?'

John Climacus

c. 580 Constantinople — Mount Sinai 650

One of the guides of both Eastern and Western monachism

A much sought-after spiritual leader whose teachings were followed for many centuries, John Climacus was the abbot of Saint Catherine's monastery on Mount Sinai.

Having left Constantinople at the age of 16, John became a monk at Saint Catherine's monastery on Mount Sinai, where God appeared to Moses as the burning bush, and which, from the earliest Christian times had attracted many holy men and ascetics. John left the monastery 19 years later in order to devote himself to contemplation and asceticism in the absolute solitude of a desert cave, where he lived for some 30 years. Soon, his reputation for saintliness brought him disciples and, towards the end of his life, at his disciples' insistence, John returned to Sinai to become their abbot, but died shortly after. As a result of his life and his writings Mount Sinai became the principal centre for the diffusion of Hesychasm – the achievement of divine quietness through the contemplation of God in uninterrupted prayer.

His works

John Climacus wrote many tracts mainly to meet the demands of his disciples. His work on progressive asceticism, *The Holy Ladder*, became so famous that the Sinai leader was nicknamed Climacus (from the Greek *klimax* meaning 'ladder').

The theory

The Holy Ladder that Jacob saw in his dream links heaven with earth. Jesus refers to it when He talks of open skies while the angels go up and down. John Climacus did not regard the movement as only upwardly unidirectional: God comes down to meet his creation, just as the latter goes up to meet Him. The Ladder has 30 rungs; the upper degrees are humility (25th) and *hesychia* or peace of mind and body which only perpetual prayer (27th) can bring. Above *hesychia* is the stage of *apatheia* where all passion is extinguished, all that is wordly is regarded with indifference and which is 'heaven inside the spirit', the last stage before union with God is reached. Although John himself was extremely learned, he did not greatly prize erudition without personal experience, and it is personal experience that he wanted to emphasize in his description of stages. This practical side to his works coupled with the aphorisms that are sprinkled throughout it have made him a very popular religious author not only in the East, but also in the West, from the Middle Ages until the 17th century, where he found favour with the Jansenists.

> 'I am amazed that he who has not tasted the fruits of heaven can be mistrustful of those of the earth.'

John Damascene

c. 640 Damascus — near Jerusalem 741 (?)

Arab and doctor of the Church

Considered one of the last of the Greek Fathers, John left his mark on Byzantine spirituality and liturgy.

John, a Christian Arab, was called Mansour ('Victorious') like his grandfather who had been an important official in the Byzantine Empire and who took part in the surrender of Damascus to the Muslim Invaders. John was a financial administrator but at the same time he protected his fellow Christians. He later left Damascus, withdrawing to the monastery of Mar Saba near Jerusalem, where he dedicated himself to contemplation, preaching and the completion of his works. Faithful to Christ the Redeemer, he was a vigorous defender of image worship, opposing the Iconoclasts who rejected any worship of images. He died in the monastery at the age of about 100. He was anathematized soon after his death but was reinstated by the 7th ecumenical council in 787. He is venerated by both the Catholic and Orthodox branches of Christianity and was declared a doctor of the Church by Pope Leo XIII in 1890.

His works

Apart from canons, which are hymns sung during vigils or religious festivals and which are still in use in Orthodox liturgy, and three tracts *Against the Iconoclasts,* his works include: *Fount of Knowledge,* chronologically the first of the great theological exposés on which, five centuries later,

Thomas Aquinas based his own works. In *Fount of Knowledge* the doctrines of the Greek Fathers and the controversies which came after them are synthesized, as well as the works of the councils. It is divided into three parts: 'Dialectic' founded on Aristotle's works as transmitted by the Neoplatonists, 'History of Heresies', and most importantly, 'Exposé or Orthodox Faith', which was used for a long time as the principal authority on the subject.

The theory

As the inheritor of a long-standing Christological tradition, John of Damascus defined the Son, Word of God, as the very archetype of humanity, transcending his own transcendence through love. 'Suffering and dying in His flesh', Christ takes on our suffering and our death, and by His resurrection any separation between God and humanity is abolished. Human nature, which was created in view of its future deification, is perfected for Christ, and in Him. Through the mystery of the sacraments, humankind is transfigured by this godly energy. This is why the icon, which is originally the image of the Transfiguration, is the symbol of true unity regained. The liturgy then becomes the tangible manifestation of deification; it was John Damascene who gave it its definitive form.

Christ

'Complete, He takes charge of me completely. Complete, He unites with me completely in order to give me complete salvation.'

John of the Cross

1542 Fontiveros, near Avila — Ubeda 1591

Poet of the 'dark night'

One of the greatest mystics of all time, John was also a profoundly lyrical poet.

John's father died when he was two, leaving the family in poverty, but he still managed to get an excellent education at a Jesuit school. At the age of 20, he entered the Carmelite order, and studied for four years at Salamanca university. Disillusioned with the lax morals of the order, he was about to leave when he met Teresa of Avila who persuaded him to carry out the same reforms to the whole branch of the order as she was trying to accomplish in the female. There was great resistance to these reforms and to the founding of the Discalced (Barefoot) Carmelites in which he took part and John, who had taken the name John of the Cross, was imprisoned in 1577 and subjected to such a severe prison regime that he went through a period of terrible inner trauma (the 'dark night'). He escaped in 1578 and in 1582 became prior of the Carmelites in Granada but was soon again involved in the internal disputes within the reform movement. He was made destitute by the provincial, Nicholas Doria, and sent to Ubeda where he died. John of the Cross was canonized in 1726 and proclaimed a doctor of the Church in 1926.

His works

Fear of the Inquisition made John of the Cross have most of his manuscripts destroyed. His works were not published until 1618, and the first critical edition did not appear until 1912. John of the Cross is firstly one of the greatest Spanish poets. *Spiritual Song* was partially composed in a dungeon. His tracts, *The Ascent of Mount Carmel* and *The Dark Night*, are didactic commentaries on his poems.

The theory

John of the Cross is essentially a spiritual guide on the narrow path of perfection which leads to the mountain on whose summit the soul rediscovers its Creator and melts in this love. But before this, the soul must go through two purifying nights, the active night of effort, followed by the passive night, or 'dark night', where the soul, denuded and without any comfort, abandons itself to the workings of God. In fact, faith can only be found at the heart of the mystic night, at the end of the ultimate purification, which only operates in the 'horror of complete darkness'. What John of the Cross proposes is his personal experience of God's love, both painful and glorious, which he sums up when he writes 'Love does not consist of feeling great things, but of experiencing great need and suffering for the Loved One. Yet, John of the Cross does not talk about himself, because he has renounced the self. His direct and exemplary account has had immense repercussions right up to the present day.

> **'The soul must empty itself** . . ., it must always remain as though stripped bare and in darkness depending on faith alone, using it as a guide and a light.'

Judaism

The first monotheistic religion

From the prophets of Biblical times to the Cabalists of the Middle Ages, there has been a succession of interpretations of Jewish Law.

The word Judaism comes from the tribe of Judah, denoting the religion of Israel, God's chosen people. In answer to Yahweh's call, Abraham, the first Patriach, left Sumeria with his family, and c. 1760 BC, settled in Canaan, between the Jordan and the Mediterranean, adopting the local language, Hebrew. Joseph, Abraham's great-grandson, became Pharaoh's minister and brought the whole clan to settle in Egypt, where they were unfortunately enslaved. Freed by Moses, they went to conquer Canaan.

Moses was really the true founder of Judaism, but once his people became settled they were influenced by surrounding religions. Upholding the purity of the faith, was encouraged by the Prophets in the name of Yahweh, who was worshipped in the unique holy centre of the Temple of Jerusalem. The temple was built by Solomon, the son of David, who was the first king of a state which in 930 BC split into Israel (in the north) and Judah (in the south). After the temple's destruction by Nebuchadrezzar in 587 and the Babylonian captivity, Jerusalem once more became a centre of Judaism, even in the Hellenistic period which saw the revolt of the Maccabees (from 168 BC) and the Roman period, until the final destruction of the temple in AD 70. The ensuing Diaspora meant the dispersion of Jewish communities throughout the Mediterranean basin, then into Europe; one of the largest and most influential of these communities was in Egypt, concentrated especially around Alexandria.

The descendants

As the Law did not permit the offering of sacrifices outwith the temple, the Jews gathered together in synagogues, which were regular meeting places for the study of the Torah and the Talmud (see **Bible**), run by Rabbis, the community's religious leaders. Contact with Islam introduced a speculative, more mystical trend into Judaism in the 12th century, led by Maimonides. In the same period the esoteric or Cabalist movement emerged. Although it was at first a purely speculative movement, the Cabala was behind the active Safed school in Galilee, dominated by Isaac Luria (1534–72). The prophetic Safed school later inspired the messianic heresy of Sabbatai Zen (1626–76) who incited crowds to follow him in an attempt to reconquer the Holy Land. Zen later embraced Islam when forced to choose between conversion and execution. In the 18th century, Hasidism brought about a small scale return to this earlier fervour.

Moses

'There are things hidden, and they belong to the Lord our God, but what is revealed to us belongs to us and our children for ever: it is for us to observe all that is prescribed in this law.'
(*Deuteronomy* 29, 29)

Jung, Carl Gustav

1875 Kesswil, Switzerland — Küsnacht, Switzerland 1961

Explorer of the depths of the psyche

Jung gave contemporary humankind a method of self-knowledge which allows them to exploit hidden potential

Jung was the son of a Protestant minister. He studied medicine at Basel and began his career at the Burghölzli, the psychiatric clinic at the University of Zürich. In 1907, when he was the director of the clinic, he met Sigmund Freud and the two men became friends and collaborators; but with the publication in 1912 of Jung's *Symbols of Transformation* in which he rejected Freud's reduction of psychic energy (libido) to the sexual impulse, the split between the two men became inevitable. From then on, in order to distinguish it from Freudian psychoanalysis, Jung called his own doctrine 'complex psychology'. Jung was then living at Küsnacht on the shores of Lake Geneva, where he remained until his death. Although still practising, he began to devote more and more time to his personal research in which he sought confirmation

for the theories he had formed about Western and Eastern mysticism, medieval alchemy and ethnography, for which he had travelled in India, Africa, and the United States. Moreover, he corresponded with many great experts on China (R. Wilhelm), on India (H. Zimmer) and with the philologist and religious historian K. Kerenyi. Even during his lifetime, Jung earned a reputation as a religious leader, a position to which he had never aspired.

His works

In Jung's vast and complex body of writings some texts are clearly orientated towards the spiritual. The most remarkable of these are: *Transformations of the Soul and its Symbols* (1953) which was a reworking of the 1912 *Symbols of Transformation; Dialectic of the Self and the Unconscious* (1964); *Commentary on the Mystery of the Golden Flower* (1979); and most importantly, *My Life* (1966).

The theory

Jung's work is so wide-ranging and exceeds by so much the field of psychotherapy, that there is a modern-day tendency to see him as the founder of a new humanism, based on a detailed analysis of the psyche's innermost depths. Some of his concepts, like that of the 'collective unconscious' which feeds the individual unconscious with 'archetypes' — in particular those of the *Anima* and the *Animus* which introduce the image of the opposite sex into the psyche — are very close to Hindu or Buddhist psychology. They end in the 'process of individuation', or the individual's realization of his or her potential which is no longer centred on the *ego*, but on the self (*Selbst*) and is comparable to what mystics call the image of God in the Soul.

The necessary transformation

'Nothing has been achieved as long as the individual's character has not changed itself.'

Invisible truth

'All of us such as we are, spy on that tarnished mirror in which figures parade in an obscure mystery, looking in order to draw the invisible truth from it.'

Kabir

1440 — 1518

Famous saint and mystic

Although he followed no religion himself, Kabir is one of the most popular and remarkable religious leaders in Indian tradition.

Despite his extraordinary popularity, we know virtually nothing of Kabir's life, except that he was a low-caste Muslim weaver and as such despised by society, and that he lived in the Hindu holy city of Benares, which at that time was under Muslim rule, as was all north India. His posthumous glory was so great that he was adopted by Hindu tradition which portrays him as the son of a Brahman widow who was brought up by Muslim parents, and the disciple of a Vishnuite master. Kabir was almost certainly illiterate and never wrote anything, but his *Words*, in the form of short songs were transmitted orally, then gathered together into different compilations such as the *Adi Granth*, the Sikhs' holy book (16th century).

Teachings

A witness of the bitter conflicts between Hinduism and Islam, Kabir has often mistakenly been seen as someone attempting to reconcile different systems of belief. In fact, he rejects both of the above faiths, is against all religion, all revealed Scripture, and attacks the hyprocisy of followers who 'in markets and public squares become absorbed in meditation.' For him, only inner revelation exists; the only source of religious knowledge is personal experience, which enables the individual to go beyond illusory duality and return to the original state of being which is one of pure beautific spontaneity. Although Kabir may have come into contact with Hindu saints and the Sufis, he never mentions them and only recognizes the *Satguru* or 'inner One'.

In direct and abrupt language, *Words* tells of the spiritual experience of a man of the people, an unmoveable defender of the Unity of the Being whom he sometimes calls Allah, sometimes Ram (*Rama*) and who is 'the same in all the bodies'. His passionate conviction that the mystic path was unique has brought him followers not only amongst the mass of the people, but also from the cultured. The *Words* were never forgotten and indeed were highlighted by two of Kabir's greatest admirers, Rabindranath Tagore (1861–1941) and Gandhi (1867–1948).

Kabir is venerated by both Hindus and Muslims for the purity of his experience which surpassed any religious segregations. He was also the first great poet to write in the Hindu language.

> **The Other is me**
> 'He whom I was going to look for, has come to meet me. And he whom I called the Other, has become me.'

Kierkegaard, Søren Aabye

1813 Copenhagen — Copenhagen 1855

Aware of the fragility of our existence

A unique and mysterious personality, Kierkegaard regenerated the Protestant Church through reinternalizing faith.

Kierkegaard's relatively uneventful, brief life was spent almost entirely in Copenhagen. By the time of his birth, his father was already quite elderly and embittered by the deaths of many close relatives, including his second wife. He gave his son a rigorous and austere education, dominated by the image of Jesus crucified. As a student, Kierkegaard began to lead a pleasurable life but his mother's death in 1834 and a series of mysterious events which he called the 'earthquake' (in fact the discovery of the curse which hung over his family), brought on despair that never left him. In 1838 his father died, and Kierkegaard, who by now had finished studying divinity, became engaged to Regine Olsen, whom he loved passionately. For some mysterious reason, he later broke off their engagement, and also refused to become a minister, preferring instead to begin

> **'What is a Christian?** From beginning to end, he is a scandal, the divine scandal.'

> 'It is impossible to stress **existence** with more insistence than I have done.'

writing the books in which his vocation as Christianity's witness gradually becomes more clear. He also attacked the institutions which had finally betrayed the faith. In 1843 his first work *Either-Or* was very successful, but there was public outcry and indignation at his extremist stance, and he was soon at the centre of a scandal.

His work

His works are both autobiographical and philosophical, and relate the various stages of his inner experiences. They begin in 1843 with *Either-Or*, which contains *The Diary of a Seducer*; followed by *Philosophical Fragments* (1844) and *Postscript to Philosophical Fragments* (1846); and include other works with meaningful titles: *Fear and Trembling* (1843); *The Concept of Anxiety* (1844); and *On Despair* (1849).

The theory

Kierkegaard's philosophy was little known and even less understood in his day, because he denounced the progressive rationalization of Christianity and foretold of the crisis it would have to go through. This kind of philosophy electrified 20th century philosophers. It reminded believers that true Christianity can only happen from within. He wanted the central importance of the individual reinstated and the deliberate choices each of us makes in forming our future selves affirmed. Kierkegaard's firm choice of internalizing and its requirements, makes him one of the greatest modern mystics. He is also regarded as one of the founders of Existentialism.

Koran

A message transmitted directly from God

The Koran was revealed to Muhammad so that he might pass it on to his followers. Recited continually, it governs all aspects of Muslim life.

When Muhammad first received the Divine Revelation, he was obliged to recite the text dictated to him by his vision, thus *qur'an*, meaning 'recitation', was the name given to the Muslim holy book. The text in its original form was transmitted to the Prophet's first followers who also recited it before transcribing it on to pieces of leather or carving it on to camel bones. After this initial period, Muhammad stopped having visions and had no more for three years; then they came at regular intervals and Muhammad dictated their content to his secretary. His followers gradually assembled these fragmentary texts into a more coherent book form. After Muhammad's death, it became necessary to establish a complete, standardized version of the text. Abu Bakr, the first caliph, began by gathering together the oldest collections of *suras* but it was not until the Caliph Othman (644–656 bc) that a definitive version was decided upon, to the exclusion of all others. Tradition has it that, following this

decision, all other unofficial versions were destroyed. The Vulgate established by Othman therefore constitutes the original text to the Revelation and remains unchanged to this day.

The suras

The Koran consists of 6226 verses which are divided into 114 chapters or *suras*. These *suras* are neither arranged chronologically nor grouped by subject matter, but are listed in order of decreasing length, thus rendering interpretation extremely difficult. The shortest, which are often reduced to juxtaposed incantations or to messages of intense religous fervour, go back to the original prophecy at Mecca, and describe Muhammad's overwhelming religious experience; they are urgent and dramatic in tone, for they announce the universal judgment that is to be feared by the impious and by sinners alike. The later and longer *suras* reflect the inability of the Meccan population to understand the Prophet's message, and compare this to a similar hostile attitude which met his predecessors Noah, Abraham, and Jesus. Finally the Medina *suras* denounce the enemies of the Prophet as enemies of God who are no longer to be persuaded into conversion but to be converted by the sword; they also lay down the foundations of the new, evolving Muslim society.

Although this text remains unchanged (and indeed to change it would be impossible), in parts it is extremely concise and the meaning can be obscure. Over the centuries, the Koran has been interpreted in a multitude of ways, in particular the *Hadith* or traditions dating from the Prophet's own era, which, due to their frequently divergent nature, have contributed to the divisions within the Islamic religion.

What is the Koran?

'In truth, the Koran is a revelation from the Lord of the world placed in your heart by the Holy Spirit so that you might be amongst those who sound the alarm.' (*Koran* 26, 192–4)

Krishnamurti

1895 Madanapalle, Madras — Ojai, California 1986

An areligious spirituality for today's world?

According to Kirshnamurti, it is only within oneself that one can find the absolute, unconditioned Truth, which is Eternal Life.

Jiddu Krishnamurti was born in southern India to Brahman parents. While he was very young his mother died and he and his brother Nitjananda (died 1925) were adopted by Annie Besant, the president of the Theosophical Society (see **Theosophists**) who believed the 13 year old Krishnamurti to be the future 'World Teacher,' the reincarnation of great past religious leaders. At the age of 16, he was already leading the international order of the Star of the East which was founded by Annie Besant, who sent her protégé to complete his studies at Oxford and Paris. But the young man soon refused the messianic role that had been forced upon him and declared that as he had achieved 'liberation' through his own efforts, he had become 'Truth incarnate'. Krishnamurti dissolved the order in 1929, and broke away from the society completely. From then on he used Ojai in California as his home base, travel-

ling from there on lecture tours which attracted audiences of thousands. Every year he went to Brockwood Park (England), Saanen, near Gstaad (Switzerland) and Madras (India). He was also president of four foundations in Britain, the United States, and India, which have their own schools.

His works

At the present time, a transcription of his lectures and interviews is under preparation for publication. Amongst the works already available are: *The Revolution of Silence* (1972), *The Awakening of Intelligence* (1975), and *Tradition and Revolution* (1978).

The theory

Krishnamurti constantly declined the role of guru or religious leader. He systematically rejected all religions because he believed that people took refuge in them and that they presented an obstacle to the personal search for truth. Starting from the premise that no matter how far it has advanced materially, humanity remains violent and savage, divided within and against itself and capable of self-destruction, Krishnamurti considered that change was only possible through the evolution of the individual. In consequence, he asked his audiences to take responsibility for themselves, and adopted the attitude of a researcher starting out from 'unknowledge'. He joined them in their search in order to help them shed their prejudices and attain self-knowledge.

Towards liberation

'What is important is not what happens after death, but the liberation of the conscience, which is immortality.'

Lamas

The religious leaders of Tibetan Buddhism

The lamas belong to four maor monastic orders, and are only called upon to teach once they have been fully consecrated at the end of a long training period.

The word *lama* in Tibetan does not refer to the simple monk, but means 'superior', and corresponds to the Sanskrit *guru* meaning 'a leader capable of transmitting initiatory teachings'. The process of becoming a lama is long and arduous. Years of study must be completed at the monastic universities, followed by successive initiation rites and long periods of solitary retreat (three years, three months and three days). The lamas, who do not always live in monasteries, but sometimes in hermitages, are considered to be the visible manifestations of the universal Buddha principle. As such their disciples owe them respect and must have absolute faith in them. A lama is an experienced guide, before eventually becoming a religious dignitary; it is therefore necessary to differentiate between ecclesiastical hierarchy and spiritual progress.

The four schools

The lamas belong to the four great schools which emerged in Tibet during the 10th and 11th centuries. These schools spread throughout Mongolia as well as in the different Himalayan states of Ladakh, Nepal, Sikkim, and Bhutan. Since the invasion of Tibet, they are also represented in various forms in the West. In 1056 Domton, the first Tibetan disciple of the great Indian guru Atisa, founded the monastery of Radeng, to the north of Lhasa. It was to

become the centre of the first great Tibetan monastic order, the Kadam-pa, 'Linked by the Doctrine', a title which underlines their strict observance of monastic rules. They led an ascetic life, devoted to study and meditation. This school was later to give birth to the Gelug-pa order. In the 12th century, the Kagyu-pa order ('Transmitters of the Word') appeared. The name stresses the importance of a transmission which, through the intermediary of Marpa, the Translater (1012–96) who was the master of the mystic poet Milarepa, goes back to the great Indian Siddhas, Naropa (1016–1100) and Tilopa (988–1069), who are said to have received the teaching from Vajradhara, the celestial Buddha. The school created by Gampo-pa (1079–1153), one of Milarepa's main disiciples, split into six branches. The best known of these are the Brug-pa school which was founded in 1180 and can almost be described as the national church in modern day Bhutan, and the Karma-pa order, founded by a disciple of Gampo-pa, which used to be very active in eastern Tibet, but today is centred on Sikkim.

In 1073 a disciple of the translator Dogmi (922–1072), created the Sakya-pa order, named after their first monastery. From the 13th century this order played an important role in politics, but had to give way to the leaders of the new Gelugs-pa school, known as the 'Yellow Hats', as opposed to the other schools who were

> **Reverence due to a lama**
> The lama has received his inherited wisdom through a long line of gurus which goes back to the Buddha Shakyamuni and he proposes to transmit this treasure to his disciples. In his own lama, the disciple reveres all the gurus of his line (*John Blofeld*)

Milarepa, *Tibetan poet and mystic, founder of the Kagyu-pa monastic order. Detail from fresco, Tashilunpo Monastery, seat of the Panchen Lama, Shigatse, Tibet*

known as the 'Red Hats', because of the different colours of their ceremonial head wear.

The Gelugs-pa order ('Followers of the Virtuous Path') resulted from the restoration of strict discipline by Tsong Kha-pa (1357–1419) at the monastery of Ganden near Lhasa, then at Drepung in 1416 and Sera in 1419. By the end of the 15th century, Drepung was the largest monastery in Tibet, with 1500 monks. The Gelugs-pa order which gives precedence to philosophical study, has the Dalai Lama as its head. This title, which comes from the Mongol *Ta-le* meaning 'ocean' (implying 'of wisdom'), was conferred by King Altan Khan on Sonam Gyantso (1543–88); the latter was considered to be the reincarnation of his two predecessors, and he became the third Dalai Lama. Tenzin Gyatso, is the 14th. He was born in 1935, proclaimed in 1940 and inaugurated in 1950. He had to leave Lhasa in 1959 because of political troubles, taking refuge in Dharamsala in the Indian area of the Himalayas.

The fourth great monastic order, Nyingma-pa (the 'Followers of the Elders' (tantras)) is completely different from the others in that the monks are not obliged to be celibate, nor does the order possess any hierarchical organization. It was among the first orders to establish a monastery in Tibet, and is based on the teachings of Padmasambhava. during the religious persecutions of the 9th century, isolated yogis, or small communities dispersed in the mountains, managed to keep the tra-ditions alive. Later, because of the priority given to solitary meditation and mystical research, the Nyingma-pa monasteries attracted only a small number of monks, some of whom were married and lived within the monasteries with their families. The order keeps traditions which probably ante-date Buddhism and includes the school of meditation known as the 'Great Perfection' (*Dzogtchen*), close to Ch'an. Some of their writings are *terma*, ancient texts of an esoteric nature which were hidden during periods of persecution and rediscovered and revealed from the 11th century onwards.

The Tulku

Belief in the reappearance of the great lamas was first evident in the Kagyu school in the person of Dusum Khyen (1110–93), a disciple of the founder Gampo-pa, who became the first Karma-pa. The 16th was Ranjoun Rigpai Dorje (1924–82). In the Saskya-pa school, the great lamas are believed to be the reincarnations of the bodhisattva Manjusri and are known for their erudition. The Dalai Lamas are worshipped as emanations of the Bodhisattva of Compassion, Avalokitesvara, in Tibetan Tcherenzi, the protector of Tibet. Incorrectly called the 'Living Buddhas', the Tulku 'bodies of incarnation' are not considered as reincarnations, which would be contrary to the Doctrine, but, in accordance with the concept of *bodhisattva* (see **Mahayana**), as beings produced by the compassion of great religious leaders.

Lanza del Vasto

1901 San Vito dei Normanni, Italy — Lalonguera, Spain 1981

Contemporary mystical prophet

Lanza del Vasto was the founder of a new kind of spiritual community.

Giuseppe Giovanni di Trabia Branciforte's father came from ancient Sicilian nobility, and his mother was Flemish. Both his childhood and his education were very cosmopolitan. His studies at the University of Pisa orientated him towards the Catholicism of St Thomas Aquinas, an ancestor. He had all sorts of different jobs and wandered around the country before leaving for India. In 1937 his meeting with Ghandi, who gave him the name *Shantidas* (Servant of Peace) was a turning point in his life. Published in 1943 *The Pilgrimage to the Source* was very successful. With his wife, whom he called 'Chanterelle', Lanza created his first community, called the Arch, at Charente. It was dedicated to working the land, but also to a rigorous spiritual life. The Arch moved about several times before settling at La Borie-Noble, to the south of the Cévennes. Several groups later left the Arch to set up new sister establishments.

'You want a better, more fraternal, more just world? Well then, start building it: who is stopping you? Build it inside yourself and around you, build it with those who want it. Build it small, and it will grow.'

Although it is perhaps best known for its active policy of non-violence, the community founded by Lanza del Vasto was and still is a centre for intense inner purification, based on love for others, the worshipping of nature, and the reassessment of humble daily chores.

His works

His works are very diverse, including poems, plays, and especially writings on spirituality and Christian exegesis, the better known of which are: *The Pilgrimage to the Source* (1943), *Vinoba, or the New Pilgrimage* (1954), *Principles and Precepts of the Return to Evidence* (1945), *Approaches to Inner Life* (1963), and *The Spiritual Trinity* (1970).

The theory

Lanzo del Vasto decided to create a brotherly community for spiritual training in the West, close in essence to early monachism, but answering the needs of contemporary society. It was based on Gandhi's principle of *ahimsa*, which is not only non-violence, but also respect for others, voluntary poverty, and obedience; this was achieved through blending Christian faith and charity, and Hindu wisdom and renunciation as demonstrated by the Mahatma. If Lanza del Vasto's books outline the principles on which he based his acts, the most important aspect of his work was the personal example he set, which numerous disciples followed.

Lao Tzu and Taoism

c. 570 — 490BC

The 'Hidden Sage' of China

Lao Tzu is traditionally thought to be the author of the Tao-te-ching, the most frequently translated text in the Chinese language whose obscure nature makes it impossible to compile one definitive version.

Although it is impossible to separate Taoism from the name Lao Tzu, we know virtually nothing of the man and certain Sinologists have gone so far as to question his very existence. Lao Tzu means 'Ancient Master' and the only biography we have of him dates from the 1st century BC, but is very misleading. He is supposed to have been born in the 6th century BC, and been an archivist and astrologer in the Chou administration. He was apparently visited by the great Confucius himself, but is said to have snubbed him openly. Lao-tzu was aware of the decline of the reigning dynasty which made him decide to leave for the uncivilized West. However, at the frontier the guard asked him to write down his teachings, so Lao Tzu, who at the time was between 160 and 200 years old, wrote the *Tao-te-ching* and disappeared, never to be seen again. Ssu-ma Ch'ien, the historian who records this tradition concludes: 'Nobody knows whether this is true or not; Lao Tzu was a hidden Sage'. This in part explains why history makes no explicit reference to him. Although Lao Tzu may have lived in the 6th century BC, the *Tao-te-ching* dates from no earlier than the 3rd century BC. However, some verses pre-date this time, and are the key parts of the work which really express Lao Tzu's philosophy.

The theory

The *Tao-te-ching* is divided into two books which have 37 and 44 brief chapters in verse. The title, which is probably a later addition, is usually translated as 'The Book of the Way and of Virtue', but *tao* more precisely describes the original passive principle, whereas *te* is the spiritual and magical energy put at its disposal. The actual text is often paradoxical and enigmatic because of its brevity. It is mainly addressed to those concerned with meditation and the pursuit of mystical knowledge, and many of the sayings can be understood on several different levels, which accounts for the *Tao-te-ching*'s reputation as an inexhaustible source of knowledge.

In itself, *tao* is indefinable:

'That which is without name is the origin of Heaven and Earth
That which is named is the Mother of ten thousand beings'.

Although *tao* itself is inactive, it is the primordial cause of all action and can only be defined negatively like *wu*, which is absence, non-being or not-having, as opposed to *yeu*, having, which defines the

---

Becoming a Child again
'He who knows himself to be male, but behaves like a female, is the Ravine of the world. Constant virtue never leaves him. He becomes a little child again.' (*Tao-te-ching*)

Emptiness
'Aspire to complete emptiness, and be calm. In the face of the seething agitation of beings, only contemplate their return.' (*Tao-te-ching*)

sensory matter created by the above. Hence the esoteric phrase: 'Tao gave birth to One. One gave birth to Two. Two to Three. Three gave birth to 10 000 beings'. Tao divides itself without becoming less intact; it is Emptiness, but that emptiness is filled with possibilities. Where there is nothing, like in the hub of a wheel or the hollow centre of a vase, lies potential. One who conforms to tao is a saint; like tao, he can only be free if he is totally empty; like tao, he never acts but allows things to happen. Having brought about his return to the source, he rediscovers child-like spontaneity, and nothing in life or in death can frighten him, for he has overcome them as well as all other contradictions. Taoism is presented as total non-action, in which it is diametrically opposed to Confucianism. It is mystical knowledge intended for sages who have withdrawn from the world and can contemplate it from afar. Three such sages were the 'fathers' of Taoism: Lao Tzu, Chuang Tzu and Li Tzu, to whom the *True Classic of the Perfect Emptiness* is attributed.

Neotaoism

The face of Taoism was to change over the centuries, becoming popular religion on the one hand, and mystical and alchemical knowledge on the other. Taoism as a religion began with the divination of Lao Tzu in the 2nd century. It embodies certain elements of ancient Shamanism. Its founder, Chang tao-ling instituted a succession of 'Celestial Masters' in AD 150, in west China,

while in the east, the 'Yellow Turban Revolt', was endangering the Han dynasty. The Taoist religion was directed by magician and healer priests who presided over ceremonial rites including exorcism, confession, the worshipping of ancestors, and several divinities, and the celebration of the equinox and solstice. It still survives in modern day Taiwan, where the 63rd Celestial Master lives in exile.

Neotaoism also became the search for immortality, not the spiritual immortality Chuang Tzu talked of, but physical immortality, the final apotheosis resulting from practices meant to encourage long life. These practices revolved around a particular breathing technique already alluded to in the *Chuang Tzu*, but which later became a method destined to encourage the growth of the immortal soul contained in each individual. This was accompanied by a certain diet, sexual practices which avoided the loss of vital energy, the use of drugs and talismans, and finally the imbibing of an 'elixir of life' which was obtained through alchemical processes. These ideas and experiments, which included a cosmic physiology of the human body, had a far-reaching effect on Chinese medicine. But this esoteric and sometimes magical Taoism is also based on a particular form of meditation whose aim is to encourage the vision of inner light which shows the presence of tao. It remains Chinese mysticism at its most typical for body and soul, microcosm and macrocosm are not separate entities, but inter-react and must finally harmonize.

Tao

'Tao is the secret base common to all mankind.'

'Tao itself does not act, yet everything is made by it.' (*Tao-te-ching*)

Luther, Martin

1483 Eisleben, Thurungia — Eisleben 1546

The first and greatest reformer of the Christian Church

Luther was deeply affected by the drama of sin and redemption; the strength of his convictions attracted many followers.

Luther's family were originally peasants, but had moved up to join the lower middle classes. In his youth he was influenced by the severity of his father and the sensitivity of his mother who was very superstititous. At the age of 14 he was sent to study at Magdeburg and Eisenach, then when he was 17 to the University of Erfurt, to study law, a career chosen for him by his father. But a terrifying thunderstorm during which lightning uprooted an oak tree close to where he was standing, prompted his vow to become 'really Christian', and he entered the monastery of the Eremites of Saint Augustine. Through the austerity of the life he imposed upon himself, and his asceticism, Luther tried to find the certainty of salvation, but was totally unable to attain a state of inner peace. He was ordained a priest in 1507 and began to give lessons at the Wittenberg monastery. From there, in 1510, he was sent on monastic business to Rome, where he was shocked and outraged by the corrupt Renaissance papacy. At 29, Luther was a doctor of theology and sub-prior of Wittenburg where he began to teach courses on the Bible, thus extending his knowledge of the

Scriptures and the Church Fathers. It was while he was meditating on a passage in Paul's Epistle to the Romans that the solution to his anxieties finally came to him: justification is by grace through faith alone not by works, and also by absolute confidence in Salvation.

The reformer

From 1516 onwards, Luther preached the necessity of a theological renewal, and the following year in his Ninety-five Theses stood up against the practice of the sale of indulgences, outraged that a financial price should be put on the remission of sins. At this point he had no desire whatever to break away from the Church; his intention was to encourage internal reform. Therefore he was most surprised at the reaction of the Church, and at the positive response to his proposals in general.

Denounced in Rome and accused of heresy by several theological opponents, Luther agreed to appear before Cardinal Legate Cajetan in October 1518. It was then that he stated that the infallibility of the pope could not override the Scriptures, reaffirming this statement the following year at Leipzig. On 15 June 1520 Luther was excommunicated, and the break was made final by the publication of his three 'great reformatory writings'. In April 1521 he was summoned before the diet at Worms where, despite the risk of execution, he was still unwilling to recant. He was given a triumphant reception by the crowds but on 26 May was declared a political and

---

Freedom of faith

'I want to preach, I want to talk, I want to write, but I do not want to force anyone, for faith needs to be voluntary and free, and to be received without fear.' (1522)

In the middle of the fray

'My God carries me away, my God chases me in front of Him, He does not lead me, I am not my own master, I aspire to rest and here I am in the middle of the fray.' (1519)

ideological outlaw of the empire. For almost a year he was hidden at Wartburg Castle by the Elector of Saxony. Although this was a period of self-doubt, he used the time to compile some of his works.

Lutheran ideas had already electrified the whole of Germany, often with extreme consequences, as in the case of Müntzer, the fanatical leader of the German 'Peasants' War'. Refusing to see the Scriptures condone violence, Luther had to act by lending his support to the Princes' repression and by recognizing the State Church controlled by them. At about the same time, the reformer had to fight against the Humanists who had supported him at first, and against Swiss reformer Zwingli's symbolic interpretation of the Eucharist. But he was principally occupied with teaching and the organization of the new Church which he provided with a liturgy, choral *Hymns*, the *Small* and *Large Catechisms*, and finally a complete translation of the *Bible* (1534). In 1534 Luther left his monastic order and the following year married a former Cistercian nun, Katharina von Bora, with whom he had six children.

Defending the Reformation against Rome occupied Luther until his death. In 1530 he sent his friend Melanchthon to act as Lutheran spokesman at the diet of Augsburg. Melanchthon read out the *Augsburg Confession*, one of the great documents of the Reformation. In 1537, in the Smalkaldic Articles, Luther only emphasized the differences between the Lutherans

and the Catholics. Although his last years were clouded by conflicts between his disciples, he still led a peaceful life: he was overweight and he developed his favourite ideas drinking beer with his friends, who gathered his words into the *Table Propositions*.

His works

He left a vast body of work in which it is possible to trace the evolution of the man and his reforms. The three great reformatory writings of 1520 are: *On the Liberty of a Christian Man*, *Appeal to the Christian Nobility of the German Nation*, and *A Prelude concerning the Babylonish Captivity of the Church*. In *De Servo Arbitrio* (1525), Luther speaks out against Erasmus, reaffirming the superiority of grace over everything else. In 1529 the *Small* and *Large Catechisms* were published; the former remains one of the cornerstones of Lutheran spirituality. It was also at this time that Luther's translation of the Bible appeared, one of the first great works in the German language. He also wrote polemic and educational tracts for the new community, and some 42 hymns.

The theory

The reason for the instant triumphant reception given to Luther's theories is that they answered many of the Christians' questions. Luther had only discovered these answers at the end of an extremely long and painful struggle, and these experiences fill the pages of his works. For him, because of original sin, human nature is invincibly led by its sexual appetite. Hope of salvation can only come as a result of absolute faith in Redemption and in personal union with the Redeemer. Thus internalized, Christianity no longer has any need for a rigid ecclesiastical hierarchy which claimed to be the sole source of salvation and truth, and which alone benefited from the practices and credulity of the pious.

What is Luther?

'The doctrine does not come from me, and I have not been crucified for anyone.'

Justification of faith

'I understood . . . that the passage (from the Epistle to the Romans) meant this: the Gospel reveals God's justice, whereby Merciful God justifies us by faith. Then I felt reborn, I felt as though I was entering Paradise.' (1515–16)

Mahayana

The 'Great Vehicle'

The Mahayana school of Buddhism was born in India and spread primarily to the north and west, from Tibet to Japan, through China and Korea with the bodhisattva of infinite compassion as its ideal.

Mahayana practice was perhaps a direct result of the split (from about 370 BC) between the 'Elders' (*Thera*) and the 'Great Assemblists' (*Mahasamghika*), but it was also the product of a slow evolutionary process which took Buddhism towards new metaphysical and spiritual developments. These are largely due to the great philosopher and ascetic Nagarjuna (1st–2nd centuries), founder of the Madhyamika school, or 'Middle Way', and to Asanga (4th century), head of the Yogacara school, founded on the existence of consciousness which could be mastered through yoga. The Mahayana has its own holy texts (*sutra*), the most important being *Lalitavistara*, a legendary life of the Buddha, *Saddharmapundarika* (Lotus of the Good Law), *Lankavatara*, and above all *Prajnaparamita*, teachings of supreme wisdom which are central to all Buddhist schools (see **Amida Worship, Shingon, Ch'an, Tendai, Zen**). The concept of emptiness (*sunyata*) is all-important in Mahayana Buddhism; it is seen to be the essence of all phenomena and also the root cause of their existence. In Mahayana Buddhism the bodhisattva ideal, which we already know from the Hinayana school in which it played a less important role than the saint or arhat, is revered (see **Buddhism**).

The boddhisattva

Having reached Enlightenment, the bodhisattva can become a buddha and enter Nirvana, but he prefers to stay on earth to help others liberate themselves. These models of wisdom became the object of worship by both the laity and monks, especially when they were incarnated by popular figures like Avalokitesvara, who personified perfect compassion, Maitreya, the Buddha who is yet to come, or Manjusri, the master of knowledge. These maha-bodhisattva are considered as emanations of the five directions in space and correspond to the five elements: Aksobhya (the 'Unshakeable'); Amitabha ('Unmeasured Light'); Amogasiddhi ('Infallible Realization'); Ratnasambhava ('Origin of the Jewel'); Vairocana ('Resplendant'). The five historical Buddhas, of which Sakyamuni is the penultimate, are dependant on them. This superposition of spiritual instances spread throughout the whole universe, gave birth to a complicated cosmological system which was to be further developed by the Vajrayana school, which grew from Mahayana Buddhism and is the third and last phase of the doctrine's development.

Human Anguish
'Like an artist terrified by the horrible monster he has painted, the common man is appalled by *samsara* (endless cycles of births and deaths).' (*Mahayanavinsika*)

Salvation of all Beings
'My life with all my rebirths, all my possessions, all the merit I have acquired or will acquire, all this I give up without hope of personal gain, in order to further the salvation of all beings.' (*Santideva*, 7th sutra)

Maimonides

1135 Cordoba — Fostat, Cairo 1204

The upholder of Jewish law

A major influence on Jewish thought, Maimonides was a spiritual leader at a time of extreme persecution.

Rabbi Moses ben Maimon was introduced to Talmudic study by his father. While he was still a child, Cordoba was conquered by the Almohads, who gave the Jews the choice between leaving the town and conversion to Islam. Moses's family went to Morocco where religious persecution was less severe, then on to the Christian kingdom of Jerusalem, and finally settled in Egypt, where Moses became Sultan Saladin's personal physician. He was elected overall leader of the Jewish communities, and campaigned successfully for them to be allowed to settle in Jerusalem and all of Palestine.

His works

He wrote in Arabic and apart from several scientific volumes on medicine and tracts intended to bolster flagging faith, his principal works are: *Mishneh Torah*, (c. 1180) (The Repetition of the Law), a concise examination of the Israelite tradition and philo-

sophical meditation on the roots of Judaism, and *Guide of the Perplexed* (c. 1190), which was intended mainly for those intellectuals who felt themselves caught between ancient Jewish culture and the new Arabic and Jewish philosophies which were emerging at that time; it supports the substantial similarity of philosophy and religion.

The theory

Persecuted and forced to flee from country to country in his search for religious freedom, Maimonides typifies medieval Judaism through his desire to preserve his Jewish identity and culture from the contamination of new philosophies, namely the Greek and Arab ideas that were being promulgated at that time.

As the spiritual leader of all the Jewish communities, Maimonides trained many disciples, lecturing not only on the Talmud but also on philosophy and the sciences. He was and is one of the most prominent figures in Jewish esoterism. His theories had a profound effect on 13th century society, provoking enthusiasm in some and consternation in others, particularly those who had already been influenced by the mystical tendencies in the Cabala.

In his *Letter to Moroccan Jews*, Maimonides exhorts his fellow Jews to remain faithful to Yahweh and the community, but he nevertheless acknowledges that an enforced conversion could not be a crime in God's eyes if it was accompanied by a secret allegiance to Judaism. This was to be the attitude of the Marranos in Spain three centuries later. From the 14th century onwards, Maimonides's influence began to wane, but at the end of the 18th century 'enlightened' Jews rediscovered and re-evaluated his works, and to this day he is acknowledged as one of the foremost authorities on Jewish thought.

Moral conscience

'In fact, every man has it in him to be fair . . . whether he be wicked, wise or a drunkard. And nobody can constrain him or dictate his behaviour, nobody can drag him on to the path of good or evil. The choice of path shall be made by him alone, with full realization of what he is doing.'

Mani and Manichaeism

216 near Ctesiphon, Southern Babylonia — Gundeshap, Belapet

274 or 277

The struggle of Good against Evil

Carried by his missionaries from the Atlantic to the Pacific, Mani's teachings influenced both Muslim esoterism and Cathar doctrine.

For centuries, the only information about Manichaeism came from reports made by enemies of the movement, in particular Saint Augustine, but the discovery of the sects' manuscripts have enabled a more balanced picture of the Manichaean system and its founder to be built.

Mani's father had joined a Judaeo-Christian sect in which they lived until Mani was 24. He was only 12 when an angel foretold his mission, which he himself began in 240. Shortly after this date, he left to preach the new doctrine in India, then throughout the whole empire. At first he was protected by the Emperor Shahpur I, but his successor, Bahram I, succumbed to the pressure of the Zoroastrian clergy and condemned him and his teachings. After Mani's

---

From the Manichaean Psalter

'Since I went into Darkness,
I have had to drink water
which I have found bitter.
I have carried a load
which is not mine.
I have been amongst my enemies.
Beasts surround me.
The load I carried was
that of the Powers and the Principalities.'
(Psalm 246)

---

death as a martyr, the new religion continued to spread westwards to the Roman Empire, and eastwards to China. It survived in north Africa and central Asia for many years, becoming the inspiration for several spiritual movements.

The theory

Mani declared himself to be the last great prophet after Adam, Zoroaster, the Buddha, and Jesus. The 'Church of Truth' had its own canonical books, some of which are known today. In them it is possible to discern not only elements of Iranian and Christian thought, but also the teachings of Buddhism and Hinduism. Manichaeism was presented in the form of a gnosis, which was dependent on a sophisticated cosmology; as a religion it was founded on the existence of two principles which are locked in eternal battle: God or Light, and Matter or Darkness, which is also concupiscence. After a series of dramatic episodes and successive creations, man appears, but falls prey to the powers of Darkness by coupling and procreating. The soul, which in itself is Light, is forced to wander from existence to existence. It is a prisoner and can only be freed through absolute self-control, and the renunciation of all violence. Only the 'elect', those who impose this kind of regime upon themselves, will be emancipated at their deaths. At the end of the world, there will be a general cataclysm which will last for 1468 years, burning and devastating the visible world. The last parcels of light (those souls which adhere to Manichaeism) return to God, while the forces of evil are sucked down into a bottomless gulf. Such a clearly dualist conception of the universe could not fail to attract many followers over the centuries, especially those to whom purity was an ideal.

Maximus the Confessor

580 Constantinople — Lazi, Colchis 662

The theoretician of humankind's capacity of deification

Maximus was venerated by the Western church as well as the Eastern and died a confessor of the faith. His theological and ascetical works permeated Byzantine spirituality.

Maximus was secretary to the Emperor Heraclius, restorer of the Byzantine Empire. At the age of 50 he withdrew to the Chrysopolis monastery near Constantinople where he eventually became abbot. He declared himself to be a staunch adversary of monothelitism, a limited resurgence of 5th century monophysitism, which recognized the existence of two natures in Jesus, both of which came from the same source of energy; this doctrine was upheld by Heraclius in an attempt to appease the Eastern populations of the empire. In 645 Maximus called a council at Carthage which condemned the heresy, and afterwards went to Rome to have this decision ratified. But in 653 Heraclius's successor had the pope arrested and

---

Man, God's game

'We ourselves, by the unfurling of our present nature . . . deserve to be called God's game.'

God is always willing to become **man** in those who are worthy.'

---

deported, and Maximus was hauled off to Constantinople where he was tortured but still refused to recant. He died in exile. However, his doctrine on the deification of man, linked to orthodox Christology, triumphed at the 5th Ecumenical Council of Constantinople less than 20 years after his death.

His works

Maximus's *Mystagogia*, a mystical and symbolical interpretation of the sacraments in the manner of Dionysius the Areopagite, and his *Ascetical Works*, devoted to modes of contemplative life, have become classics in the Eastern Church.

The theory

In his theory of the deification of man, as a result of the intervention of Christ who came to realize 'God's plan' on earth, Maximus supports the belief that although divine status can only be achieved after a long struggle, it is still a natural accomplishment for a man who has discovered his own reality. From then on he is driven by a force much more powerful than he, but which was already present in him; the soul then realizes that the only way to know God is to join with him. Maximus's originality is more evident in his views on the Creation as a divine game, views which contain elements of Hinduism. Man's role in the world can only be defined once it has been understood. Through participation in the multiplicity engendered by the infinite fecundity of the divine One, Man is destined to find the latter through Grace.

Menno Simons and the Mennonites

1496 Witmawsum, Friesland — 1561 Wüstenfelde, Germany

The direct descendants of the 16th-century Anabaptists

Found chiefly in the United States and Canada, the Mennonites prefer to live outwith society which they consider to be immoral.

Pacifist Anabaptism emerged in 1525 in Switzerland as a result of the dissidence of some of Zwingli's disciples, who wanted to break immediately with the political authorities of the new Reformed Church. From Switzerland the movement spread through the Hapsburg Empire, attracting survivors of the Müntzer, Hoffman, and 'kindgom of Münster' revolutionary groups concentrated particularly in the Netherlands.

Menno Simons

Menno Simons was first a Catholic priest, then he converted to Anabaptism. Gradually he became the leader of the pacifist element in the movement, outspokenly condemning the excesses of his predecessors and calling for the implementation of the principles outlined in the Sermon on the Mount, not only in the Netherlands but also in Rhennish and northern Germany, and even in Switzerland. From 1536 to 1559 Menno worked as an itinerant evangelist, reorganizing communities that had been disbanded, checking on the purity of their 'assemblies', and giving a prominent role to the ministers of the faith.

After his death, almost all the remaining Anabaptists had been converted to his principles; they called themselves 'Mennonites'.

In the Netherlands, while the more liberal urban Mennonites were gradually integrated into the existing social order, their rural counterparts were fiercely independent and convinced pacifists who refused to bear arms or take oaths, most of the latter emigrated to Russia in the 18th century, although from the 17th century onwards (and particularly in the 19th century) there had been mass emigration to the United States and Canada, where the members cleared virgin territory and built their own communities. The most conservative branch of the Mennonites, the *Amish*, popularized by cinema and photography, are remarkable not only for their archaic clothing and refusal to use all modern machinery, but also for their scrupulous honesty, their assiduous work ethics and their charity to others. They have no contact with any of the other different Mennonite groups. There are estimated to be about 700 000 of them, of which 300 000 are concentrated in the United States.

Moreover, it was the influence of the Dutch Mennonites which inspired John Smith (died 1612), the English Congregationalist pastor, to found the first Baptist community. After his death the movement was introduced in England by Thomas Helwys (1550–1616), and was soon exported to the North American colonies where Roger Williams founded Providence in 1636, around which the state of Rhode Island was to develop.

Milarepa

1040 Tibet — Tibet 1123

The Tibetan national hero

The influence of Milarepa, an ascetic who lived in a cave, is still evident in Tibet today.

We know of his life through the narrative written by his disciple Rechung, who had lengthy discussions with Milarepa towards the end of his life. When his father died, Milarepa was stripped of all his belongings by close relatives. After his mother pushed him into exacting some form of vengeance, Milarepa studied witchcraft and succeeded in wiping out his enemies. Then, overcome with horror at the crime he had committed, he began to look around for a spiritual master. He found Mar-pa (1012–96), translator of sacred texts he had discovered in India and a disciple of the great siddha Naropa (see **Tantrism**), who subjected him to terrible trials in order to purify him of all dishonour. Milarepa then returned to his native village where, amidst the ruins of the family home, he discovered the bleached bones of his mother, and learned that his sister had been forced to become a beggar. In accordance with his master's wishes he left to live as a hermit near the Himalayan summits, vowing to come down only when he had reached a state of enlightenment. It was at this time that he took the name Milarepa, which means 'dressed in cotton'. His extraordinary asceticism, his miraculous powers and inspired poetry combined to bring him many disciples, including Gampo-pa (1079–1153), founder of the Kagyu-pa monastic order (see **Lamas**). Thanks to Milarepa, Buddhism took definitive root in Tibet,

where the poet–ascetic is still considered to be the most perfect expression of spirituality.

His works

The *Gourboum* (Hundred Thousand Songs) are poetic improvizations on the various stages of Milarepa's spiritual life, which were compiled by his disciples. They are seen as sacred, equal to the Buddhist sutras.

The theory

While Milarepa rejected the magical practices of the archaic indigenous religion, he also disregarded all devotion to the Buddhist Scriptures. For him, only severe asceticism held any value, for its aim was Enlightenment, the discovery of the Being's true identity. The *Gourboum* express the slow progression of the renunciant (who is still under the influence of evil forces which he will gradually turn into positive energy) towards the final victory which will bring him spiritual sons who want to follow in his footsteps.

> 'I am a yogi who sings of elation,
> And does not wish for any other joy.'

> **Milarepa on himself**
> 'A solitary, naked old man,
> A hymn springs from my lips,
> Nature for me is a book.
> A steel-tipped stick in my hand,
> I cross the moving Ocean of life,
> Master of Spirit and Light.'

Monachism

Life devoted to God

In all religions, to live in God but be in the service of all people, is the monastic ideal. Monasteries, centres of prayer and contemplation, were perfect environments for producing religious leaders.

In every era, and in every country, men have withdrawn from the world in order to dedicate their whole lives to God: these are the monks (from the Greek *monos* meaning 'alone'). However, although he may be alone, the monk does not feel cut off from the rest of humankind; he prays for them and hopes he may serve as an example. As well as hermits, or anchorites, coenobites — monks who live in communities — have always existed.

In Christianity

In Judaism there were certain monastic trends including the Essenes sect and, later, various ascetic Jewish communities around Alexandria who may have been the example upon which the first Egyptian Christian monks based themselves. But Christian monachism comes directly from the words of Jesus: 'If someone wants to be my disciple, let him take up the cross and follow me', which the first Christians put into practice, often gathering in small communities isolated from the world. From the 4th century onwards this trend became very popular. Christianity, which at first was a religion of martyrs, lost much of its heroic fervour when it was made the official religion of the empire. In order to live more perfectly men withdrew into the desert, in the Near East and especially in Egypt. Here

they lived as hermits, giving themselves over to extreme and rigorous asceticism like Saint Antony (c. 250–356), the 'Father of Monks', while Saint Pachomius founded the first monasteries devoted to prayer and communal work. The three vows of obedience, chastity and poverty have to be taken before entering the monastery (see **Desert Fathers**). In the 4th century Basil of Caesarea gave them the rules still in use in the Eastern Church today. These institutions were led by a guide and a treasurer, under the overall authority of a bishop. They played an important role in the religious life of the Byzantine Empire, maintaining their autonomy and authority while the secular clergy were dependent on imperial power.

Apart from the large monasteries, there was an impressive number of isolated ascetics, like the 'Stylites' who spent their lives perched atop columns. In the Mount Athos peninsula, in northern Greece, where hermits and coenobites were present from the 10th century onwards, certain archaic forms of contemplative life have survived. The monks in this area are held in particularly high esteem by the Orthodox Church, and the bishops are always chosen from amongst them.

The West did not delay in following the example of the East, but coenobitism was soon the predominant trend in monasticism. In what was still Gaul, Saint Martin, who preached in areas that were still pagan, founded Ligugé near Poitiers (c. 363). Then, after he became Bishop of Tours, he founded Marmoutiers on the other side of the Loire, not far from the episcopal city. After he had visited the monasteries of Palestine and Egypt, John Cassian founded the Saint Victor abbey at Marseilles (c. 415). In the 6th century Benedict of Nursia established the rule which was to become the overall authority while monks, in particular the Irish, evangelized pagan

Saint Benedict *receiving a gift of flour for his monastery and the monks listening to a reading from the Scriptures during their meal. Fresco by Sodoma, Monte Oliveto Maggiore abbey, 1505–08*

Europe. The founding of Cluny in 909, and Cîteaux in 1098, and the deeds of Bernard of Clairvaux gave an extraordinary boost to monachism, which developed over the centuries into a multitude of orders corresponding to the diversity of vocations. Renewed interest in the life of the hermits was behind the creation of the Chartreux order in France and the Camaldolese in Italy in the 11th century. Throughout the Middle Ages monasteries, situated as they are away from society, were centres of intellectual as well as spiritual life, which preserved ancient wisdom.

The development of urban society from the 13th century brought about the creation of the mendicant orders: the Friars Minor or Franciscans (see **Francis of Asissi**), and the Friars Preachers or Dominicans (see **Dominic of Guzman**). They established their monasteries in town centres, while the monks travelled around the country preaching. During the 16th century, in response to the needs of the Counter-Reformation, several active orders or regular clerics were created, the most famous being the Society of Jesus (see **Ignatius Loyola**).

Throughout the Ancien Régime most of the education system was run by the religious orders which in medieval times had also created universities, like the Sorbonne, founded by Robert of Sorbon in 1253, and which was a faculty of divinity until the Revolution (1789). But from the 16th century the majority of monasteries slipped progressively into decadence. This was caused, on one hand by forced entry into orders and, on the other hand, by the commendatory system which allowed non-resident abbots, and sometimes lay people, to control the monasteries' finances to the detriment of their vows. In 1792 all monastic houses were closed down. They reappeared in the 19th century and today there are 200 000 Catholic monks worldwide of which 12 000 are Benedictine, 5000 Cistercian, 38 000 Franciscan, 15 Dominican and 25 000 Jesuit.

In Islam

While Islam is opposed to monachism in principle, from the 8th century onwards Sufism gave birth to spiritual communities which became brotherhoods in the 11th to 13th centuries (see **Tariqa**). Several have survived and are still influential today. The most famous is that of the Mau'lawiya (Whirling Dervishes) founded by Djalal ad-Din Rumi. In these brotherhoods the disciples, who in general do not live together permanently but come on retreat, gather round their leader, the sheikh.

In Hinduism

Brahmanic India has rarely experienced coenobitic life. On the other hand, it was a common occurrence for a pious Hindu to withdraw into a forest and spend the remainder of his life as a hermit; and the sannyasin broke all contact with the world and lived as itinerant monks and beggars.

Shankara in the 8th century, and Ramanuja in the 12th century created two orders, both of which were based in monasteries (*matha*) and had a monastic rule rather like those in the West. This also applies to the 'Ramakrishna Mission', founded in 1897 by Vivekananda. There are now 80 mission centres in India and abroad whose monks are called *swami*. Finally, disciples often gather round a guru, forming communities known as ashrams; certain disciples are renunciants, or *sadhu*.

In Buddhism

From the earliest days of the Buddha's preaching career, Buddhism has essentially been a monk's religion. The mendicant

---

The Christian monk

'The monk is one who is separated and yet joined to everyone.' (Evagrius of Pontus, 4th century)

'Monastic poverty is the wet nurse of philosophy.' (Basil of Caesarea, 4th century)

'Here are the angels of the earth . . . chastity enables them to act in all things as if they had no body at all, as though heaven were already theirs, as though they had already attained immortality.' (John Chrysostome, 4th century)

monks (*bikshu*) are itinerant ascetics who gather together during the three-month rainy season and who practise absolute poverty, chastity, and compassion towards all beings. Like their leader the Buddha, they survive on donations from the faithful and in return they preach the doctrine. In the *sangha* (community) the caste system was abolished. As soon as he is admitted to the novitiate, the future monk chooses a spiritual director who will clarify the sacred texts and guide him in his meditation exercises. This education which is founded on the development of personal intuition, has been passed down from generation to generation and can be traced to the Buddha himself. In all Buddhist countries, the education given by monks is greatly respected, whether it be in the village school or in one of the important universities like Nalanda in India in former times, or those of Tibet which housed many hundreds of students.

It was monks who spread the doctrine throughout South-East Asia, China, Tibet, and Japan. Soon permanent monasteries appeared, especially in Tibet where the leaders of the great orders (see **Lamas**) also held secular power. In China where Buddhist monachism used to play a social and political role, the monasteries which were closed down during Mao's revolution are now re-opening their doors and attracting a new following. In Japan the monastic orders are still very popular, and the role of the monk is often comparable to that of the priest in other religions. In Thailand and Burma it is still customary for laypersons to follow a temporary novitiate in a monastery, and to return for short periods of retreat over the years. Buddhist monks do not take irrevocable vows, but are always free to return to secular life. According to the rule, they may keep only a few personal possessions: three pieces of clothing, a bowl, a comb, a fan, and occasionally a parasol or umbrella. On the other hand the monasteries are never locked, and apart from the hours of liturgical office and during periods of retreat, the monks are allowed to occupy their time as they will. There are also a small number of nuns. Buddhist religious and spiritual leaders have invariably been monks.

Buddhist monastic ideal

'Liberated, liberated; having reached the other side, help others to reach it too; comforted, comforted; having attained perfect nirvana, help your fellow men attain it too.' (Vinaya)

Tibetan monks

'The clerical education produced a small literate élite, a large number . . . of amiable and jovial people, and a few mystics who spent their lives in continual meditation in their desert hermitages.' (Alexandra David-Neel *Tibetan Mystics and Magicians*)

Moses

c. 13th century BC

The mediator between God and his chosen people

Israel's guide and lawgiver, Moses is also considered by Christians and Muslims to be an exemplary religious leader and mystic.

Moses's historicity may be questionable and it is doubtful that he was the author of the Pentateuch (see **Bible**), although contemporary studies tend to show that tradition has preserved texts like the Covenant and the Decalogue which constitute the Law of Israel just as he gave them. But he is characterized as the leader and spiritual guide of his people.

According to Exodus and Deuteronomy, he was born in Egypt and brought up in Pharaoh's court, and went on to become the defender of his exiled and oppressed people. In the Sinai desert, where he had to take refuge at the age of 40, he received orders from Yahweh, who appeared to him in the burning bush. On his return to Egypt he roused the slumbering national consciousness of the Isrealites, and convinced

---

Moses in Deuteronomy

'There has never yet risen in Israel a prophet like Moses, whom the Lord knew face to face; remember all the signs and portents which the Lord sent to him to show in Egypt to Pharaoh and all his servants and the whole land . . .'
(*Deuteronomy* 34, 10–12)

Moses and his people

'This whole people is a burden too heavy for me. I cannot carry it alone.' (*Numbers* 11, 14)

---

them to return to their true homeland. Having brought them across the Red Sea, he led them to the foot of Mount Sinai, on whose slopes he acted as an intermediary when Yahweh made a covenant with Israel and gave his Law, the Decalogue. But when they wanted to enter Palestine the Israelites turned back and were forced to wander in the desert for a further 40 years, during which time it became increasingly difficult for Moses to allay the fears of his people and to deal effectively with the growing internal strife. After 40 years, they settled at the oasis of Cades, remaining there for 37 years before setting off on the march that took them to the valley of the Jordan. However, Moses died before he could do any more than gaze upon the Promised Land that his people were finally about to enter.

The theory

Moses was not only a leader of humankind and Israel's lawgiver, he also mediated between God and his chosen people. He had spoken with Him and during their talk God had revealed His name and some of His mystery: 'I am who I am', which is the translation of Yahweh. Moses was progressively initiated by God and was the carrier of the Divine Light which he was to transmit to his followers. In the Bible he is portrayed as the true founder of Judaism; it was he who instituted all the traditional rituals, centred on the Ark of the Covenant which contains the 'tablets of the Law', and created a powerful priesthood to enforce it. He is considered as the first of the great prophets by Christians, Muslims, and Jews; as the man who saw the Lord face to face and brought back some of the Divine Light to shed upon humanity, he has been an unending source of inspiration to artists such as Michelangelo in the Renaissance, and thinkers like Freud in the 20th century.

Muhammad

c. 570 Mecca — Medina 632

The prophet

Muhammad passed on to humanity the word of God which had been revealed to him by the angel Gabriel. He founded a new religion which today has half a billion followers.

Muhammad in Arabic means 'praised', 'glorified'. He was born in Mecca where the dominant tribe was the Qurayish. Mecca is situated in the barren Hidjaz valley, and as no agriculture was possible, the town economy depended on the Yemen–Syria caravan trade, and the pilgrimage to the Ka'bah, the sanctuary housing the sacred Black Stone. At that time, the Ka'bah, a 'house of God' was overrun with various pagan idols. Muhammad's father died when he was a child, and the future prophet was brought up by his grandfather, then by his uncle, who took him on his business trips, most notably to Syria where he is said to have met with the Nestorian monks. Bahira, one of these monks foretold Muhammad's destiny, and is mentioned in the Koran. As an impoverished orphan, Muhammad entered the service of Khadijah, a rich widow who organized caravans. He soon became her steward and trusted

confidant until she proposed to him and they were married. At this time he is said to have been 25 years old and she 15 years older. They lived happily together for 20 years until Khadija's death, a marriage which produced three sons who died in childhood, and four daughters, including Fatima, who married Muhammad's adopted son Ali. It is only through Fatima that Muhammad's bloodline was continued.

God's word

Although he was a respected and prominent member of the community, Muhammad's nervous and fiery temperament made him dissatisfied with his religion. Like many of his fellow citizens, he found it increasingly difficult to accept the prevalent polytheism of his day, and was attracted to the ideas spread in Arabia by Jews and Christians. He often retreated to a mountain cave outside Mecca, where he would lose himself in asceticism and meditation. One night in the year 610, Muhammad felt as though a strange being had gripped him by the throat and was commanding him to read a roll of cloth that appeared to be covered in symbols. When he awoke, it seemed to him that during this dream, a book had been written in his heart, and he saw the angel, later identified with Gabriel, in the distance. Terrified and convinced he was going mad, he went home to Khadija, who reassured him and became his first convert. Muhammad gradually became accustomed to receiving God's messages in visions, which he passed on to a small group of disciples including Ali, his other son-in-law Uthman, and his future fathers-in-law Abu

131

Bakr and Omar, who later became the first four caliphs. After three years of more or less regular visions, the Revelation ordered him to begin his public career.

In passionate language the Prophet told of God's wrath, and of the imminence of Judgment Day, but his prophet statements were met with scorn. Because they endangered the city's religious and therefore economic interests, the Muslims, 'Those who give their souls to God', were cruelly persecuted. In 619 Muhammad lost both his wife and his protector, Abu Talib, who was also his uncle. Abu was replaced as the head of the clan by another of the Prophet's uncles, but unlike his predecessor, he had no affection for Muhammad. It was at this time that Muhammad had his most famous vision in which the angel took him by the hand and made him mount the winged mare Boraq, who transported him to Jerusalem, where he prayed in the ruins of the Temple. From there, he was taken before the throne of God, who gave him the five daily prayers to be enforced on the Muslims.

The 'Holy War'

Muhammad was already in contact with the people of Yathrib, the future Medina (*Medinat al nabi* means the 'town of the Prophet'), and they invited him to mediate in their internal disputes. Preceded by his Meccan followers, Muhammad arrived at Medina on 24 September 622, the year of the Hijrah (Emigration). He soon showed himself to be a capable politician and military leader, and in March 624 won a significant victory over the Meccan troops at Badr, which helped confirm the authenticity of his mission. There was already a thriving Jewish community in Medina whose approval Muhammad sought, as he preached monotheism and accepted the legitimacy of all the previous biblical

prophets and patriarchs including Jesus. But the Jews disagreed with his interpretation of the Scriptures, and he had to seek his allies elsewhere. The Jews were either put to death or expelled from the town, while his supporters disposed of the newly-formed Arab opposition.

Once he had clearly defined the rules of the new faith, Muhammad, now a respected leader with an army of faithful followers, enjoyed absolute power. He had gradually developed and amplified his religion, which is demonstrated by the Medina suras in which the laws for the new society are set out. The religion had also become more Arabic in tone; from this time on it was centred on Abraham, father of the Semites, and his son Ismael, the forefather of the Arabs. Ismael is believed by the Arabs to have founded the Ka'bah, the mystical shrine towards which the Muslims now prayed, whereas in the past they had always directed themselves towards Jerusalem. The Revelation began to attack the Jews who had persecuted the great prophet Jesus and vilified his mother, but who had failed to put him to death as a ghost had been crucified in his place.

The Meccans had to give way to the superior strength of the Muslim army; in 630 the Prophet's forces occupied the town. By the time of his sudden death in 632 at Medina, the whole of Arabia recognized his authority. To succeed him, he left on the one hand his daughter Fatima who was married to Ali and had two sons, and on the other several wives, who included the daughters of his advisors Abu Bakr and Omar. Two distinct factions were to emerge from this group of people engendering a power dispute that is still active today (see **Islam**). The complete Revelation is set out in the Koran, and is complemented by the Hadith, written records of Muhammad's oral teachings (see **Koran, Hadith**).

Müntzer, Thomas and the Anabaptists

c. 1489 Stolberg, Harz — Mülhausen, Thuringia, 1525

The radicals of the Reformation

The Anabaptists rejected all civil and religious authority, and aimed to create a new evangelical society, to prepare for the impending return of Christ.

The Anabaptists get their name from one of the pecularities of their doctrine which forbids the baptism of children; adults may only be baptized once they have made a profession of faith. They represent a current which pushes the freedom born of the Reformation to the extreme, by only recognizing the personal relationship between the soul and God, and claiming to institute an egalitarian theocracy. The movement, which attacked the existing social order, soon spread in Germany, Switzerland, and Holland, and was persecuted by both reformers and Catholics.

The league of the elect

The first group of Anabaptists seems to have been the one which gathered around Thomas Müntzer in 1521 in Saxony. Müntzer met Luther at Leipzig in 1519 and began to preach rebellion against secular power and the creation of a new evangelical society at Zwickau. Denounced by Luther,

Müntzer had to flee, and in 1523 founded a 'League of the Elect' at Allstedt, which joined the bloody revolt called the Peasants' War. The rebellion was crushed in 1525, and Müntzer decapitated. But one of his followers, Melchior Hoffmann, preached Anabaptism in Holland, northern Germany, Scandinavia, and the Rhine valley, insisting on the urgency of conversion while awaiting the parousia (second coming of Christ). As it put the seal on the status of 'elect', he too was baptized in 1530 at Strasbourg, which he stated would be the site of the parousia. He gave several successive dates for the event, but died in 1543, without having seen his prophecy come to fruition.

After hearing Hoffmann preach, Bernard Rothmann, an ex-Catholic priest from Münster, Westphalia, declared it his intention to turn the city of Strasbourg, to which Anabaptists from Germany and Holland were flocking, into a celestial Jerusalem. The leaders of the Dutch movement, John Mathijs (died 1534) then John of Leiden, established a theocratic dictatorship which was entirely given over to violence and lust. The bellicose Münsterites were destroyed in June 1535 by an alliance of Protestant princes and Catholic bishops. John of Leiden was burnt at the stake and his followers tortured and massacred.

Only the pacifistic sect of Anabaptism survived, a sect which developed from a quarrel between Zwingli and some of his disciples. The disciples left Zürich and went to south Germany and Holland, where Menno Simons became their leader.

Mysteries

Rites revealed only to the initiated

Reserved for select initiates who were born through antiquity, the mysteries played the role of secret spiritual guides.

While it is acknowledged that the influence of the mysteries was considerable, it is almost impossible to evaluate the exact extent of that influence, as a rule of secrecy and silence was strictly observed. Nearly all are of eastern origin: Egyptian (Isis and Osiris), Phrygian (Cybele and Attis), Phoenician (Adonis) and Persian (Mithras), but from the Hellenist period onwards, the mysteries spread to the Graeco-Roman world in the form of a religion of salvation which offered immortality to its adherents. It was therefore a question of a return to archaic practices which had been gradually eliminated by manifestations of these religions. We remain ignorant as to the crucial phases of the secret rituals, about which we possess only fragments of information.

Eleusinian Mysteries

In much earlier times, in ancient Greece, secret societies already existed, devoted to the mysteries revealed by various deities including Zeus in Crete and Dionysius. None of them ever became as famous as the Eleusinian Mysteries, which were celebrated for roughly 2000 years. Almost all of Greece's élite, in particular the writers and philosophers, and later a number of Romans, were initiated into this secret society. The sanctuary of Eleusis, founded in the 15th century BC was destroyed by Alaric, King of the Goths. We are dependent on two sources for all we know about the mysteries:

the Greek and Roman authors, who rarely allude to them, and the details transmitted by the Church Fathers, which must be treated with some degree of scepticism. In Greek, the plural *ta mysteria* comes from the verb *myo*, 'to close the mouth', which gives *myesis* meaning 'initiation' and *mystes* meaning 'the initiator or initiate to the mysteries', which refers to the absolute obligation of ritual silence. The Greeks believed that the most sacred teachings could only be communicated to those who had passed from being profane to being divine through the rites of initiation. Thus not only the oracles but also many poets and philosophers used symbols, allegories, and enigmatic language, which was only accessible to fellow initiates.

The Eleusinian Mysteries originate in the myth of the goddess Demeter. Having lost her daughter Kore (Persephone), who was kidnapped by Pluto (Hades), god of the underworld, and having found out that it was Zeus who had approved this act, Demeter decides not to return to Olympus. Taking on the appearance of an old woman, she stops at Eleusis, where she agrees to look after Demophon, the queen's last-born

---

Olympiodorus

'Like Kore, the soul goes down in the world of generation . . . it goes back up towards its true origin with Demeter. The aim of initiation is to make souls go back up to this finality, there where they made their first descent or beginning.'

Sophocles

'Thrice happy those mortals who, after having contemplated the mysteries go to Hades; only they can live there; for the others, there will be nothing but suffering.'

Eleusinian Mysteries
Eleusis bas relief showing Demeter and her daughter Persephone on either side of the young Triptolemus, an Eleusinian Prince; c. 440 BC (Roman replica, Metropolitan Museum of Art, New York; original in the National Museum in Athens)

135

child. In order to make him immortal, she hides him in the embers of the fire at night. The queen finds out and, horrified, interrupts the process that would have made her son immortal. The goddess shows herself in all her splendour, lamenting the blindness of men, and demands that a temple and an altar be built where she would teach her rites to mortals. Then, obtaining Zeus's permission for Persephone to return, and thereafter spend only the four winter months with Pluto, Demeter returns to Olympus, and the barren land begins to flourish once more. But from then on, a benevolent Olympian goddess was to reign in the underworld and would welcome initiates. Since then, the two goddesses of the fertile earth have been worshipped at Eleusis.

This basic myth allows us to grasp the probable meaning of the mysteries; after the necessary purification, it seems to have been a case of a process of regeneration, of a radical modification of the human condition, thanks to which the initiate rediscovered his lost immortality which had become merely a possibility. Thus, the mysteries gave the most spiritually advanced what the official religion could not; they were the complement, and their attraction and the secrecy that surrounds them are easily understood.

The candidates to Eleusinian initiation (open to all Greek speakers, men and women, including slaves, provided that they did not have the stain of murder on their hands) first had to take part in the 'lesser mysteries' in the spring, which were purificatory rites directed by a mystagogue,

before participating in the 'greater mysteries', which took place in the autumn and lasted eight days; they included a ritual bathe in the sea, a ceremonial procession from Athens to Eleusis, followed by a day of fasting and purification. After the high priest had given a speech, the mysteries culminated in the sudden revelation of brightly lit objects, the *epopteia*, which was only available to those who had been initiated the preceding year.

The resting place of the blessed

The character of these objects has never been disclosed, nor have we been able to decode the few formulae which history has preserved for us. Yet, the high priest's declaration during the night of the *epopteia*, 'in a blinding fire' : 'noble Brimo gave birth to Brimos (the Powerful), a sacred male child', can only mean the initiate's second birth, as Demophon immortalized by Demeter. Moreover, according to an ancient text, the trials leading up to the epopteia seem to have simulated the soul's experiences immediately after death as it wanders in darkness beset by all sorts of terrors, before being blinded by a sudden light and glimpsing the resting place of the blessed. Everything leads us to think that it was a question of a process of death followed by a rebirth, a theme found in most traditional religions. Because of this, the mysteries can be compared to the Egyptian initiation rites at Abydos, as well as to the peregrinations of the soul described in both the *Egyptian Book of the Dead* and the *Bardo Thodol* in Tibet.

Mysticism

The highest form of spirituality

At its innermost, most intimate expression, mysticism is the search for personal union with God. Regarded with suspicion in the West, in the East it is venerated as an ideal way of life.

Mysticism comes from the Greek *mystikos* meaning 'to do with mysteries', which in turn came from *mystes* meaning 'the initiate or initiator to mysteries'. The original connotation must not be forgotten when one deals with mysticism. In the most usual sense, mysticism is distinguishable from formal religion in that it is the personal search for the hidden God who is in each individual's heart, but who can only be revealed after a long interior journey ending in the complete denial of the self. This is a phenomenon which transcends all religions and rational limits, and can only be explained from within. It has to be experienced to be believed. In fact, it is a question of a mystery.

The path of mysticism is only open to the select few who feel called to it, and respond to that calling. There are dangers involved, for not only could this meeting or union be illusory, but, by its very nature it transcends the normal human state, and, as it were, breaks apart the normal confines of human existence. Mysticism has also aroused the ire and mistrust of religions, which the mystic, albeit unwillingly, compromises since his experiences do not bow to rules and regulations, or to the Church authorities. Resistance to mysticism is apparent in all three monotheistic religions, particularly in Christianity and

Islam. During their lifetimes, most mystics were victimized and humiliated, and often condemned like Meister Eckhart, or reduced to silence like Jakob Böhme, or persecuted like John of the Cross, or even martyred like Hallaj, although this may have meant that they would be held up as an example to believers after their deaths.

The mystic's voyage

The path of mysticism is long, and strewn with difficulties and obstacles. It begins with an urgent calling felt in the heart of hearts which is followed by a conversion bringing the mystic to look inwards and discover his 'holy core', or the presence of God in himself. Such an absolute certitude only comes at the end of a long and patient period of asceticism, through prayer and orison of which Angelo de Foligno wrote: 'Through orison, you are illuminated, through orison, you are united with God'.

At this stage, the help of a spiritual guide is indispensable, but later, the mystic must continue his journey alone. It is possible that he might go through the unproductive periods of doubt and sometimes despair, which were so effectively described by Saint

---

Dionysius the Areopagite (5th–6th centuries)
'The mystic is brought up on the supernatural beam of godly darkness, above all that is sensory and intelligible. If, when we see God, we understand what we see, we are not looking at God but one of the things which come from Him, which we cannot know.'

Hallaj (c. 857–922)
'If I call you . . . No, it's You who calls me. You! How could I have talked to You, if You hadn't talked to me?'

John of the Cross. Such trials correspond to the obstacles that separate the soul from God, and will continue to do so until it reaches a state of voluntary deprivation, inner emptiness and silence at the heart of which the Voice can be heard, during the inner ecstasy born of sudden illumination.

Much emphasis has been laid on the psychophysiological accidents which have occurred, but apart from the fact that they can, and have, also happened to those who were not looking for union with God, mystics themselves see them as epiphenomena resulting from human weakness and not as proof of the authenticity of their experiences. This also applies to the so-called supernatural powers which can only be obstacles and even traps. Confusion may arise because of the language used by mystics in an attempt to relay their uncommunicable experiences. Much mystical vocabulary is drawn from the language of lovers, justified by the fact that mysticism is love, but love of God and of all that is divine in others and in creation, which only the

mystic can perceive. It is important to make a distinction between true mysticism (as above) and the modern usage of the term: in common parlance, mysticism denotes an anti-rationalist, sentimental and often inconsistent attitude, or even an irrational or fanatical attachment to a particular doctrine or a party.

The Eastern experience of God

The frame of reference we have used to try to define the mystical phenomenon as it appears in the West cannot be applied to the great Eastern traditions of Buddhism and Hinduism. There is no opposition and no true distinction between the religious person and the mystic in these two creeds; moreover the term mysticism has no exact equivalent in the East, where religion is seen as an experience of the divine, and fusion with God. The man who is 'living free', who has renounced his 'self', is still revered and admired as a model for others. His quest is metaphysical as it does not aim at simple unity with a personal god, but at a return to the primordial One. In these religions, the path of mysticism can be approached through tried and tested disciplines, which are often very exacting; these include a long apprenticeship under the guidance of a spiritual leader, progress on the path being marked off by successive initiation rites. This applied to the yogas, Tantrism, Tibetan Vajrayana, Chinese Ch'an, and Japanese Zen.

No matter what their differences may have been, most of the world's great religious leaders have been mystics. The teachings it was their mission to spread, only took on their full value once they had become personal experience; it is only after having walked the path themselves, that they became qualified to guide others.

Angela of Foligno (c. 1260–1309)
'Nothing is necessary to us but God. To find God is to receive our soul in him.'

Meister Eckhart (c. 1260–1327)
'Let this eternal voice shout in you as it will, and be a desert of yourself and all things.'

Ramakrishna (c. 1838–66)
'To be able to hear the divine calling, for grace to flow abundantly, it is enough to love something dearly, music, the sun, or a little child.'

Nagarjuna

c. 150 Vidharba — Nagarjunikonda, South India c. 250

The most profound of the Buddhist thinkers

With his doctrine of emptiness, Nagarjuna gave Buddhism a new impetus which is still evident today.

The only details of Nagarjuna's life are found in two narratives written some time after his death; the older of the two was translated into Chinese by Kumarajiva in 405. Son of a Brahman family, Nagarjuna was born in South India. While still a child, he studied the *Veda* (see **Hinduism**) and taught himself the rudiments of all the sciences, including magic. At a tender age he converted to Buddhism and took monastic vows. Having mastered all Buddhist canon, but still thirsting after more knowledge, Nagarjuna went to the Himalayas. There he met an ancient monk who taught him the Mahayana sutras, then the king of the serpents (*nagaraja*) handed over the *prajnaparamita* to him. The latter was Buddha's authentic revelation which he did not believe could be understood in his lifetime. This legend is obviously used to connect the Mahayana with Sakyamuni's teachings.

A philosopher of genius, Nagarjuna was soon considered as one of the Buddhist's greatest leaders. The doctors of Nalanda university, a centre of Buddhist spirituality from the 5th to the 12th centuries, claim him as their forefather. In the same way, in Ch'an, strongly influenced by his doctrine of Emptiness, he is considered as the 14th patriarch after the Buddha.

His works

He was a prolific writer, and apart from the Mahayana school's basic texts, he wrote *Madhyamakasastra* (Middle Path) and *Mahaprajnaparamitasastra* (Great Virtue of Wisdom); Tantric texts like *Sutra samukaya* (Compendium of Sutras); *Catuhstava* (a collection of four hymns); and, finally, works on spiritual guidance including the famous *Suhrrleka* (Letter to a friend).

The theory

According to Nagarjuna, 'Buddha's teachings refer to two sorts of truth: relative conditional truth and transcendant, absolute truth.' The first, that of illusory appearances is produced by ignorance and hides the ultimate truth which leads to deliverance, but defies linguistic definition. Phenomena, because they are impermanent, can only be devoid of substance; recognizing this leads to Enlightenment, as well as the understanding that 'nothing differentiates samsara from nirvana'. The doctrine of Emptiness is not nihilistic, it institutes the 'Middle Path' which neither affirms nor denies. It is not even a philosophy, but the formulation of the highest spiritual expression.

Emptiness

'In truth, all things are inexpressible, empty, calm, and pure. All those who see them this way are worthy of being called buddhas and bodhisatras.'

Neoplatonists

The inheritors of Plato's ideas

These philosophers developed mystical extensions of Plato's theories, and were the last spiritual guides in antiquity.

Founded by Plotinus (205–270), this school marks the end of classicism and was active until the start of the 6th century. Based on a particular interpretation of Plato's *Parmenides*, it recognized the existence of an uncommunicable and absolute principle which was called the 'One', or 'Good'.

A disciple of Plotinus, whose biography (*Life*) he published, Porphyry (234 Tyre — Rome c. 310) was an extremely prolific author, with more than 60 books attributed to him, although we only possess a few of them. He came to study Platonism in Athens but was attracted by the reputation of Plotinus, whose disciple he became in Rome. However, Plotinus's teachings incited him to such protracted states of nervous tension that he even contemplated suicide. Plotinus advised him to travel, so he went to Sicily. After the death of Plotinus, he returned to Rome to take his master's place.

Although he was a Neoplatonic philosopher, Porphyry retained his Eastern attitudes, and throughout his life was troubled by questions of a religious nature, which often conflicted with his belief that

religions were directed towards lesser deities, whereas philosophy transcended them all and was the true cult of the supreme and only God. Only the philosopher could hope to escape from the endless cycle of births and deaths. This stand led Porphyry to attack Christians. For him, Jesus's distorted teaching painted an unworthy and absurd picture of God. His tract *Against Christians* (268) lent weight to the argument for persecution, but was destroyed under Constantine. Pardoxically, his other works, including *On the Abstinence of the Flesh, On the Return of the Soul* and especially *Isagogus* (an introduction to Aristotle's *Categories*) had a profound influence on Christian spirituality through the esoterism, as well as in Arabic Neoplatonism. We can therefore conclude that his original theories on the unity and activity of the One 'definitively marked Western philosophical thought'.

Iamblicus

Iamblicus (c. 250 — c. 330) was one of Porphyry's Syrian disciples. After studying in Rome, which was no longer the intellectual capital of the empire, he returned to his native country and opened up a school. With him, Neoplatonism became even more Easternized, incorporating the doctrines of Pythagoras whose disciple he claimed to be and whose *Life* he wrote. Because of his attempts at reconciling various different contributions in the hope of breathing new life into paganism, his works are rather fragmented. While in *On the Science of*

Porphyry

'The One, who is above substance and being, is neither being nor non-being, but rather acts, and in himself is pure action in that he is the Being, the Being who is before being and like the idea of Being.'

Divine Iamblicus

'Iamblicus, an enthusiastic dreamer and subtle metaphysician, who was adored by his disciples like a supernatural dreamer, who worked wonders, commanded demons and spoke to the gods . . .' (A. and M. Croiset)

Mathematics in General he exposes the close relationship between the soul and mathematics as the transition of the sensory to the intelligible, in *The Egyptian Mysteries* he draws together the elements which had already inspired his masters, Pythagoras and Plato, and becomes the outspoken champion of theurgy. He considered theurgy to be a necessary sacramental practice, as one can only deify oneself through one's own wisdom and by responding to the signs chosen by the gods to permit one to communicate with them. 'Iamblicus the Divine' was considered to be more of an inspired thinker than a true philosopher by his successors.

The end of the school

In the following century, the most important Neoplatonist was Proclus (412–485). Born in Constantinople, he studied in Alexandria and Athens, where he was introduced to 'Plato's mystagogy' by Syrianos, the head of the Neoplatonic school, whom he succeeded in 438. Although of a pious and ascetical nature, Proclus was nonetheless devoted to the welfare of his disciples, leaving an impressive amount of work which constitutes the last stage in the development of pre-Christian philosophy. In his *Elements of Theology*, structured as methodically as a treatise on geometry, Proclus exposes the famous Law of the return to the One. The One, reflecting itself, develops, multiplying itself again and again to infinity, each new entity producing a number of inferior entities. All these new beings are retained within the sphere of the One and by a circular movement must return to their source.

Damascius, born in Damascus in 485, was the last head of the school until its closure by Justinian in 529. Neoplatonism survived in Alexandria with Olympodorus (6th century), one of the last representatives of the Orphic tradition.

Neoplatonism and Christianity

It was also from Alexandria that Neoplatonism spread to influence Christian thought. The majority of the great theologians were inspired by this final stage in Greek philosophy. Origen and Plotinus shared the same mentor, Ammonios Saccas. These theologians held Christianity to be the crowning glory of Greek thought in the Neoplatonic form they had come to know.

During the centuries that followed, Neoplatonism found favour with various different thinkers: Johannes Scotus Erigena (810–870), an Irish philosopher who spent much of his life in Paris, Meister Eckhart and Johannes Tauler, the great Rhenish 14th century mystic, certain Renaissance Humanists like Marsilio Picino or Nicholas de Cusa, and at the start of the 20th century, William James and Henri Bergson. In other words, Neoplatonism as a mystical and metaphysical current has unceasingly nourished the underlying layers of Western spirituality.

> **Porphyry**
> 'The wisest of philosophers . . .' (Saint Augustine)

New Testament

The basis of the Christian faith

The New Testament not only exposes Jesus's message, it also traces the development of the nascent Church. It is a sacred book whose authority is recognized by Protestant, Catholic and Orthodox Christians.

At the start of the Christian era, the New Testament was added to the Old Testament, which Christians called the Bible. The New Testament contains 27 books in Greek: the four Gospels; the Acts of the Apostles; 13 Letters by Paul, three attributed to John, two to Peter, one to James, one to Jude; the Letter to the Hebrews; and finally the Book of Revelation. Testament here alludes to the covenant made between God and His people which was renewed by the coming of Christ; Jesus himself confirmed this during the Last Supper when he held up the cup of wine and said, 'This is my blood, the blood of the covenant, shed for many'. The New Testament was not intended to replace the Old Testament, but rather to complete it.

While we are sure of the dates between which Paul's Letters were compiled, AD 51–67, much speculation surrounds the ages of the other books. The gospels are thought to have been written between AD 70 and 90/95, Acts between AD 80 and 90, and Revelation at the end of the 1st or beginning of the 2nd century AD. The other Letters are believed to have been written between AD 60 and 90.

From Judaism to Christianity

Some Letters are particularly precious as they reflect the diversity of the teachings central to the primitive Church; thus the Letter of James, 'brother of the Lord' makes no mention of redemption through Jesus, but predicts the 'imminent coming' of God's kingdom. This demonstrates the view of the Judaeo–Christians, who had still not broken completely with Judaism, and is attested to by the information supplied by the Acts of the Apostles. The Letter to the Hebrews, which was formerly attributed to Paul, stresses the continuity between the Old and New Testaments and is also addressed to this milieu. It would seem unlikely that the New Testament could have been compiled before the middle of the 2nd century, but it was preceded by a longstanding oral tradition which the Apostles and their successors continued. A definitive list of the 27 so-called 'canonic' books, considered to stem directly from this teaching, was not compiled until the 4th century. Some texts, now known as 'apocryphal' were excluded at that time. Recent studies of apocryphal texts have shed new light on the making of the New Testament.

> 'I tell you this, unless you turn round and become like children, you will never enter the Kingdom of Heaven.' (*Matthew* 18, 2–3)

> 'I do not speak on my own authority, but the Father who has sent me has Himself commanded me what to say and how to speak.' (*John* 12, 49–50)

Nichiren

1222 Kominato — Ikegami 1282

The last reformer of Japanese Buddhism

An ardent patriot, Nichiren wanted to make his country the centre of the Doctrine as he perceived it and spread it throughout the world.

The son of a fisherman, Nichiren entered a monastery at the age of 15. He left on a long study voyage which took him to Mount Hiei near Kyoto, the most important Tendai monastery, where he remained for ten years. He disapproved of Tendai interpretation of the Doctrine, and of the passion for Amida worship which was rejecting Sakyamuni in favour of Amida. He believed that the true spirit of the Doctrine was to be found in the *Lotus of the Wonderful Law*, a Tendai canonical text. But because he also believed that not everyone would be able to understand this text, Nichiren declared that its very essence was in its title and that it corresponded to the Buddha's state of Enlightenment. He was convinced that his country could only redeem itself if it returned to the Good Law which he would communicate to the world. He wanted to convert both the government and the people, and began to publish numerous warnings and to preach in the streets of Kamakura, condemning all the other schools. His vehemence was such that he was exiled to the Izu peninsula in 1261. Once pardoned,

he resumed his attacks. Condemned to death, he only just escaped execution in 1271, but was banished once more. Within three years he was back at Kamakura and with his disciples went to live on Mount Minobu, to the west of Fuji, which has since become a popular shrine.

The theory

Founder of the Hokke sect ('Flower of the Law') Nichiren left a vast body of work which is rather muddled and repetitive. The clearest texts are *Ways of Upholding Justice and Stabilizing the Nation* (1260) and the *Tract which Opens Eyes* (Kaimokusho 1972). In them, Nichiren promulgates the 'Three Great Secrets': the first is represented by a mandala based on the sutra's title; the second is the formula 'Homage to the *Sutra of the Lotus of Perfect Truth*; the third makes Japan the platform for the worldwide spreading of the Law. Nichiren's school, which numbers some 7 million followers, gave birth to the Nichiren-shu sect, founded by Nikkan (1246–1333), which from 1930 became known as Soka Gakkai, famed for its ultra-nationalist views.

'What is happening now was predicted by Sadaparibhuta (in the *Sutra of the Lotus*). Nichiren is the **Sadaparibhuta** bodisattva. (1271)

Nikodimos Hagioritis and the Philokalia

1748 Naxos — Mount Athos 1809

The reviver of the prayer of the heart

As the author of Philokalia Nikodimos was the instigator of the 19th century Russian spiritual revival.

Born on the island of Naxos and baptized Nicholas at the age of 27, he took monastic vows under the name Nikodimos, and entered the Dionysius (after Saint Dionysius) monastery on the Athos peninsula, hence the nickname 'Hagioritis' (of the Holy Mountain). There he took advantage of the renewed interest in theological study which began in the middle of the 18th century. He was totally devoted to perpetual prayer, and on the rare occasions he left Athos, it was in pursuit of further knowledge. He took his final vows in 1783 and went on to live in several different monasteries and hermitages. His contribution to the Greek Orthodox Church was so great that he was canonized by the patriarch of Constantinople in 1955.

His works

Nikodimos left some 30 theological texts, reworkings of ancient Eastern writings and translations, notably of Ignatius Loyola's *Spiritual Exercises*. But his fame is mainly due to the publication in 1782 of his massive Philokalia (in Greek 'love of the Good and the Beautiful' which in this case refers to divine splendour), on which he collaborated with Makarios, Bishop of Corinth. In this work 'we see how, through a philosophy of active life and contempla-

tive life, the spirit purifies itself, is enlightened and made perfect'. Described by its author as 'the treasure of sobriety, the safeguard of intelligence, the mysticism of mental prayer, the infallible guide of contemplation, the familiar and enduring memory of Jesus', this collection of the writings and sayings of the ascetic Church Fathers from Evagrius of Pontus to Gregory Palomas, breathed new life into the Orthodox spiritual renaissance. The Philokalia was particularly influential after 1793 when it had been translated into Russian with the title *Dobrotolyubie*, by Paissy Velichkovsky (1722–94), a native of Kiev who travelled extensively in Russia, Moldovia, and Walachia before settling in Athos.

The theory

Summing up the works of his predecessors, Nikodimos outlined the method to follow in order to achieve union with God. Constant repetition of Jesus's name enables the mind to take refuge in the heart, where it sees its 'impure face' and must learn humility and to recognize its faults. The mind can then detach itself from the world, and throw off evil thoughts: it will soon be in a position to converse with the inner Word, to contemplate and then enter a blessed state.

The prodigal son

'Just as the man who comes home after a long absence cannot contain his joy at seeing his wife and children again, so the mind, when it unites with the soul, overflows with joy and inexpressible delight.'

144

Nisargadatta Maharaj

1897 Bombay — Bombay 1981

A great contemporary guru

The teachings of this Indian merchant spread throughout India and have been translated into several languages. A growing number of Westerners are attracted to his theories

The son of a farmer from the Bombay region, Nisargadatta, who was then known as Maruti, was an office worker, but opened his own business selling *bidis* (Indian cigarettes). He married in 1924 and had one son and three daughters. His quest for religion began in childhood, and led him to meet Sri Siddharameshwar Maharaj in 1923, who was part of the Navnath tradition, that is to say leaders who, whether they were family men, shopkeepers or farmers, devoted themselves to the spiritual emancipation of others. Siddharameshwar gave one piece of advice to his disciple: 'You are not what you think you are . . . Find your true self'. After three years, Nisargadatta found his 'true self'. In 1937, after the death of his spiritual guide, Nisargadatta left on a pilgrimage, abandoning his family and possessions. But another of the disciples convinced him that he should return home to Bombay, where he began to work again to provide for his family. Any free time that he had was devoted to listening to the people who came from far and wide seeking his advice.

It was in these conditions that he was 'discovered' by M. Frydman, a Westerner who had already heard Ramana Maharishi and Krishnamurti speak. Frydman collected

Nisargadatta's conversations into *I Am* (1973). The publication of this book brought a steady stream of visitors to Nisargadatta who answered their questions with endless patience.

The theory

Nisargadatta never actually wrote himself, but his conversations and discussions were published in European languages from 1982. His theory, modelled on the great *Vedanta* tradition (see **Upanishad**), appears very simple, but is radical and revolutionary for our era. It stresses the idea that we are victims of an illusion, that reality is not what we think it is. The world in which we live is the product of erroneous knowledge, obscured by our desires and by our *karman*. We must therefore become what we are, which according to Nisargadatta is nothing less than 'Being-Conscience-Beautitude', that is to say attached to and indistinguishable from God. In other words, from this very moment we can break the cycle of deaths and rebirths, we are already free: it is therefore enough to realize this fact through a long voyage of self-discovery.

The ego

'A man should be in constant rebellion against himself, for the ego shrinks and deforms like a concave mirror. It is the worst of tyrants for it totally dominates you.'

The guru

'The guru's role is only to teach and encourage. The disciple remains completely responsible for himself.'

Occultism

The study of the secret

Although occultism was not built on solid foundations, it played an important role at the end of the 19th century and the beginning of the 20th.

Although the term 'occultism' (from the Latin *occultus* meaning 'hidden', 'secret') was not used until the end of the 19th century, it originates in *De occulta philosophia* (1510) by the German Humanist, Heinrich Cornelius Agrippa von Nettesheim (1486–1535), one of Goethe's models for Faust. Agrippa was also the forerunner of and model for modern occultists in the sense that his work shows a pseudo-synthesis of initiatory teachings (see **Esoterism and Initiation**) from very different sources: gnosis and Gnosticism, Cabala, hermetism, alchemy, astrology, magic etc., all of which join to make a magico-philosophical system for interpreting the universe, which is presented as the rediscovery of long-lost knowledge.

Modern occultism

It was this knowledge that the Theophysical Society (see **Theosophists**) in England purported to have brought back to life. An occultist movement was beginning to evolve in France at the same time. The ground had already been prepared by the peculiar work of Fabre d'Olivet (1768–1825), *Langue hébraïque restituée* (1816) (The Hebrew Language Restored) and of Eliphas Lévi

(1810–75), *Dogme et rituel de haute magie* (1856) (Dogma and Ritual of Magic). In the last years of the 19th century and the first of the 20th, occultism had some success in intellectual and fashionable circles. It was represented by a select number of initiated authors including Saint Yves d'Alveydre (1842–1909), Grillot de Givry (1874–1929), Mark Haven (Dr E. Lalande 1868–1920) and especially the most active member known as Papus (Dr G. Encausse 1865–1916), the driving force behind the group which brought together doctors, writers, and artists. Papus restored the 'Martinist order', which is arbitrarily linked to Saint Martin, and was also instrumental in the creation of other groups, including the Cabalistic Order of the Rose Cross, and the Universal Gnostic Church. It was in this milieu that René Guénon was to develop his own theories which later led him to denounce the movement as totally opposed to authentic tradition.

Both naive and confusing, occultism never engendered a real spiritual renewal, but it was nonetheless extremely attractive to many people who were reacting against materialistic and sectarian scientism. Occultism reasserted the value of traditions and drew attention to the importance of myths and symbols, and as such indirectly inspired a rich current of thought which still exists today.

R. Alleau
'Occultism is worth paying attention to . . . as it has highlighted the existence of a spiritual undernourishment at the heart of the intellectual and material comfort in Western society.'

Origen

185 Alexandria — Caesarea, Palestine 253 or 254

The most learned and original of the early Church Fathers

Having attempted to make Christianity into a mystical philosophy, Origen was at the centre of a controversy whose echoes linger to this day.

Origen was born into a Christian family in Alexandria. When he was 17 his father and spiritual director was martyred, and Origen was to remain fascinated by martyrdom throughout his life, for in Greek *martyr* means 'witness'. He later published an *Exhortation to Martyrdom*. In 202 the young man had to take his father's place and provide for his family. The Bishop of Alexandria assigned to him the task of training catechumens, but he did not neglect his own philosophical education, becoming a pupil of Ammonius Saccas, who was later Plotinus's master. Like his contemporary Clement of Alexandria, Origen saw in Christianity a new philosophy which owed much to its predecessor, Greek philosophy, of which it was the crowning achievement. But he was also an ascetic and used to an extremely harsh way of life, even going as far as self-mutilation; this was probably the result of a too liberal interpretation of the Gospel which states: 'There are eunuchs who have made themselves so for the Kingdom of Heaven'.

The influence of Origen's teaching even reached pagan circles, and the dowager Empress Severa, mother of Alexander, expressed a desire to hear him. However, the audacity of his views alienated him from his bishop, who found an excuse to condemn him when Origen had himself illicitly ordained a priest in Palestine, when he was already a eunuch. He then settled permanently in Palestinian Caesarea, where he carried on preaching and teaching for a further 20 years. He died, his health broken by the imprisonment and torture he had suffered during Decius's persecutions.

His works

Origen left a considerable amount of writings, all of which are based on the teachings to which he developed his whole life. His works consist principally of *Commentaries on the Holy Scriptures*; *Homilies* based on his analyses of biblical texts; and *Hexapla*, which contained the Hebrew text and its various Greek translations. This immense work of exegesis was partially founded on the writings of the Jewish philosopher, Philo of Alexandria, and was intended to uncover the meaning of spiritual writings inspired by the Holy Spirit. It later became a model text for all theologians. But Origen also wrote *De principiis*, a tract in which he synthesizes his ideas and spiritual experiences. This work was later banned by several councils because it did not comply with their standards of orthodoxy.

The theory

According to *De principiis*, all spirits were created equal and united in divine contemplation but some of them, future human-

> **Origen**
> 'In every soul there is a sense of the spiritual, and the image of God.'

> **To Daniélou**
> Origen 'left his mark on Eastern theology just as Saint Augustine, the only genius with whom he can be compared, left his on Western theology.'

kind, became bored and gradually distanced themselves from God, and were finally incarnated. This explained the Fall; matter, therefore, is not the cause but the consequence; being born of choice, it is the generator of freedom. It is freedom which allows humankind to regain what has been lost, but one existence alone would not be sufficient to bring about this union with God, and the spirits are forced to wander at length through different worlds which correspond to their level of advancement. Nevertheless, they all move towards the same goal, the rediscovery of original unity or Oneness, unity with God which is not enforced but chosen freely.

Therefore while the author puts forward a gnosis, and a doctrine of salvation, he also refutes gnostics, in that he restores humankind's free will; humankind is no longer the victim of a wicked demiurge, but the product of a Loving God, who allows him that freedom. Origen specifies that this esoteric theory should only be taught to 'spiritual' people. In *De principiis* he defines the path to be followed by those to whom God has given wisdom and science. Their search must begin with the articles of faith promulgated by the Apostles, but they must go on to understand the profound echoes and to grasp the continuity of the latter. Then, faced with the truths of faith that have been affirmed but not explained, like the relationship between the Holy Spirit and the Son of God, or the origins of human souls, angels and demons, the spiritual people must apply themselves to defining the content of the articles of faith through the active use of the understanding of faith turned towards the contemplation of invisible realities. This is the only way they can progress in the meditation of divine mysteries.

Origen's condemnation in the end is due less to the audacity of his philosophy which did not conform to Orthodoxy, than to the excesses of his followers like Evagrius of Pontus. In his *Gnostic Centuries*, Evagrius supported the belief that Christ's spirit was the same as other men's, the only difference being that he remained joined to God, and was the creator of the sensory world destined to show fallen spirits the way to salvation.

In the 4th century, Gregory of Nyssa and Saint Jerome both relied heavily on Origen's theories. Because of their subsequent condemnation, his teachings were marginalized by the Church proper, but they were never totally forgotten, and in the 12th century, Bernard of Clairvaux still quoted from Origen. His inspired ideas have acquired new relevance today, perhaps because they exceed the doctrinal theology and incorporate elements also found in the mysteries of antiquity and Asian traditions, although realistically, Origen could not have been acquainted with them. Such chance meetings lend his works an aura of worldwide significance.

Saint Jerome

'After the Apostles, I consider Origen as the great leader of the Churches; only ignorance could deny this fact. I would willingly accept the slanderous accusations that have been levelled at him, if I could have his profound intellect.'

Orphism

Initiatory current in Greek spirituality

Orphism was an underground movement throughout antiquity, the response to a desire for profound mystical knowledge.

The esoteric doctrine known as Orphism appeared in Greece in the 6th century BC and was centred around the figure of Orpheus, the Thracian demigod.

A healer and musician who charmed wild animals and descended into the underworld to bring back Eurydice, Orpheus can be compared to the ancient shamans, and Orphism is without doubt a revival of pre-Hellenistic rites and beliefs, intended as a reaction against the politico-religious system of the city.

The myth

Founded on a cosmogony similar to those of Egypt and the East, Orphic mythology depicts the universe as being born from a cosmic egg. The brilliant Phanes, who is also Eros, god of Love, is the 'firstborn', that is, first to come out of the egg. As Phanes was androgynous, he was able to give birth to the first generation of gods himself. An Orphic myth explains the origins of humankind and its condition: Dionysus-Zagreus, son of Zeus, inherits the right to rule the world, but is captured and subsequently devoured by the rebelling Titans. In retaliation Zeus strikes them down with a bolt of lightning and the human race is born from their ashes in which there are divine elements inherited

from Dionysus, but also the Titans' marked propensity for evil.

Humankind therefore, had to rid itself of the evil parts of its nature, leaving only divine parts. To accomplish this, Orphism advocated an ascetical way of life based on ritual purification and numerous prohibitions. Its followers refused to take part in the bloody sacrifices of the official cult and abstained from eating of all kinds of flesh, which they saw as a result of murder; they dressed in white, avoided wearing wool as it came from an animal, and also refused any contact with a corpse. These prescriptions were a direct rejection of all that was held dear by the official cult from which the Orphics had broken away.

Orpheus, the founder of the initiation rites, particularly those of Dionysus, was associated with and involved in the Eleusinian Mysteries.

Today, Orphism's role in antiquity is better understood due to the discovery of Orphic books which were buried with the initiated and intended to serve as a passport to the other world. As a religious and philosophical movement it inspired Pythagoras, Plato, who used Orphic myths in his works, and also the Neoplatonists at the start of the Christian era. Orpheus was even adopted by the first Christians, giving birth to the 'Good Pastor' figure.

Golden Page of Thourion

'Now I come begging to Persephone, the spirit, that through her grace she deigns to send me to the abode of the Blessed. Happy and Blessed, you will be a god, not a mortal.'
(W.K.C. Guthrie)

149

Orthodoxy

The true Christian doctrine

A mystical theology of humankind's return to God, Orthodoxy was illustrated by a long line of religious leaders and, because of recent revival, by a succession of great religious thinkers.

The word orthodoxy (from the Greek *ortho-doxos* meaning 'correct opinion') is applied to the Eastern Church with its Greek language liturgy which is considered to have preserved the Christian heritage of the first centuries, as opposed to the Western Church, termed 'catholic' meaning universal, due to its more expansionist ideals. The date of the separation between the two churches is normally given as 1054, the year in which the Roman legate and the patriarchate of Constantinople came into direct confrontation for the last and irrevocable time. Although this decision was made final in 1054, the division between the Eastern and Western Roman Empires had existed for some time, brought about by the pretensions of the Roman Church, founded by Peter, to supremacy over the other four Eastern patriarchates of Constantinople, Antioch, Alexandria, and Jerusalem. Constantinople, nicknamed the 'second Rome', became the capital of the Byzantine Empire and soon rose to dominate the other three. However, Orthodox Christianity has never been ruled by one single power; supreme doctrinal authority belongs to the councils, and the Church is governed collectively by the patriarch and the synod, or assembly of bishops.

The division between East and West was also the result of divergent dogmas, but even more due to the existence of distinct concepts of spirituality and mysticism on each side. Despite several attempts which continued until the 15th century, reconciliation remained an impossibility.

Orthodoxy today

After 1453, the year of Constantinople's capture by the Turks, while the patriarchate survived, the Eastern Church was divided into many more autocephalies or independent Churches. The majority of the new Churches were Slavic, which saw the patriarchate as merely an honorific primacy. At the present time, the Orthodox Church with its 160 million followers is represented by the Greek, Russian, and

---

Clement of Alexandria (2nd century)
'The Word of God became a man so that you could learn from a man how man can become God.'

Evagrius of Pontus (4th century)
'Anyone who prays is a theologian.'

Maximus the Confessor (8th century)
'The mystery of the Incarnation of the Word contains within it the meaning of all sensible and intelligent creation.'

Serafim of Sarov (19th century)
'Find inner peace and thousands will flock to your side.'

Sylvain of Athos (1866–1938)
'For the man who prays in his heart, the whole world is a church.'

Balkan Churches, but because of mass emigration from these areas, orthodoxy is also evident in the United States and even Japan and North Africa. The patriarch of Constantinople has not only managed to maintain unity within a dispersed Church, but he also accepted in principle a reconciliation with Rome, made more possible by the memorable meetings between Pope Paul VI and the patriarch Athenagoras in 1964–7, and by the lifting of the anathemas laid down in 1054.

Orthodox spirituality

The Byzantine spiritual ideal was embodied in the life of prayer and contemplation led by the Desert Fathers, whose direct descendants are the monks; it was based on the mystical theology of the Greek Church Fathers, who were strongly influenced by Neoplatonic philosophy. Byzantine spirituality blossomed in the great monasteries like those of Saint Catherine at Mount Sinai, Stoudion at Constantinople and Mount Athos in northern Greece, and spread all over the East. In the Eastern Church, only the monks are considered to be truly 'spiritual' for they have exchanged wordly life for a celestial state comparable to that of angels. Only monks can practise asceticism in preparation for *metanoia*, the soul's conversion and transformation, and thus attain *apatheia*, the pacification of passion, and *hesychia*, repose in God in solitude and silence, thanks to the 'prayer of the heart' (see **Hesychasm**). The monks are the spiritual fathers of the Christian community, providing it with both bishops and all its great doctors. These doctors, from Symeon the New Theologia (10th century) to Gregory Palamas (14th century) developed the dogma of the Trinity and glorified Christ's Incarnation and Resurrection. They also highlighted his Transfiguration as the promise of humankind's own transfiguration — as experienced by Serafim of Sarov and described by his disciple Motovilov — as well as the role

of the Holy Spirit, present in the Church and the hearts of the faithful. The outcome of this theology is the 'deification' of humankind, which is recognizing God's presence within and uniting with it. This can only be obtained after willing engagement in a long purificatory struggle, because 'God can do everything, except force man to love Him'. While God is unknowable and inaccessible, He nevertheless transcended his transcendence through love, 'God suffers and dies in his flesh' in order to convince humankind of His 'mad love' (Maximus the Confessor). Religious life finds fulfilment in the sacraments, particularly in the Eucharist 'the true transference of vital deificatory energy' as well as in the liturgy, which are a foretaste of the blissful union to come. There was a brilliant renewal of Orthodox spirituality in 19th-century Russia, following the translation of Nikodimos Hagioritis's *Philokalia* into Russian and also as a result of the spiritual role played by the Starsi. This renaissance took a messianic turn with Soloviev, but was soon compromised by the 1917 Revolution. It was carried on by Bulgakov, Berdiaev, and Vladimir Lossky (1903–58), whose works tried to minimize the differences between East and West in order to let the Church of the future, the Church of the Holy Ghost, become manifest through Christ. This mystical and popularized spirituality is demonstrated on a day-to-day basis in *Tales of a Russian Pilgrim*, and is summed up concisely in the definition given of saintliness: 'What is saintliness? It is nothing less than the first man's innocence resurrected in the sinner.'

The language of creation

'Everything around me seemed so beautiful: the trees, the grass, the earth, the birds, the air, and the light, everything seemed to be saying that it existed for man, that they were proof of God's love for man; everything was praying, everything was singing to the glory of God!'

Padmasambhava

8th century India

The 'Great Guru'

Padmasambhava introduced Buddhist doctrine into Tibet and exorcized its demons.

Padmasambhava ('born of the Lotus') was born in the extreme north-west of India, now Pakistan. He was already an accredited Tantric master at the Nalanda university when he was called to Tibet by King Thi-Srong Detsan (740–786). Buddhism had doubtlessly arrived in Tibet one century before, during the reign of the first king, Stong-Btsan (c. 610–649) who had married two Buddhist princesses, one from Nepal, and the other from China. However, it was only under Thi-Srong Detsan that the new religion began to spread. Thi-Srong Detsan invited the highly educated monk Santirakshita to his kingdom, where he began construction of the first Buddhist monastery, but could not complete his task because of the interference of demons from the ancient indigenous religion. These demons were most probably the priests themselves. Santirakshita, who was a philosopher, did not have the means to fight them, and advised the king to call in Padmasambhava who was a Tantric siddha, and therefore, an exorcist.

His journey to Tibet was a triumphant march. One by one the demons were beaten and one by one they had to swear to become loyal protectors of the Doctrine. The Samye monastery was opened in 779, at the same time as Buddhism was declared the state religion and the first seven Buddhist monks ordained. A few years later, the last representatives of Ch'an, the Chinese school of Buddhism which had been very influential, were expelled, and the Vajrayana school, or Indian Tantric Buddhism reigned supreme.

The 'Great Guru'

After the persecution of Buddhism which accompanied the collapse of the monarchy (842), a popular form of the religion survived which remained faithful to the teachings of the 'Great Guru' whose writings were hidden and not discovered until several centuries later (see **Bardo Thodol**). Padmasambhava is closely linked to the oldest Tibetan monastic order, Nyingma-pa. Throughout Buddhist Himalaya, the Great Guru, or Precious Jewel (*Lopon Rinposhe*) is worshipped as the Lama par excellence and is even considered by some to be the Buddha's reincarnation. His birthday, the tenth day of the fourth month of the Tibetan calendar (end of June/beginning of July) is celebrated with sacred dances, particularly at Hemis in Ladakh.

Paul

Early 1st century Tarsus, Cilicia — Rome 67(?)

The 'Apostle' of the Gentiles

Originally a persecutor of Christians, but then the most ardent convert, Paul travelled tirelessly, spreading the Word.

Born of Jewish parents who had become Roman citizens, Paul was also known as Saul (his Jewish name). We know about his life from his letters and above all from the information given in the Acts of the Apostles. Paul went to Jerusalem to study at an early age, and was there just after Jesus's death. He was instrumental in the martyrdom of Stephen, the first deacon, and appointed himself persecutor of the Christian refugees at Damascus but, on the road to Damascus, he was struck down by a vision of Christ. Once he had converted and been baptized, Paul retreated into the desert spending several years in prayer and meditation before returning to Jerusalem where he was received with suspicion by the Apostles. We then lose sight of him until AD 44, when Barnabus went looking for him in Tarsus to ask him to preach Christianity to the pagans at Antioch. From then on, Paul became an itinerant preacher, touring the pagan lands of Cyprus, Asia Minor, Macedonia, and Greece. On his return to Jerusalem he was only able to escape the fury of the Jews by reminding them of his status as a Roman citizen. He was taken to Palestinian Caesarea where he was held prisoner for two years before being sent to Rome for judgment. He was probably acquitted as evidence shows that he made a further voyage to Spain and the East. He was arrested a second time and brought back to Rome, where he was beheaded.

His works

We have 13 of Paul's Epistles or Letters, addressed to the different Churches he had founded. Apart from advice on church matters the Letters are an extremely important exposé of the Christian faith, as they were written before the actual completion of the Gospels.

The theory

Speaking principally to pagans, Paul gave a universal character to Christ's message. Taking the Resurrection as his starting point, he affirmed that salvation and the promise of the after-life no longer depended on deeds — as Christ's coming had abolished the old Law — but on faith in Jesus, the 'new Adam' who had paid for our sins with His life. Salvation is dependent on God's mercy, which he bestows on the chosen ones. While Paul's theory of Redemption is the rock on which much of Christianity had been built, it has not always been accepted without question: some have even gone so far as to accuse him of perverting the simple message of Christ.

> 'There is no question here of Greek and Jew, circumcised and uncircumcised, barbarian, Scythian, slave and freeman; but Christ is all, and is in all.' (*Colossians* 3, 11)

153

Pelagius and Pelagianism

Between 350 and 354 Ireland — Palestine or Egypt betwee
423 and 429

Western Christianity's first great heretic

*Pelagius defended the theory of free
will and was a staunch opponent of
Augustine. Their dispute has had
repercussions throughout the history
of Christianity.*

Born in Ireland, Pelagius was educated in
the East where he became firmly convinced
of the validity of Origen's doctrine of free
will. In 401 he settled in Rome, leading an
austere life and lecturing on humankind's
natural dignity and the absurdity of original
sin to his numerous disciples. To escape
Alaric's invasion, he fled to North Africa
where he met Augustine, who later condemned Celestius, one of Pelagius's disciples, on the grounds that his teachings
were heretical. Pelagius travelled to
Palestine where he was very well received.
However, through the effort of Augustine,
Pelagius himself was condemned by Rome
in 417, then again by a council at Carthage
in 418. He was banished along with numerous Italian bishops who supported his
views. Under the leadership of Julian,
Bishop of Eclanumin Campania, they continued to defend Pelagianism with fervour

'It is not much to set an example to pagans;
what is much better is to set such an example
that even the saints can learn from you.'

until it was finally condemned in 431
lose track of Pelagius in 418 and I
presumed to have died some years la

His works

Pelagius's doctrine is explained in
tracts: *Tract on the Trinity* and *Eclog
Liber* (Book of Testimonies or Extracts
his *Commentaries on the Letters of Saint Pa
well as in *Letter to Demetriad*.

The theory

According to Pelagius, humankin
Creation's masterpiece, because it w
humankind alone that God gave rea
awareness of his acts and the freedo
choose between good and evil. In f
choosing good, humankind deserves
vation. Pelagius also rejects everything
could hinder this freedom, includin
physical and hereditary determinism
especially original sin, which woul
God's condemnation of his own work
itself, which is only fleeting disobedien
no way alters freedom. However, Pel
was an ascetic and strongly believed
in choosing to commit evil, human
breaks the contract which joins it to
while the man who chooses the virt
path lives united with Him. After Pelag
death, Julian of Eclanus defended the
imacy of concupiscence against attac
Augustine, maintaining that it wa
manifestation of the freedom God wa
the human race to have. Accordin
Julian, only reason which is particul
people can control desire, which in ani
is instinctive.

Philo of Alexandria

20 BC Alexandria — Alexandria AD 45

The greatest representative of Hellenized Judaism

Philo of Alexandria had great influence on the roots of Christian thought.

Philo belonged to a wealthy and prestigious family who lived in Alexandria, which at that time was one of the principal centres of the Diaspora (see **Judaism**). He received an excellent education (both Greek and Jewish) in an extremely cultured Hellenized Jewish milieu. The only fact about Philo that can be reported with certainty is that he led a deputation to Emperor Caligula, sent by the Alexandrian Jews to ask for exemption from having to put statues of the emperor in their temples. Although he only obtained a few concessions, Philo showed his courage and his strong attachment to Judaism, and he always supported his fellow Jews especially in his written works like *Apology of the Jews*. He is usually depicted as an erudite contemplative who dedicated his whole life to the compilation of his works.

His works

Apart from the occasional text, the Philonic corpus is essentially composed of three groups of commentaries on the Pentateuch (the first five books in the Bible): *Exposition of the Law, Allegory of the Sacred Law,* and *Questions and Solutions* (on Genesis and Exodus), which are completed by three philosophical tracts: *On the Slavery of the Insane, On the Freedom of the Sage,* and *On Providence.*

The theory

As a contemporary of Christ, Philo developed a synthesis between biblical revelation and Greek philosophy by means of allegorical interpretations. This form of exegesis, which did not detract from faith but joined Greek ideas on God, humankind and the world to it, served as a model for the first Christian thinkers, Clement of Alexandria and Origen, and thereafter, for the Church Fathers. Philo took up the theory of the Word already sketched out by Jewish theologians, and greatly enriched it by means of Platonic concepts. According to him, the Word becomes the mediator between humankind and God. Philo's influence on Judaism was just as important in that he uncovered the hidden and deeply spiritual meanings in religion which were the result of a personal experience of ecstasy brought about by God's intervention in the human soul.

Philo's works also represent an important source of historical data. Through them we not only know about the ideals of the pious and sophisticated Diaspora Jews, but also about the existence of the *Therapeutae*, Jewish ascetics who lived together in communities, who were probably the inspiration for early Christian monasticism.

Mystical ecstasy

'As long as our intellect shines and, like the midday sun, pours light into every corner of our soul, we remain within ourselves, but, when it begins to set, then ecstasy naturally begins to happen inside us; we are possessed, seized by divine fury.'

Plato

c. 428 BC Athens — Athens 347 BC

The founder of the first school of philosophy

A disciple of Socrates, Plato and his school of philosophy have been an inexhaustible source of inspiration for Western philosophers, theologians and mystics.

Coming from an aristocratic family which claimed to have descended from the last Athenian king, Plato seemed destined to take up a career in politics, but at an early age, his personal tasks led him towards poetry. At the age of 20, he was involved with the Sophists when he met Socrates. This meeting inspired him with so much enthusiasm that he burned his poetic efforts and decided to devote his life to philosophy. For eight years, he was one of Socrates's constant companions, until the former's death in 399 BC. From Athens, he fled to Megara where he took lessons from Euclid. In 396 BC he had to take part in the Battle of Corinth at which the Athenians were beaten by the Spartans. Athens lost all its attraction for Plato and he left for Egypt where he studied astronomy, religion, and institutions. He travelled on to Tarente in southern Italy which was governed by the Pythagorean Archytas, an accomplished philosopher and statesman, on whom Plato was later to model himself. He was invited to Syracuse by Dionysius the Elder but fell foul of the tyrant ruler and was sold at Aegina, where fortunately he was bought by a friend.

> **Plato**
> 'To reach absolute truth, we must use pure thought.'

The Academy

On his return to Athens, Plato, who had witnessed the dramatic fall of Athenian power, opened the first school or Academy of philosophy in the Academos gardens near the town gates. The Academy's intention was to train politicians who would be able to run the city according to just and reasonable principles. The Academy was an immense success overnight. Plato was invited back to Syracuse in 366 BC, and again in 361 BC by Dionysius the Younger who had succeeded his father, but both visits were ill starred, and he was only rescued through Archytas's intervention. When he returned to Athens, he composed his last works, *Timaeus*, *Crito*, and *Laws* which remain unfinished. He died in his 80s having appointed his nephew Spousippus, and not his best pupil Aristotle, as his successor. Disappointed, Aristotle left for Asia but on his return to Athens, he founded his Lyceum which was to compete with Plato's school. Apart from several politicians the Academy also numbered the orators Lycurgus, Hyperides and maybe Demosthenes. It was to be active for nearly 1000 years until an edict by the Emperor Justinian closed it down.

His works

We have his complete works which are presented in the form of 28 *Dialogues*, during which the teacher Socrates has his interlocutor discover truth in and by himself. While they preserve the spontaneity and variations of real conversation, the *Dialogues* contain rigorous, thorough and sometimes extremely dry, analyses. The longest of them, like *Republic* or *Laws* are devoted to the description and government of the ideal town: others, like the *Banquet*, *Phaedo*, and *Phaedrus* give an idealistic picture of Socrates or recall the end he met.

The spiritual teachings were never systematically exposed in any one work, but are contained in the critical and metaphysical dialogues in which allegories and myths are often used to suggest the inexpressible.

The theory

The Platonic corpus only represents his public lectures; these were complemented by an oral tradition which because it was esoteric, has remained secret, but of which, we find traces in the works of Plotinus and the Neoplatonists.

Athens was in the throes of a grave crisis which was both moral — because of the Sophists — and political. Plato tried to remedy that situation by giving a sound metaphysical basis to justice and virtue, producing his system of 'Ideas' which allow the passage from the sensory to the intelligible, from existence to essence, typified in mathematics. If the maieutics practised by Socrates can succeed, it is because we have within ourselves the memory of a former, but forgotten existence. These memories or reminiscences, the Ideas, are behind everything that is conceivable to the spirit. We have contemplated them before we were born, a theory illustrated by the famous myth of the cave, in which we are imprisoned in such a way that we can only see the distorted shadows of reality on the cave's walls. Only the person who has managed to shrug off the fetters of existence will be able to leave the cave and look at things as they really are, and at the sun which lights them up. The aim of life therefore, is the liberation of our immortal soul, through inner harmony, and aspiring towards the Absolute.

No other philosopher has had such a dramatic effect on the West. Not only did he illuminate all the Greek philosophy that was to come after him (the last school of antiquity was that of the Neoplatonists) but he also moulded Christian thought in the first few centuries of its existence. In Christian terms, Plato's Ideas became the eternal divine truths, and his description of birth in this world as a fall, became the original sin. According to Christians, Plato was one of their precursors, perhaps even the most important precursor. This is certainly one of the principal explanations for the survival of his works in their complete form. Through the Byzantine Empire, Platonism also influenced Islamic philosophy, particularly the Arabic Sufi movement. Traces of Platonic thought can even be found in the speculations of the Hebraic Cabala.

Saint Augustine

'Plato was the wisest man of his era, who spoke in such a way that all he said became great . . . if just a few words were omitted, he would be a Christian.'

Meister Eckhart

'Plato speaks of a purity which is not of this world nor yet outside this world, which is neither in time nor eternity, neither outside nor inside.'

Plotinus

205 Lycopolis Magna — Campania 270

Antiquity's last great mystic

With Plotinus, Plato's philosophy became a doctrine of salvation or Neoplatonism, which illuminated the last centuries of paganism and the first of Christianity.

We do not even know if Plotinus, who was born in Egypt, was Roman; the education he received in Alexandria was Greek, but had a distinct Eastern flavour. At 28 he decided to 'give himself to philosophy', becoming the disciple of Ammonius Saccas who professed eclectic Platonism.

At that time, the study of philosophy was a form of asceticism, an initiation into a superior spiritual life reserved for the select few. Plotinus spent 11 years with this great teacher who had also taught Origen, and had to swear never to reveal the content of the doctrine. In 242 he wanted to learn about Persian and even Indian philosophy. It is not impossible that he had already discovered them at second hand in Alexandria, which would explain some of the more audacious passages in his works. To become better acquainted with Eastern thought he followed Emperor Gordien III to the East, but the imperial expedition was a failure, and Plotinus left for Rome in 247.

He became a sort of spiritual adviser to the cultural circles of the capital. He practised extreme austerity, based on contempt

---

Plotinus's last words

'If you want to contemplate God and beauty, let your soul become beautiful and godly.'
'I try to make what is godly within us rise up to the God who is in the Universe.'

---

for the body; he lived surrounded by his pupils, whom he taught that 'escaping the world' was necessary to each individual dedicated to the search for truth who wanted to unite with God. His disciple Porphyry was appointed to edit his works, and later wrote his biography. However, the strict regime and constant tension he imposed on his pupils was finally to distance them from him. After having dreamed of founding Platonopolis, the city of philosophers, Plotinus withdrew to Campania where he lived in solitude and ill-health until his death.

His works

It was only at the behest of his pupils that Plotinus decided to commit to paper a teaching which had until then been entirely oral, and which was mainly in the form of his answers to the questions of his pupils. His brief tracts, of which there are 54, were collected into a coherent whole by Porphyry, who grouped them into six books — the *Enneads*, each of which contained nine tracts. The first book is mainly devoted to humankind, the second and third to the physical world, the fourth to the Soul, the fifth to Intelligence, and the sixth to the One. Thanks to Proclus, Augustine, and the Neoplatonists, Plotinus's works made an impression on a whole current in Christian thought; they were used as a guide by mystics and nourished philosophers' wildest speculations.

The theory

Taking Plato's works as his starting point, Plotinus taught a complete system for the interpretation of the world, humankind, and God. From the superabundance of the One, the pure light which is absolutely simple and self-sufficient, emanates or diffuses — Plotinus says it 'proceeds' — a second substance which in no way detracts from the One, and is at once Being, Intelligence, and the intelligible world. Like the Word, Intelligence, which is a vision of the One, produces the All-Soul, which gives life to all animate things without splitting itself, remaining intact in the heart of each person.

Individualized, the soul succumbs to the attraction of matter which is a confused corruption of the primordial Light and the causes of all evil. The return to our true and original status, the enraptured contemplation of the One, can only be achieved if we abandon our body which Plotinus sees as both prison and tomb. This is the only way to understand how 'Life spreads in the Universe and the individial at the same time . . . The soul must contemplate the All-Soul; however, in order to rise to this contemplation, the soul must be worthy and noble, be free from error, have got rid of those objects which fascinate vulgar beings and be plunged deep in meditation . . .'

Musical harmony and beauty on the one hand, and love on the other can be the first rungs on the ladder leading to Light, of which they are the imperfect reflections.

Hegel

'All of Plotinus's philosophy takes us towards virtue and the intellectual contemplation of Eternity.'

But only philosophy leads to the final rung, at which the soul, detached from itself, resides in God. 'Such is the life of the gods and godly and blessed men . . ., the flight of the spirit towards the One.'

An admirable experience

Although it appears abstract, Plotinus's doctrine is actually the result of personal experience which he describes in his writings: 'Often, waking from my body to myself, having become exterior to all things but interior to myself, seeing then extraordinary beauty, having the certainty of belonging to the best part of reality, having become one with the divine, having been established in him, having established myself above all other objects of intellection, after this repose in the divine, falling from intellection to reason, I ask myself how it is possible that once before, and now again, I can come down thus and how my soul can have found itself in my body, if it is what it appeared to be in itself, although it was in the body.'

This exemplary description of a spiritual ascension, comparable to that of the great Christian mystics, particularly of John of the Cross was to shine brightly throughout the last pagan centuries and to influence the first Christian authors and even Islamic mysticism. It also attracted many spiritual philosophers and was carried on in the works of Hegel and Bergson.

Prophets of Israel

Those inspired by God

Addressing the chosen people in Yahweh's name, the Prophets reminded the people of Israel of his active presence in the world, as well as in the hearts of humankind.

The word prophet comes from the Greek *pro* meaning 'before' and *phemi* meaning 'I say'. Today the word describes someone who by divine inspiration can predict the future, in particular those the Bible more aptly calls *nabi* (inspired) or *roeh* (visionary). For the Jews, the Prophets were God's mouthpieces, chosen by Him to communicate his wishes. They therefore carried on the work of Abraham and Moses, considered by tradition to be the first prophets who founded a long line which extended throughout the centuries. The Prophet's status in Isrealite society has varied according to the circumstances and personality of each one. While the majority denounced both civil and religious authority, others seem to have played an official role.

Elijah

In David's time (11th century BC) Nathan appeared, then in the 9th century BC, Elijah

---

The Tree of Jesse
'Then a shoot shall grow from the stock of Jesse and a branch shall spring from his roots.
The spirit of the Lord shall rest upon him,
a spirit of wisdom and understanding,
a spirit of counsel and power,
a spirit of knowledge and the fear of the Lord.'
(*Isaiah* 11, 1–3)

---

alone defended Yahweh from the cult idols and shady power deals. Persecuted Queen Jezebel, Elijah withdrew into th desert. Having predicted the extinctio of the unholy Ahab ruling dynasty, entrusted the task of continuing the missic to his disciple Elisha. Legend quickly la claim to Elijah who is said to have risen in the sky on a fiery chariot, and will reappe at the end of time. Elisha also battle against encroaching idolatry and, like h master, performed miracles.

Amos and Hosea

In the 8th century BC prophetism reach its apogee. Yahweh, through the voice his Prophets, sent message after message his people whose ingratitude and infideli merited chastisement. Amos outspoken denounced the greed for riches whi oppresses the poor, and the hypocrisy of t clergy. He warned the people who believ themselves to be the chosen ones impending divine revenge, the 'Day Yahweh' when Israel would fall, for it h not respected the rights of widows a orphans. Hosea, who had forgiven his w after she had been unfaithful to him, dr on his personal experience to create image of the relationship between God a His people which was to become popul He unfailingly fought syncretist tendenci believing any compromise between t pagan divinities and the one God to whc Isreal owed everything, to be an absolu impossibility.

Isaiah

Generally believed to be the greatest of Prophets, Isaiah was born c. 700 BC Judah and began his 50 year public minist in 740 BC. A brilliant poet, in his verse describes the threats hanging over Isr which were already beginning to come tr and predicts gloomy times ahead for the whole nation. He is not to be confused with the second Isaiah, who lived amongst the exiles while Cyrus was threatening Babylon. He also announces the end of hardship and in mysterious terms predicts the coming of a messiah, the 'Servant of the Lord,' the 'Man of pain' who will redeem the human race.

Jeremiah

Born c. 650 BC, Jeremiah was a sensitive and tender visionary who accepted the mission thrust upon him unwillingly and with trepidation. His mission was soon to prove dangerous, as he had to foretell the taking of Jerusalem, a city everyone thought impregnable. This event took place in 587 BC. Persecuted by his contemporaries, in spite of himself Jeremiah expresses the weariness of the righteous and his despair, but also his faith and hope in God.

Ezekiel

Almost a contemporary of Jeremiah, Ezekiel is perhaps the most extraordinary of the Prophets. He was called to prophethood during an ecstatic trance in which a chariot whose wheels turned at a fantastic rate appeared to him and he was surrounded by fantastic creatures, half-man half-bull, who dictated God's orders amidst roaring waters. More of these hallucinatory visions followed and the prophet translated them into a kind of oracle to which he added commentaries to make them more accessible. Ezekiel lived in a particularly dramatic period, punctuated with the disasters he had predicted. He was exiled to Babylon with the nation's élite in 597 BC. There he announced the revival of Israel, which through a renewal of faith would be blessed by God. Ezekiel insists on personal responsibility, each individual being judged according to his deeds. After the return from exile, the Prophet's role became secondary. Later, during the struggle against Greek then Roman occupiers, prophetism was to give birth to apocalyptic literature (see **Revelation**).

The prophetic books

The Prophets were first and foremost eloquent orators who used a passionate and vivid language studded with images and parables. With exhortations and threats they swept their audiences off their feet. Only gradually did they or their secretaries, like Baruch, Jeremiah's secretary, transmit their oracles. In the form in which they appear in the Bible, these oracles often seem to be reworkings of older texts; thus in Isaiah, only the first part of the book is Isaiah's own work. Normally, four great prophets, Isaiah, Jeremiah, Daniel and Ezekiel are distinguished from the 12 lesser prophets Hosea, Joel, Amos, Obadiah, Jonah, Micah, Nahum, Habakkuk, Zephaniah, Haggai, Zechariah, and Malachi.

For the Christian Church the Prophets particularly foretold the coming of the Messiah and the suffering he would have to bear before he could reign in glory while for Muslims Adam, Noah, Abraham, and Moses are recognized as the predecessors of Muhammad, the 'Seal of the Prophets', meaning the last and most important of all.

Ezekiel

'You shall know that I am the Lord when I open your graves and bring you up from them, O my people.' (*Ezekiel* 37, 13)

Protestantism

The Reformation's dissenters

The principle of 'universal priesthood' which made every Christian a priest gave rise to several sects which were on the fringes of the Reformed Churches.

In its religious sense, the word 'protestant' first appeared after the diet of Speyer (1529) when Lutheran princes and towns protested against the demands of their Catholic adversaries. Since then the word Protestantism has become an umbrella term covering the collection of diverse currents, stemming from the Reformation which have certain commonalities inherited from the 16th century reformers: absolute primacy of the Word of God as it appears in the Bible, the direct relationship between the believer and God through prayer and the Scriptures, and justification by faith alone. That the Reformation contained the seeds of its future splinter groups was evident from as early as the 16th century with the illuminist and millenarian movements which, in their desire to immediately institute God's kingdom on

---

Protestant mysticism

It 'is not the occupation of monks. It is made up of ministers turned towards the cure of the souls, of laypersons engaged in the battle against injustice and persecution, steeped in town and country life and sowing the seeds of a more conscientious and religious life.' (Raymond H. Leenhardt)

'A faith without frontiers.' (Hromadka)

Earth, revolted against the existing social order and had to be repressed by the Reformers themselves.

Religious unity which until then had been guaranteed by the Catholic hierarchy was shattered; nothing stood in the way of the new movements which emerged during the period of relative freedom following the Reformation which the reformers themselves were to end. Lutheranism, Calvinism, and Anglicanism, submitted to political power and became institutionalized. Those who wanted more radical reforms continued to oppose these new, but now, official Churches.

The European dissenters

In England from 1560, the Puritans, who called for a purer liturgy, were soon persecuted. While they triumphed under Cromwell and the new Republic (1649), the Restoration in 1660 was their undoing and they were only tolerated after the 1688 revolution. However, many of them had chosen to emigrate to the American colonies where the Pilgrim Fathers, who arrived on the *Mayflower* in 1620, established an austere and rigoristic theocratic State.

Back in England, the movement which defended the autonomy and independence of each congregation or local community engendered Baptism, founded in 1609 by the Englishman John Smith in Amsterdam, and brought over to England in 1612; the message later reached North America through Roger Williams. The Baptist Church has more than 30 million members worldwide today, 26 million of which live in the United States.

In the middle of the 17th century, George Fox in England created his Society of Friends. The Quakers, as they became known, left in droves for New England, where they founded the State of Pennsylvania in 1682.

In the 18th century, there was renewed interest in Lutheranism thanks to the Pietist movement expounded by P. J. Spener, while in England John Wesley, founder of Methodism called for a return to piety. This movement also reached the United States, where in 1987, there were 14 million of the 40 million Methodists worldwide.

The American dissenters

In the United States, which has been a hothouse for all manner of sects, a revelation received by John Smith gave birth to the Mormons or Latter-Day Saints.

Another millenarian Church, Adventism (from the Latin *adventus* meaning 'coming'), was the result of the sermons of an autodidactic farmer, William Miller (1782–1849), in which he predicted that the second coming of Christ would take place in 1843 or 1844. Although their hopes were never realized, there are still more than 1 million Adventists in the world today. After Miller's prediction failed to come true, Ellen G. White (1827–1915) declared that while the date of the second coming could not be pinpointed with any certainty, this did not mean that people should not prepare themselves for it anyway. The Seventh Day Adventists, for whom Mrs White was a prophet, prepare by respecting Saturday as a day of rest, blessed by the Lord, and by following numerous dietary prohibitions (for example abstinence from meat, alcohol, and tobacco). For them, the imminent coming of Christ will be followed by the millennium, during which the elect will live in heaven with Christ. After this period, the resurrection will take place and the bad will be destroyed while the good will be immortal and return to live in an earthly paradise.

After having waited in vain for the return of Christ between 1873 and 1878, Charles Taze Russell, an American, founded the International Students of the Bible movement which split into further groups after his death. The principal branch directed by J. F. Rutherford, took the name Jehovah's Witnesses in 1931 and was organized like a fighting body. The Witnesses await the coming destruction of the world during the battle of Armageddon as described in the Book of Revelation. Led by Jesus, who is not God's only son, but the principal lieutenant, the forces of Good will definitely wipe out Satan and the forces of Evil. All bad people will be annihilated and the good with Jesus will enjoy the messianic kingdom of a renewed earth. There were almost 3 million Jehovah's Witnesses in 1987.

In 1879 in Boston, Mary Baker Eddy (1821–1910) founded the Christian Scientist Church. She wanted to 're-establish the lost element' in Christianity, and to this end put into practice certain reharmonizing techniques which she believed were capable of curing the ills of both body and soul. Today there are roughly 2 million Christian Scientists.

Starting from 1865, William Booth (1829–1912) undertook to evangelize the miserable, poverty-stricken London masses. In 1878 he created the Salvation Army, which is famous for its charitable works. In 1987 it was made up of more than 25 000 'officers' spread across 86 countries, and its creed was followed by some 3 million people.

This is a brief overview of the principal splinter groups which emerged from the prophetic current released by the work of the Reformation. Members of these movements consider their founders to be religious leaders.

Pythagoras

c. 6th century BC Samos

The first man to call himself a philosopher

*This lover of wisdom spread
an esoteric doctrine which is
reflected by spiritual thinkers
throughout antiquity.*

While his existence in history is unquestionable, Pythagoras soon became (perhaps even during his lifetime) a legendary, somewhat mysterious figure. He is thought to have spent a great deal of time travelling, seeking initiation to the secret doctrines of Greek as well as foreign religions, particularly the esoteric doctrines of Orphism, from which it is almost impossible to distinguish his own teachings. When he was c. 40 years old, he settled at Crotona and created a religious and political community, on which many others in central Italy and Sicily later modelled themselves. Rather aristocratic in nature, these communities fell apart after successive attacks by the democrats. Pythagoras died in the fire which swept through the building he shared with his disciples. The latter saw him as a divine reincarnation, either son of Apollo or of Hermes, which gave Pythagoras the ability to remember his previous lives.

Golden verses (attributed to Pythagoras)
'And if you manage, after having abandoned your body in the free ether, —
You will be an immortal god, incorruptible and forever free of death.'

The theory

Pythagoras's teachings and theories were transmitted orally and reserved for select followers who had been sworn to secrecy, therefore we only know a small part of them revealed in the works of later authors. The Pythagoreans were divided into two groups: the *akousmatikoi* or 'outer circle', a warrior brotherhood led by Pythagoras's son-in-law Milo of Crotona, whose task was to defend the school; and the *mathematikoi* or 'inner circle'. Members of the latter were initiated into the secret doctrine of numbers as the foundation of the universe, knowledge which could be applied to such diverse subjects as astronomy, architecture and musical theory. The inner circle disciples dressed in white and observed numerous prohibitions. It was only after having passed an entrance exam and completed a three year study period, followed by five years of silence and austerity that the postulants were admitted into the presence of the leader. They then received the revelation of the *tetraktys*, 'the powerful and mysterious decade,' 'the source and root of Eternity', the basic principle of the cosmos, made up of the first four numbers.

According to Pythagoreans, the immortal soul is imprisoned in the body like a tomb, and is submitted to a perpetual transmigration. Salvation is only possible if all the ties created by successive incarnations which have dragged the soul into corruption are cut, an act which requires absolute conversion to the divine element. With Plato, this conception of the soul was to be diffused throughout ancient philosophy, particularly in the works of the Neoplatonists who were also Neopythagoreans.

Quietism

A total submission to the will of God

Quietism rendered all other forms of devotion more or less useless; in consequence it was condemned by the Church.

The term evokes the tranquil state of the soul which, passively submerged in God, awaits His command. Forms of quietism have always existed, particularly with mystics like Meister Eckhart, who have continually aroused the suspicions of ecclesiastical authorities; however, historically speaking, this name describes the movement which surfaced during the revival of mysticism in 16th and 17th century Spain and spread to Italy where it met with strong opposition. The *Guía Espiritual* (1675) (Spiritual Guide) written by Miguel de Molinos (1628–96), a Spanish priest, was read throughout Europe until its condemnation in 1687 by Rome, where its author died in prison.

A French devotee

Madame Guyon (1648–1717) who led a life of excessive austerity, soon converted to Molinos's way of perfection. In her *Moyen court et très facile de Faire oraison* (1685) (Short and easy way to Pray) she recommended total passivity of the soul, the loss of all desire, even for salvation, of all fear, even of Hell; therefore, by implication, good deeds and the sacraments had no real meaning. After five years of travel and preaching, Madame Guyon settled in Paris, where the doctrine of pure love attracted Fénelon, Archbishop of Cambrai and, initially, Madame de Maintenon, but Guyon's eccentricity in declaring herself the 'bride of Christ' and the renewer of the Church was disturbing and she was imprisoned for a time in 1687.

Bossuet's hostility

Seeing that the movement was becoming popular both at court and with the royal family, Madame de Maintenon decided that a special inquiry was necessary. Several prelates, including Bossuet and Fénelon, were given the responsibility of examining the problem and to this end, held a conference at Issy in 1694. However, they were unable to reach an agreement. In 1697, while Fénelon in *Explication des maximes des saints* (An Explanation of the Maxims of the Saints) defended pure love, Bossuet in *Instruction sur les états d'oraison* (Instructions on the States of Prayer) warned against any form of mysticism founded on personal experience alone. In 1699 Bossuet obtained Rome's condemnation of a movement he felt undermined the unity and authority of the Church. Certain linguistic excesses, and especially the quarrel between Bossuet and Fénelon, have caused the original ideas of a woman who was a real mystic to be underestimated.

In Protestant countries, Guyon's influence was still remarkable. In the 18th century, she was to inspire a renewal of personal piety which manifested itself in Spener's German Pietist movement, then in Wesley's English Methodism.

> '(**Madam Guyon's**) mysticism is the mysticism of annihilation. The person must go into the darkness of the senses and knowledge in order to meet God as he really is.'
> (J. Lacoudre)

165

Ramakrishna

1836 Kamarpukur — Daksinestivara 1886

The great 19th-century Hindu mystic

Ramarkrishna's personal experiences revealed to him the unity of all spiritual paths.

Son of a poor and pious Bengali Brahman, even in childhood, Gadadhara Chatterjee, more commonly called by his religious name Ramakrishna, was fascinated by mysticism and would lose himself in an ecstatic trance. At the age of 19 he assisted his brother who was a priest in a temple dedicated to Kali at Daksinestivara. When his brother died the following year, Ramakrishna took his place. His devotion to the goddess made him long passionately to see a vision of her. He was in such despair that he was on the brink of suicide when finally, Kali showed herself to him, and he dedicated the rest of his life to her. At the age of 23, his family forced him into marriage: in a trance, Ramakrishna picked out a little five-year-old girl, whom he married five years later, but with whom he lived in a state of perfect chastity.

Initiated by a Tantric ascetic who saw in him a divine reincarnation, Ramakrishna achieved perfect union with God; a second guru taught him the *Vedanta* which enabled him to reach a state of fusion with the Brahman, in which he remained for six months, and which he was able to re-enter at will during the more or less continuous ecstasy he experienced afterwards. At a later date, when he was studying with a Muslim and then a Christian, Ramakrishna had the same experience. Soon he had followers of his own, attracted to him because of his radiant joy, his gentleness and his humility. By his very presence, he facilitated entry to their inner divine dimension. The disciples stayed together after his death, worshipping his widow who lived until 1920.

The theory

Ramakrishna's teachings were entirely oral, but were scrupulously noted down by his followers. Although perfectly spontaneous, his theories are connected to those of all the great Indian mystics, but different in that he does not identify himself with the Divinity; he sees himself as a worshipper and servant living in close union with the One. Moreover, from personal experience he knew that all religious paths, if they are followed with ardour and perseverance, lead to the same ultimate goal. Thus he never tried to wean his followers from their original faiths, but encouraged each individual to follow his own path to its end.

Ramakrishna uncovered the divine presence in each human being: according to him the instability and suffering in the world were caused by humankind's refusal to live in God. Ramakrishna's influence was very important during the Hindu renaissance, but it was only through the efforts of his favourite disciple Vivekananda that his doctrine spread to the rest of the world in the years after his death.

The one God

'There is only one God but his names are countless, and countless are the aspects under which He can be considered. Name Him with any name and worship Him in the form you like best, you are sure to reach Him.'

Ramana Maharishi

1879 Tiruchuzli — Tiruvannamalai 1950

Modern India's great guru

For his disciples Ramana's radiant appearance, even his silences, were the culmination of what they sought from him.

Born in the outskirts of Madura, South India, Venkatraman Aiyer studied at the town's American high school. He later confided to his followers: 'I have read nothing. My knowledge is limited to what I learned before the age of 14 . . . All my studying was done in former existences and I have had enough of it.' At the age of 17 he was sitting peacefully in his room when suddenly he was overwhelmed by the terrifying experience of his own death. He then 'contemplated' the divine source of his being, the immortal 'I' as opposed to the temporary and changeable 'Me'. Ramana Maharishi did not realize that this spontaneous revelation conformed exactly to the teachings of Hindu mystical philosophy until many years later. Shortly after this experience in 1896, an inner voice compelled him to give up everything and to withdraw to a cave on the side of Mount Aranachala, a sacred mountain near Tiruvannamalai to the west of Pondichery. But

'In the midst of the cavern of the heart, the **pure Absolute** shines alone.'
'**Freedom** is understanding that you are not born.'

soon pilgrims were attracted to this ascetic who was almost permanently transfigured by a state of ecstasy, whom they called *Maharishi* (Great Wise Man). Two ashrams had to be built to house the pilgrims who flocked to the mountain, not only from all over India, but also from the many Western countries to which his reputation for saintliness had spread.

The theory

Ramana Maharishi did not write anything, but his followers noted down the discussions he had with them. The Maharishi is distinguished from other great contemporary Hindu leaders in that he belonged to no particular sect, nor did he have a spiritual adviser. However, he is representative of the pure *advaita vedanta* tradition (see **Hinduism**). Living in solitude, he never sought to teach. To those who came looking for him and to question him, he invariably asked in return: 'Who are you?' thereby encouraging them to discover their true nature, the 'I' identical to 'Self' and to *atman*, which is pure reality, and to the universal principal within every human being which constitutes that pure reality. For him, the role of the guru 'who is always present in the innermost depths of "Self"' consisted essentially in 'taking the disciple back to his original state and preventing any further distancing'. In leading them to recognize the actual reality of 'Self', the Maharishi freed his disciples from the anxieties and sufferings which the illusion of a separate personal ego creates for him, evil in the world came from this egotism which excludes others.

Ramanuja

1017 Shriperumbudur — Shirangam 1137

A philosophy of divine love

Ramanuja, the great theoretician of devotion towards a personal god, exerted an influence over the development of Hinduism that is still tangible today.

Born south-west of Madras in a Brahman family, Ramanuja followed the teaching of a *Vedanta* master (see **Upanishad**), but having quarrelled with him he decided to dedicate himself to the cult of Vishnu. His piety and knowledge led him to be appointed by a great Vishnuite leader at Shirangam as his successor. Ramanuja lived there for the rest of his life, only leaving the community to spread his teaching all over India. He died at Shirangam aged 120, leaving behind him a solidly constructed monastic order. The order split into two groups after his death, one in the north and one in the south. Both are still active today.

His works

Like those of his predecessor Sankara, his works are principally made up of commentaries on the *Brahmasutra* and the *Bhagavadgita*, but he also wrote several tracts on the *Vedanta*.

The theory

Ramanuja is representative of a longstanding tradition of devotion to *Vishnu*, considered to be the supreme god who watches over the fate of the world and, in the form of an *avatar*, comes to the rescue of his followers 'each time that order falters'. This Vishnuite tradition is very active in south India, and is represented by alvars or mythical poets, and acarya, religious leaders from whom Ramanuja is descended.

To the intellectual asceticism advocated by Sankara, Ramanuja opposed worship of the Supreme Being. Although he is the infinite All, God is nevertheless a person, imminent and transcendent to his creation at the same time; he is the Principle which unites the multiplicity which also comes from Him. He can therefore be the object of worship. Only divine grace can release the human soul from the endless transmigration to which its *karma* subjects it. Contrary to Sankara's doctrine, Ramanuja believed that nature and humankind are distinct from God, although they come from Him and must ultimately return to Him. The world then is truly real; what human beings do not know is the extent of their relationship with God, which can only be revealed by the Lord Himself. Ramanuja expounded his doctrine, known as Particularized Nondualism with such expertise and talent that he remains one of the greatest thinkers in the world, even today.

'He whom the **Self** chooses can attain it. The Self reveals his innermost depths to him.'

Reformation

Christianity divided

Despite the efforts made to contain it, the movement of revolt against the established Church soon spread to 16th-century northern Europe, bringing in its wake new modes of spiritual expression.

From the 16th century, the decadence of the Church was obvious, culminating in the exile of the papacy to Avignon, and the Great Schism of 1378; European Christians were gradually turning away from a clergy that was all too often corrupt and ignorant, in search of more simple and personal forms of religious expression. Seeds of the Reformation had already been sewn in the sermons of Wycliffe and his followers in England and the political–nationalist rising of the Hussites in Bohemia which had been mercilessly crushed. The Reformation proper burst into life at the start of the 16th century when the Renaissance Humanists attacked medieval scholasticism and the new printing presses were used to publish first Bibles then the works of the reformers themselves.

In 1517 outrage at the scandalous sale of indulgences pushed Luther into starting the long-awaited rebellion. While it was definitely not his original intention, Luther was forced to break away from Rome in 1520. Initially his sermons and writings aroused enthusiasm, but he was soon outflanked by extremists like Andreas Bodenstein von Karlstadt or by social uprisings like that led by Thomas Müntzer. He acted swiftly and categorically, and the Lutheran Church went from being a popular movement to being controlled by the princes,

finally becoming the state church. From 1525 until his death, Luther organized the new Christian community, helped by his disciple Melanchthon (Philip Schwarzerd, 1497–1560), author of the *Augsburg Confession* who, in the spirit of reconciliation, attempted to temper Luther's impetuosity. By the time of his death in 1543, the Reformation had reached Denmark, Norway, and Sweden. In Germany the movement was threatened by Charles V, but with the help of France, the Protestant princes were able to keep the emperor at bay and in 1555 the Treaty of Augsburg sanctioned the religious division of Germany, giving each prince the right to impose the religion of his choice on his subjects.

Dissemination of the Reformation

In 1522 the Reformation was introduced in Switzerland by Huldreich Zwingli. More rationalist than mystical, he secularized the religion, closing down religious establishments and forbidding the celebration of mass. Relying on civil power, Zwingli went on to play a role in politics when the reformed cantons of Basel (as a result of the efforts of the Humanist colampadius, 1482–1531) then Bern, Saint Gallen, Glarus, and Schaffhausen, rose in opposition against those cantons which had remained Catholic. The Reformationist army was crushed at Cappel in 1531, but in Zürich, the level-headed and lucid Heinrich Bullinger (1504–71), managed to continue the Reformation, moving closer in spirit to Calvin's Geneva. He compiled his *Later Helvetian*

> **R. H. Leenhardt**
> The Reformation 'was not a simple protest against ecclesiastical abuses, it was initially a theological movement led by doctors in order to re-evaluate Christian doctrine and life.'

Reformation
Luther among his disciples, by Lucas Cranach the Younger 1515–86 (Lutherhalle, Wittenberg)

Confession which was accepted in such diverse countries as Scotland, Hungary, and Poland. In Strasbourg, Lutheran ideas had been accepted since 1521, causing much religious agitation. Martin Bucer (1491–1551) who undertook to maintain a united front regardless of internal differences, played an important part in the organization of the Church at Strasbourg, but Charles V called for his banishment and Bucer finished his life as a professor at Cambridge.

From 1520 onwards, Luther's works appeared in France, which during the first few years of the century, had already witnessed a return to the values of the Gospels and personal piety with the Humanists. The authorities gradually responded to the heresy's rapid growth but the measures taken, especially by royalty, were insufficient to completely wipe out the Reformation established in Geneva by the Frenchmen, Guillaume Farel (1489–1565)

and John Calvin. From Geneva, Calvinism spread into France towards the United Provinces, where it took the form of strict theocentrism, and to Bohemia, Hungary, and Poland, while in Scotland, John Knox (1514?–72) instituted the Presbyterian Church. The Scottish Church was to become popular throughout the kingdom despite opposition from the official Anglican Church.

The Anglican Church

This Church was not founded by any new religious leader but had its basis in a decision by the ruling monarch to make the Church subject to the State. The Reformation in England was initially a schism caused by the excommunication of Henry VIII in 1534, following his divorce. The *Act of Supremacy* deprived the pope of all power in the English Church, and made the king its 'unique and supreme head.' The monasteries were then secularized. But Henry VIII did not want to break definitively with the Catholic Church, and in 1539 the *Six Articles* defended the principles which the Reformation most violently attacked. During the reign of Edward VI, Henry VIII's son, the *Six Articles* were abolished; instead the *Book of Common Prayer* which reformed the ritual, and the *Forty-Two Articles* which described a faith very similar to Calvinism, were imposed. But after the Catholic reign of Mary Tudor, it was Elizabeth I who really established the Anglican Church, which is of Calvinist inspiration, despite many outward signs of Catholicism. The Reformation cut Europe in two; while it was overwhelmingly successful in the northern Germanic countries, it did not make such progress in the south, because of the Church's violent persecution of heretical minorities, and because it had enough foresight to institute its own series of reforms which culminated in the council of Trente (1545–63), giving birth to the Catholic Counter-Reformation. Most importantly, the Reformation adapted a religious life by secularizing it and ridding it of all intermediaries between humankind and God, in principle making each individual his own religious leader.

Luther

'Life is beautiful and glorious! Who can understand its beauty and abundance? It possesses everything and never suffers from indigence; it is stronger than sin, death and hell; but at the same time is entirely devoted to the service of others, full of goodness and solicitude.'

Calvin

'Prayer is a sacrifice of adoration as well as a direct communion with God through which we penetrate the sanctuary of heaven, and, admitted to God's presence, we question him about His promises.'

Revelation

Revelation of divine secrets

*Revelation, the last and most
enigmatic book of the New
Testament, has given rise to
innumerable commentaries and
interpretations. It proclaims
the imminent end of the world
and was the inspiration for
millenarian movements.*

Today the word apocalypse may be defined as total planetary devastation. This is the secular version of the end of the world, but the Greek *apocalypsis* means simply an uncovering or unveiling, and in the figurative sense 'a revelation of that which was hidden' which in this context refers to the divine secrets revealed by God. That is the original meaning of the last Book in the New Testament. It contrasts strikingly with the preceding Books both in structure (the tragic end envisaged includes dramatic scenes, heavy with symbolism which nevertheless remains mysterious) and in content, which necessarily differs from that of the Epistles. For Revelation does not refer to history but to eschatology, or the doctrine of last or final things. Tradition has it that Revelation was written by the

---

Prologue to Revelation

'It was given to him so that he might show his servants what must shortly happen. He made it known by sending his angel to his servant, John, who, in telling all that he saw, has borne witness to the word of God and to the testimony of Jesus Christ.'

Apostle John on the island of Patmos, which lies off the coast of Asia Minor; moreover this work is addressed to the Seven Churches of Asia, including Ephesus, where John died.

The prophecy

Invited by a voice calling 'Come up here and I will show you what will happen in the future', the visionary ascends to Heaven where he sees the sacrificed Lamb, symbol of Christ. The Lamb receives a closed scroll from God and breaks its seven seals one by one. The breaking of each seal releases a living plague which is to strike down the impious. The opening of the seventh seal marks the start of the world's punishment. Seven angels sound seven trumpets, then seven signs appear, including the 'woman robed in the sun, beneath her feet the moon, and on her head a crown of 12 stars'. As she gives birth to a male child who will govern all nations, she is attacked by the red dragon which, at the same time, is besieged by Michael and his angels. Although beaten, the dragon does not stop its malevolent work, and 'the rest of her seeds' are exposed to his fury. He is helped by the Beast of the Sea and the Beast of the Earth. But the Son of Man is already preparing the harvest and vintage of the world, when seven angels appear and receive seven bowls 'brimming with the wrath of God', the last seven plagues; the seventh of these is the ruin of Babylon, which is also known as the Great Harlot, and the final destruction of the world. And then, at the head of the celestial army, comes the Word of God. The Beast of the Earth and his ally, the False Prophet, are cast down into the lake of fire and the dragon, 'who is the Devil and Satan', is bound and cast into the abyss for a thousand years. During this thousand year period the good, who alone are resurrected and who need never fear a 'second death',

A woman, dressed in the sun with her feet upon the moon and crowned in stars, gives birth to a
male child while she is attacked by a red dragon with ten horns and seven heads wearing
diadems, and which itself is attacked by angels.
Commentary on the Apocalypse, *Beatus de Liebana*
Miniature from the end of the 13th century (National Library, Paris)

rule in glory with Christ. But at the end of the thousand years 'Satan will be released from his prison. He will come back to seduce all the nations on earth'. Finally, God will send down the fire which will destroy all his enemies and Satan, their seducer will also be thrown into the flames. From this time on, God's victory will be absolute. A new heaven and earth will replace the old and a celestial Jerusalem will be established on earth. God will live amongst the people bringing eternal joy to his servants.

The millennium

As soon as it was published, this work met with extreme resistance from the Church leaders. It was included with the other books in the New Testament primarily for two reasons: firstly, because it was considered to be the work of John, who was believed to have completed it towards the end of Domitian's reign; and secondly, in promising the millennium as their reward, it encouraged Christians in their faith. But the centuries passed and the end of the world did not come. From as early as the third century AD, Origen put forward the view that waiting for the millennium was pointless as it had already come about in the hearts of the Church and the faithful confessors. In the following century, Augustine, in his *City of God*, turned belief in the millennium into a spiritual allegory. From this time on, only the doctrines of *parousia*, or the glorious Second Coming

of Christ, and the Last Judgment were retained. Nevertheless, the belief that Christians were to prepare themselves for a first coming followed by a golden age has resurfaced throughout history. In the 12th and 13th centuries there were several insurrections whose participants saw Rome as the reincarnation of Babylon, while Jerusalem, though still in Infidel hands, was to be the capital of God's kingdom. Perhaps the most famous insurrections was that of the Shepherds of Hungary which took place in 1251. But most importantly, the millennium had attracted a new theoretician, a Cistercian abbot from Calabria named Joachim of Fiore (c. 1132–1202), who specified that the millennium would begin in 1260. The Age of the Spirit would then succeed the Age of the Father (the Old Testament) and the Age of the Son (the New Testament). Then the Italian Flagellant movement appeared whose members offered their self-mortification and suffering as a sacrifice aimed to bring about the coming of the Spirit. Although the fateful date passed without event, this 'redemptive' fervour caught on in Central Europe, where it became a subversive social movement based on the terrestrial creation of a celestial Jerusalem. The embers of this movement were to spark into flame again around the time of the Reformation, with the Anabaptists of Münster. Several pacifist millenarian revivals have since been recorded, particularly in the United States, with The Church of Jesus Christ of the Latter-Day Saints (see **Mormons**), and more recently with Adventism and the Jehovah's Witnesses.

Although its intrinsic, original meaning has been adapted to our dechristianized world, the word apocalypse still has the power to disturb, particularly today as we stand on the threshold of the year 2000.

The angel's warning to the author
'Do not keep hidden the words of the prophecy: for the time is near.'

Rosicrucians

Symbol of a mysterious brotherhood

Made up of initiates who were sworn to secrecy, the Rosicrucian order is believed to date back at least to the Renaissance, and to have continued its activities throughout the centuries to the present day.

In 1614 two anonymous manifestos attributed to the same author appeared in Kassel: *The Universal and General Reformation of the World* and *Fama Fraternitatis or Brotherhood of the Famous Order of Rosicrucians*. While the first was a satire directed at Lutheranism, the *Fama Fraternitatis* contained the life of Christian Rosenkreuz ('Rosy Cross') who was supposed to have spent some time in Damascus before founding a 'Holy Spirit' monastery in Germany. It is said that in 1604, 100 years after his death, his body was found intact, surrounded by symbols and initiatory devices. This apparently mythical figure is said to have been the founder of the mysterious Rosicrucian Order. He was also at the centre of a controversy particulary at the start of the 17th century, when he inspired several different works; the most remarkable of these is *The Chemical Marriage of Christian Rosenkreuz, 1454* (1616) written by Johann Valentin Andreae (1586–1654) a Lutheran author who, with his friends in the Tübingen literacy circle, was perhaps responsible for a scheme intended to make Christians take stock of themselves.

While the existence of a Rosicrucian order is impossible to prove, it does seem likely that a whole European esoteric current took refuge under this name. The movement includes utopists like the Englishmen Thomas More (1480–1535) and Francis Bacon (1561–1636), and the Italian Tommaso Campanella (1585–1639) who were directly inspired by Joachim of Fiore (who was perhaps the Rosenkreuz prototype), and alchemists, naturalists, and mystics like Paracelsus (1493–1541) and his followers including Heinrich Khunrath (1560–1605), whose Amphitheatre of *Eternal Wisdom* contains the image of a rose bearing a human form with its arms outstretched in the shape of a cross.

The Rosicrucians in modern times

At the end of the 18th century, several societies more or less linked to Freemasonry which also uses the 'Rosy Cross' symbol in some of its higher ranks, purported to stem from the Rosicrucian order but their affiliation with the ancient Rosicrucians cannot be proven. This also applies to the various late 19th-century movements which claimed Rosicrucian origins and spread an esoteric teaching which often owed much to occultism. The most important contemporary example is the A.M.O.R.C. (Ancient and Mystical Order Rosae Crucis), founded in 1909 and based in San José, California, which claims a worldwide membership of 6 million people of which 100 000 are French.

Robert Fludd

'The soul which animates the body tends to rise like a flame to the heavens. This is its instinct and its happiness. Yet, why is it that we feel such fatigue when we climb up a mountain? This is because the essence of the material body is to strain towards the earth's centre, quite against the natural tendency of the soul, and with its sheer mass, it wins easily over the spark which animates us. The soul must gather all its strength in order to rise with that spark and force the heavy mass of the body which holds it back to obey its impulse.'

Ruysbroek, Jan Van

1293 Ruysbroek — Groenendaal 1381

A great Flemish mystic

Ruysbroek was a considerable influence in his own lifetime and his teaching is still relevant today.

Born in a forest village in what is now a suburb of Brussels, Jan was brought up by his uncle, a canon in the city who obtained a prebend for him when he was ordained a priest in 1317. For 25 years, Ruysbroek carried on his ministry, fighting against the heretical 'Brothers of the Free Spirit' and writing his first books. In 1343 he withdrew to the hermitage at Groenendaal in the Soignes forest in order to dedicate himself to meditation amongst the trees he loved so dearly. There he founded a little community of Augustinian canons. His reputation for saintliness and modesty attracted numerous pilgrims. Gerard Groote, who instigated the *Devotio Moderna* (see **Imitation of Christ**) was his disciple at one time, and Tauler is also believed to have visited the community. Famous throughout Western Europe, Ruysbroek, called the 'Admirable' was almost 90 years old when he died.

Die in God

'Man was made of nothing. This is why he chases this nothing which is nowhere and in the chase drifts so far from himself that he loses his way; plunged in the simple essence of Divinity like in his own inner depths, he comes to die in God.'

'In the simple nudity which covers everything, the contemplative comes to feel himself identical to the light by which he sees.'

His works

Written in the popular Brabançon dialect but later translated into Latin, his works consist of about ten mystical books. The best known of these are *The Kingdom of the Lovers of God* and especially *The Ornament of Spiritual Marriage* compiled between 1330 and 1335, which is a commentary on the lines in Matthew's Gospel 'Here is the bridegroom, Come out to meet him.' In preparation for this loving meeting, the author deals with the three forms of religious life: active or outer life, affective or inner life, culminating in contemplative or 'superessential' life.

The theory

While Ruysbroek's mysticism is connected to the great Rhenish tradition, his works are the result of patient personal experience. The end of religious life, rest in God, can only be achieved through a gradual disowning of the self, and comes after the three stages have been completed. These stages begin with the recovery of essential purity, a sleep-like state in which the soul loses itself in God, and end with the surpassing of all dualism at which point the soul plunges into divine darkness. At this stage it is impossible for the soul to distinguish between that which comes from God, and that which comes from itself. The soul must abandon itself to the action of God within itself. However, Ruysbroek, who had had the occasion to fight heresy, was more prudent than Eckhart and issued many warnings about the pitfalls of this process. In order to avoid the temptations of isolation and quietism which can cause pride, he recommended 'communal life' and temporal activities which benefited others.

Saint-Martin, Louis Claude de

1743 Amboise — Aulnay 1803

The 'Unknown Philosopher'

At a time when the values of the Ancien Régime were crumbling, Saint-Martin was a vigorous opponent of the prevailing rationalism and materialism.

Son of an aristocratic family, Louis Claude de Saint-Martin was a second lieutenant at Bordeaux when he met Martinez Pasqualis, son of Portuguese Jews who had converted to Christianity. Pasqualis was a Theosophist, and the founder of the Cohens 'Elect' who purported to be in direct communication with angelic spirits. Once admitted to this group, Saint-Martin dedicated himself to his religious vocation. After the publication of his first book *Des Erreurs et de la vérité* (On Errors and on Truth) he moved to Paris where he played the part of the 'Unknown Philosopher', lost in the world, but cherished by it. After extensive travel in France, England, and Italy during which time he spread his teaching, Saint-Martin settled in Strasbourg where he discovered the works of Jakob Böhme who was to influence his development. He came through the Revolution unscathed, seeing in it the

necessary punishment meted out by Providence on a monarchy and faith that had fallen from glory, from which the true 'divine theology, natural and spiritual' was to be born.

His works

Three major books stand out amongst his works: *Des Erreurs et de la vérité, ou les Hommes 'rappelés' au principe universel de la science* (1775) (On Errors and on Truth, or Men called Back to the Universal Principal of Science); *L'Homme de désir* (1790) (The Man of Desire); and *Le Ministère de l'Homme-Esprit* (1802) (The Ministry of the Man-Spirit), a kind of religious testament.

The theory

Having witnessed the misery of the creature separated from God, Saint-Martin confirms that even after the Fall, man has not been able to completely forget either his basic dignity as a keystone of Creation or his responsibility for universal harmony. He must therefore regenerate himself, with the help of Christ who is both human and God; one person's regeneration will encourage others until eventually the whole world is regenerated. Indeed, for Saint-Martin, humankind plays a vital role in God's plan. He is capable of collaboration with the Creator on transfiguring his own nature.

The 'Unknown Philosopher's' teachings, representing the best of French Illuminism and Theosophism, had a discreet but profound influence on many 19th-century writers such as Chateaubriand, Joseph de Maistre, and Balzac in the religious masonic circles, as well as on the German Romantics including Franz von Baader. As a remarkable writer and one of the greatest 18th-century thinkers, Saint-Martin is still remembered in religious groups today.

A. Faivre

'The man who called himself the "unknown philosopher" today appears as one of France's major thinkers and one of the best 18th-century writers. He was also the greatest Theosophist of his age.'

'Explain things by man, and not man by things.'

Sankara

8th century

The great Indian *Vedanta* philosopher

A powerful, profound, and subtle thinker, Sankara gave Hinduism its philosophical and mystical basis enabling it to survive through the centuries.

Sankara was probably born in Kerala, south-west India, in a Brahman family. In his adolescence he chose to become a renunciant (sannyasin). He was initiated by the guru Govinda, who had been a disciple of Guadapada, and travelled around the country as an itinerant teacher, preaching the *Advaita* doctrine, the non-duality of all things, advocating personal asceticism instead of bloody sacrifice and polemizing with the Buddhists. Contrary to normal Hindu practice, Sankara founded a monastic order which is still active today. According to tradition, he died at Kedarnath in the Himalayas when he was still quite young.

His works

Many works have been attributed to Sankara. He definitely wrote commentaries on the *Upanishad*, the *Bhagavadgita*, and on the *Brahma Sutra*.

The theory

In the 8th century, Sankara was responsible for the restoration of a Hinduism whose hegemony had been threatened by two great heresies, Jainism and especially Buddhism, which at that time was in decline. Some of Sankara's ideas appear to owe so much to Buddhism that some believe he may at one stage have adhered to it, and he certainly used some Buddhist elements to renew Hindu doctrine. On the other hand, he attacked ritualists and hypocrites whom he accused of compromising the doctrine, for his real aim was to reaffirm the Revelation in its original purity, as manifested in the *Upanishad* and the *Brahma Sutra*, philosophical commentaries on the Upanishad written by Badarayana (3rd century BC).

As one of the main proponents of 'non-dual' Advaita Vedanta, Sankara only admits the existence of one principle, absolute reality or *brahman* of which all the other gods (including Siva although Sankara worshipped him) are but partial representations. Central to Sankara's doctrine was the belief that inner self or soul is part of *Brahman* and to see a difference between the two was to fall into ignorance (*avidya*) which perpetuates the cycle of births and deaths (*samsara*), while those who have freed themselves understand that the universe is a divine game (*lila*) and therefore magic (*maya*), which must be exceeded to reach its author. Today, Sankara is still considered to be one of India's greatest religious leaders.

God and Man
'One who adores a god, thinking that he is different from him does not know Brahman. For the gods, he is the same as an animal.'

Seneca

4 BC Cordoba — Rome AD 65

Nero's tutor and an accomplished statesman, philosopher, and tragedian

Seneca was the conscience of Roman society and his influence persists.

Lucius Annaeus Seneca came to Rome in his youth. He devoted himself to philosophy, particularly Stoicism while continuing to practise as an advocate. His gift in the field of rhetoric won him the position of questor, then entry to the Senate during the reign of Caligula. However, as soon as Claudius succeeded to the throne, Seneca was exiled to Corsica where he spent eight years. He was only recalled in AD 49 by Agrippina, Claudius's new wife, who entrusted the education of her son, Nero, to him. When Nero ascended the throne he was only 17 years old, and for seven years, Seneca was one of his closest advisers. Nero soon wished to rid himself of such a moral censor and Seneca, feeling his power slipping away, retired to devote himself entirely to philosophy. He lived peacefully until he was implicated in a conspiracy to depose Nero and received the imperial command to slash his wrists, which he did with perfect calm.

His works

In contrast to those of most other Roman authors, Seneca's works have survived almost intact. Not only do they illustrate philosophy at the time of the Roman Empire, but they also shed light on the teachings of the Stoics about which we previously knew very little. They include a satire, nine tragedies in which the author dramatizes a moral teaching intended to reach a very wide audience, and especially 12 moral essays, the most famous of which

are: *On Providence, On the Brevity of Life, On the Constancy of the Wise Man,* and *On Clemency.* The 124 *Letters to Lucilius* were written towards the end of his life and constitute a progressive programme of moral training. Moreover, the letters are the most precious testimony of the practice of religious direction left to us by Graeco-Roman society.

The theory

As a religious leader Seneca made a lasting impression not only on imperial Roman society but also throughout the Middle Ages up to the Renaissance and even the present day. While it stemmed from Stoicism, his philosophy reflects his experience of public life. The complex personality of the philosopher, the admission of his weaknesses, his constant search for truth and knowledge, and the uncannily modern character of some of his views, could not leave even today's reader indifferent. For Seneca, human life is of no value, except as the conquest of wisdom; everything else in life must be subordinate to this. Only the wise person has the strength to resist evil, to accept the blows of fate and suffering without losing his serenity, for, as he possesses absolute good within himself, he has become his own liberator.

> **Diderot**
> 'Tutor of the human race.'

> **Montesquieu**
> 'When some mishap befalls a European he has no other choice but to read a philosopher called Seneca.'

Seraphim of Sarov

1759 Koursk — Sarov 1833

The 'Transfigured'

Seraphim of Sarov, a humble hermit, remains one of the most popular figures in religion.

Prokhor Isidorovitch Moshnin, who later took the name Seraphim, was born in central Russia into a trading family. In his youth his father died and at the age of 15, Seraphim went to the famous monastery of Caves at Kiev, later entering the Sarov monastery in the Oka region as a novice. He was ordained a monk in 1786 and a priest in 1793. The following year he built himself a little hermitage in the forest where he spent ten years in the most austere conditions, feeding wild animals by hand. He was left crippled after a savage attack by robbers.

On his return to the monastery, Seraphim lived in absolute seclusion until the day — 25 November 1825 — an apparition of the Virgin ordered him to receive pilgrims.

The Kingdom of Heaven

'If the promise of future joy already fills our soul with such sweetness, such elation, what can we say about the joy which awaits all those who cry here on earth when they reach the heavenly Kingdom?'

Thus his life as a *starets* began. He pensed his knowledge and teaching to countless pilgrims who came looking him and founded several monasteries penitents of both sexes at Dievo. In the Virgin appeared to him one last and he was found dead kneeling on the of his cell with his head bowed and his crossed over his chest. The whole of R came to adore this holy monk who canonized in 1903 due to popular dem

His theory

Seraphim of Sarov's writings have been but we know of his profound ideas from *Dialogues with Motovilov*. In keeping with mystical tradition of the Eastern Ch Seraphim declared that any person begins to perceive spiritual reality reach the Holy Ghost and live in Him, the Apostles after the Pentecost. flamboyant grace is given to all the f ful', to all those who practise 'prayer o heart' and take part in the liturgy and eucharist. When the Christian fulfils conditions, he will rediscover real which is immortality. He will have p joy, and God's blessing; he will be ab feel God's presence, to converse with angels, and experience Christ's Tr figuration within himself, becoming Christ, glorious and brighter than the su a deification which, according to Moto Seraphim himself experienced.

Shi'ites

The esoteric branch of Islam

Shi'ism is based on the secret meaning of the Koran revealed by a series of religious leaders known as imams. Shi'ism allows ancient Eastern wisdom to be reintegrated into the heart of Orthodoxy.

The word *shi'a* describes those Muslims who recognize the 12 true imams descended from Ali, Muhammad's nephew and son-in-law who became the fourth caliph but was assassinated in 661. The imam is divinely invested which makes him 'infallible and impeccable'. He is the keeper of the Koran's 'hidden meaning' which Muhammad is believed to have communicated to Ali. He is, therefore, the only one capable of interpreting the holy text. Ali is considered to be the first imam, the second and third are his sons, Hassan and Husayn respectively. Husayn, the last of Muhammad's direct descendants, was killed in the Battle of Kerbela in 680, and is considered a martyr. The 12th imam, Muhammad, disappeared in 874 at the age of five, just after the death of his father, the 11th imam. However, he was in regular contact with a number of officials until 940. He lives in a secret place, but will return as the 'mahdi' at the end of time in order to re-establish justice: he will be the imam of the Resurrection.

The Imam

If, in the interim, the imam seems absent, however invisible he is to the senses, he is still in the 'heart of the faithful'. In Shi'ism the imam is the ultimate religious leader.

His teaching is initiatory, whereas the Prophet's was exoteric. In principle these two teachings are complementary, as they correspond to the outward meaning (*zahir*) and the hidden meaning (*batin*) of the Koran which Muhammad himself talked about in one of the Hadith. This conception resulted in a rich theological tradition to flourish, culminating in the 'Orientals' school (*ishraqiyun*) established by Suhrawardi in the 12th century and represented by Sadra Shirazi (1572–1640) in the 17th century. Shirazi founded the Shiraz school of philosophy in Persia. And finally, it was, above all, in Shi'ite circles that the mystical current known as *Sufism* developed.

Partisans of Ali and his bloodline, the Shi'ites have always been in opposition to Sunnism (see **Islam**), suffering centuries of persecution which sometimes almost forced the movement underground. Shi'ism itself split into rival sects, the largest being the Isma'ilis. It was only with the revival of Persian nationalism and the accession of the Safavid dynasty in 16th century Persia that Shi'ism openly resurfaced as the official religion. Today, apart from Iran, whose population is almost conclusively Shi'ite, the religion is professed by a substantial minority group in Iraq and by smaller numbers in Lebanon, Syria, India, and Pakistan.

The imam's Hadith
'We are the Names, the Attributes . . . the Face of God, the Hand of God . . .'

The Sunni imam
The Shi'ite imam must not be confused with the Sunni imam who leads the prayers in mosques, standing in front of the faithful and has no particular authority.
(Imam comes from the Arabic *amama* meaning 'in front')

Shingon

Japanese esoteric Buddhism

Kukai, the founder of Shingon, known as 'The Great Master of the Spreading of the Dharma' has been worshipped in Japan since the 9th century.

At the age of 15, Kukai (774–835) was already studying Confucianism and Taoism, but disappointed by their 'down-to-earth character and triviality' he was soon attracted to Buddhism and wrote *Sango Shiiki* (The Final Truth of the Three Teachings). In this work he declared that not only was Buddhism more profound than the other two doctrines, but it actually contained many of their essential elements. In 804, hoping to confirm his faith, Kukai went to China with Saicho, the founder of Tendai. There he met Huei-kuo (746–805), the seventh patriarch of the esoteric Chen-yen school ('true word') who recognized him as his spiritual son and transmitted the secret teachings to him. In 806 Kukai returned to Japan and became abbot of the powerful Todaiji monastery at Nara, but left to found the principal Chen-yen or Shingon (as it was known in Japanese) temple, on Mount Koya in 816. Kukai is considered to be the eighth Chen-yen or Shingon patriarch. The sect became extremely popular very quickly and the Koya monastery soon numbered 1500 buildings, housing a total of 90 000 monks. After creating a temple within the palace walls at Kyoto, Kukai died in 835. He was deep in a meditation that is believed to continue to the present day behind the doors of his sanctuary on Mount Koya. With his aura of mystery, and his famed magical powers, Kukai was posthumously awarded the title of Kobo Daishi, 'The Great Master of the Spreading of the *Dharma*'.

The theory

Formulated by Kukai in *Juju Shinron* (The Ten Stages of Development of the Human Consciousness), his theories and teaching are mainly based on a later *sutra*, the *Mahavairocana*, in which the Buddha revealing the Doctrine is Vairocana, the 'Great Illuminator', one of the five Mahayana Jinas. Vairocana declares the nature of Enlightenment and the heart: only the passions stop us from seizing the original purity which makes each one of us a Buddha. It is, therefore, enough to 'purify the heart and to become conscious'. The believer must bring about enlightenment not only in his heart, but also in his body, words and thoughts, which creates a need for specific practices: *mudra*, ritual gestures, *mandala*, mystical diagrams used in contemplation, and *mantra*, sacred formulae which the Shingon school uses throughout its sumptuous ceremonies. According to Kukai the other nine schools only 'brush away the dust from the doors of the heart' while, thanks to Shingon 'the treasure trove of our heart opens.'

The heart

'It is within one's own heart that one must seek Enlightenment and Omniscience. Why is this? Because the heart is naturally perfectly pure.'

Sikhs

An attempt at reconciling religion

Sikhism finally culminated in the creation of an intolerant military theocracy.

The word sikhs means 'disciples' and refers to the community founded at the start of the 16th century near Lahore in present-day Pakistan by the guru Nanak (1469–1539), in an attempt to overcome the conflict between Hindus and Muslims in India. Following on from Kabir, Nanak was inspired by Islam and instituted a monotheistic faith which could be transmitted to one and all. A husband and father, Nanak's mission had been revealed to him during an ecstatic trance. When God had given him his orders Nanak began to travel all over the country, preaching the love of God and directing his followers to give up the rites to which they had become accustomed. For his many disciples he wrote hymns and *Jap-ji*, a collection of verses which has become the Sikh credo. When he had developed the principles of his teaching, Nanak listed the practical methods by which union with the one Being, the creator and master of all things, could be realized.

A military caste

Nanak was succeeded in his role as mediator between God and humankind by nine other gurus. However, at the end of the 18th century the ninth refused to convert to Islam and was summarily beheaded. His son, Gobind Rai, swore to revenge his death. Any hope for uniting the religions was lost. Sikhism became an order of warriors founded on the cult of the sword,

and the Sikhs became a nation fiercely protective of its independence. Gobind Rai completed the *Granth* (the 'Book') which was made up of the writings of Kabir, Nanak, and the nine gurus. Gobind declared the succession of gurus at an end and invested the *Granth* as the immortal guru. From then on the *Granth* was chanted in the Golden Temple at Amritsar.

Fighting in the 18th century against the Muslim forces, and in the 19th and first half of the 20th century against British imperialism, Sikhism was almost absorbed into Hinduism. However, it has since recovered its autonomy and there are c. 6 million Sikhs today. Since the days of Gobind Rai, Sikhs have distinguished themselves from other Indian sects by wearing a sword and a metal bracelet, the symbol of simplicity. They also keep their hair and beards uncut. Absolute equality reigns among them and they all have the same surname *Singh* ('Lion').

Up until 1982 Sikhs and Hindus lived side by side in harmony. Intermarriage was not a rare occurrence, and Sikhs held important positions of responsibility in the Indian state, particularly in the army. But this situation encouraged a constant desire for an independent Sikh state, which culminated in an armed rising in 1984, and the assassination of Indira Gandhi by Sikhs in reprisal for the assault by Indian troops on the Golden Temple.

Guru Nanak

'Man is not born free. He is born to free himself.'

'Everyone repeats the name of God, but no one is capable of reaching the depths of his mystery.'

Simeon the New Theologian

949 Paphlagonia — Paloukiton 1022

One of the great Byzantine religious leaders

Recently rediscovered in the West, Simeon's works are still relevant today and could be used to further the cause of a religious revival.

Born into the provincial aristocracy in Asia Minor, at the age of 11 Simeon was sent to study at Constantinople in the hope of being admitted to the emperor's service like his uncle Basil. However, he was excluded from all governmental office and held a degenerate existence; yet his nostalgia for religious life compelled him to look around for a spiritual adviser. At the Stoudion orthodox monastery, he found Simeon the Pious, who nurtured his pupils' natural inclination towards personal experience.

Simeon then had his first mystical vision, but slipped back into his erring ways. Finally at the age of 27, he entered the Stoudion monastery as a novice, and was continually with his spiritual director, whose name he took. Because of this exclusive relationship, Simeon was told to leave the monastery. He moved to the Saint Mamas monastery, where he breathed new life into the monks' faith, and became abbot at the age of 31. Simeon was both loved and hated for his religious zeal and enthusiasm, resulting in his exile in 996; two years later

The burning bush
'I receive the fire as if I was straw and by some miracle I am suffused in ineffable dew like the burning bush in the olden days, was as fire without being burnt up.'

Immortality
'I know that I will not die, because I am inside life, and I have felt all of it flowing within me.'

he was back, but was anathematized by ecclesiastical authorities whom he exhorted to be humble and repent. He went to Paloukiton on the Asiatic shore the Bosphorus, taking up residence ruined chapel with some of his discip When the patriarch restored him to fav he refused to return to his former du Simeon, who was canonized 50 years a his death, left an account of his experie that the Eastern Church still consider exemplary.

His works

Beautifully written by the poet of 'di love', his works consist of *Catachises; Th gical and Ethical Treatises*, devoted to def ing mystical theology; *Hymns of divine* 'confessions of a visionary'; and fir *Practical and Theological Chapters*, in w Simeon, with great openness, describe most intimate experiences.

The theory

Simeon devoted himself wholehearted his functions as a spiritual adviser. render himself more accessible, he hu puts forward the example of his own s tual progress. Since he was familiar the outside world and had led a degene existence, he was able to describe dangers for others. He had perso experienced what he taught, the r towards the divine that each person ca within his heart, and because of enjoyed unimaginable blessings. His ticism is in no way disconnected from body, indeed the body takes part in it, takes part in the Incarnation of the W the body itself must be deified, and illu ated along with the rest of nature. As w his moving confessions, Simeon's c theories, which have sometimes been pared to Tantrism, lend his work overall flavour.

Smith and the Mormons

1805 Sharon, Vermont — Carthage, Illinois, 1844

A prophet in the United States in the 19th century

The 'Church of Jesus Christ of Latter-Day Saints' was founded by Joseph Smith and was later led to Salt Lake City by Brigham Young. The members of the Church prepare for the imminent coming of the Kingdom of God.

In the United States in 1820 a young boy of 14, named Joseph Smith declared that an angel had told him that a sacred book, written on golden plates was hidden in the State of New York. Smith stated that the book had been dictated to the prophet Mormon by an angel and brought to the United States by one of the tribes of Israel. The *Book of Mormon* was discovered seven years later and published in 1830. Joseph Smith went on to organize the 'Church of Jesus Christ of Latter-Day Saints'; at its head was a prophet who was assisted by a 'quorum of 12 apostles'. In 1831 the sect moved to Ohio, then on to Missouri and finally to Illinois when, in 1838, the Mormons built their refuge and city named Nanvoo. When, following a further revelation, Joseph Smith declared that polygamy was to be permitted, the Mormons had to face the outraged religious sensibilities of their non-Mormon neighbours. Smith and his brother Hyrum, along with several supporters, were arrested in 1844 and lynched by an anti-Mormon mob.

Smith's successor, Brigham Young (1801–77) who had 17 wives and 47 children, decided to transfer the Church to a place of shelter from the persecution. The exodus began on 4 February 1846. This difficult and tiring journey ended on 24 July 1847 when, having reached the Great Salt Lake, Young declared that this was the Promised Land. Salt Lake City, the 'New Zion' was founded on that site. There were violent conflicts between the Mormons and the federal government, until the Mormons abandoned the practice of polygamy in 1890. Utah, the state created by Mormons, was admitted to the Union in 1896.

The theory

Mormon theology is contained in the *Book of Mormon*, which is revered as much as the Bible and is believed to be complementary to it, as well as in several other works which contain Smith's revelations. The Mormons believe in the continuity of the Revelation which enabled Smith to restore the original Church, that of Christ and Apostles, in the hope of Resurrection. The Church is headed by a prophet who holds the 'keys to the Kingdom'. In it all men aged 12 and over enter one of the two priesthoods, the one dealing with religious matters ('Melchisedech'), and the other with temporal matters ('Aron'). An extremely close community, the Mormons are a prosperous society with 3 million members worldwide, 30 000 of which are American. While it is essentially an American sect, it does have missions in Europe, Asia, and Africa.

The Book of Mormon
'Man is what God was. What God is, man can become.'

Socrates

c. 469 BC Athens — Athens 395 BC

The 'midwife' of the soul

Socrates helped everyone to discover the truth within himself. Thus, he became the model for Western philosophers and religious leaders.

As Socrates wrote nothing himself, all we know about him comes from the eye-witness accounts published after his death by his followers Xenophon, who wrote an *Apology* and *Memorabilia*, and of course Plato, whose works must necessarily reflect the philosophy of his master to some extent. Even the caricature of him published before his death in Aristophanes's *The Clouds* (423 BC) sheds some light on the defiance that was to be his undoing.

He was the son of a craftsman sculptor and a midwife, and only left Athens in order to do his military service. Showing endurance and courage, he saved the life of Alcibiades, whom he loved, during the

---

Plato on Socrates

'His words even at second-hand and however imperfectly repeated, amaze and possess the souls of every man, woman and child who comes within hearing of them.'

The way of freedom

'And it isn't possible for them to become established among the gods; of necessity they haunt our mortal nature and this region here. That's why one ought to try to escape from here to there as quickly as one can. Now the way to escape is to become as nearly as possible like a god; and to become like a god is to become just and religious, with intelligence.'
(Plato, *Theaetetus*)

Battle of Potidaeus (432). For many years he lived in poverty and obscurity, totally absorbed in his research, and learning from physicians, geometrists, and Sophists.

The street philosopher

He already had a number of disciples when one of them consulted the Oracle of Delphi and was given the reply that his master was the wisest and most knowledgeable of all. Astounded by this judgment, Socrates saw in it a call from the gods. From then on he haunted the streets and squares questioning one and all, conversing with them and exercising a sort of authoritative power over them, which he called 'maieutics', the art of helping minds to be born, which he said came from his mother's profession. Thus he obeyed his *daimon*, his inner guide, with which he had to comply. Many young people were absolutely seduced by his philosophy and became his disciples; Plato became a disciple at the age of 20. Others were outraged: wasn't Socrates the city's bad conscience and indirectly responsible for the hardships it had just suffered, like the defeat which ended the Peloponnesian War, followed by the regime of the Thirty Tyrants? The fact that Alcibiades, a sacrilegious traitor to his country, and Critias the sceptic who, with the help of Sparta, had established the Thirty Tyrants regime, were both disciples of Socrates, had not been forgotten.

When democracy was re-established, all it took was three little-known citizens to accuse Socrates of impious behaviour and corrupting the city's youth, for him to be condemned by the judges. To his friends, who begged him to defend himself, Socrates replied: 'Until now I have been the happiest of men. The gods are preparing a peaceful death for me, the only one I could have wished for'. He refused an easy escape in order to avoid 'showing myself to strangers, proscribed, humiliated, having become the corrupter of laws and the enemy of authority.' Once he had drunk the hemlock he talked peacefully with his friends until he died.

The theory

According to what we have been able to glean from the works of Plato, Socrates's theory and teachings appear to have been essentially negative, and the Socratic dialogue aims at ridding the questioner of the character he unconsciously assumes, and of his preconceived notions, for neither his language, nor even his thoughts belong to him. All his former certainty breaks down as if he were waking from sleep, as if he were finally waking to himself. The opinions of which he was so sure now seem like insubstantial dreams, and stimulated by contact with the 'electric ray fish', with which the philosopher compared himself, he becomes aware that after all not only does he think badly, he also lives badly. So, guided by the questioner, he begins to discover the truth, and by extension, the divine element hidden within himself. All Socrates fought against was ignorance, which he believed to be the sole cause of unhappiness and wickedness in humankind. And for him ignorance was born of blindness to the self. Socrates's false naivity, his declaration that he knew nothing and therefore had nothing to learn (in this he was different to his predecessors), is a tactic but not a ruse: the interlocutor does not profit from this process of question and answer, he only helps the other person to gain self-knowledge. However, within himself the interlocutor discovers what the just, useful, good, and beautiful are, that is to say the concepts on which we can and should build our lives, and which are ingrained in us without our knowledge.

Thus, Socrates refutes both the ancient metaphysicians, because it is obvious that if the gods have hidden certain things, it would be useless and impious to go against their will, and the Sophists who were extremely popular at that time. The Sophists were the ancestors of the Sceptics for whom the only art worthy of practice and attention was rhetoric because it at least lent an aura of truth to persuasive argument.

Socrates's influence

Apart from Plato, we know very little about Socrates's other disciples, except that they went on to give birth to distinct schools, each one representing a different aspect of their master's teaching. The successors of Euclid were the best dialecticians in antiquity who heralded the logic of the Stoics; and Anthistenes, who only retained the moral asceticism in Socrates's message, opened the Cynic tradition which Diogenes amplified and which Plato called 'Socrates gone mad'. Subsequently there was a tendency to link all ulterior philosophical schools to Socrates which is in itself significant. Even more meaningful is the fact that through Plato, then Aristotle, and finally the Neoplatonists, the colourful and enigmatic figure of the sage as embodied in Socrates with his constant questions, is at the root of the history of Western philosophy. Never again would the most diverse philosophers be able to avoid that figure. In modern times Socratic interrogation can be compared to the didactic methods of Eastern masters, particularly Zen masters which confirms the traditional and global nature of maieutics.

> **Socrates before his death**
> 'The man who has renounced all pleasures of the body need have no fear about the fate of his soul.'

Soloviev and Sophiology

1853 Moscow — Uzkoe, near Moscow 1900

Messianic reformer of Russian spirituality

With his generous and ardent spirit, Soloviev continues to fascinate religious circles today.

Vladimir Soloviev was the son of one of Russia's first historians and the grandson of one of her popes. At the age of nine he had a vision of a woman 'bathed in azure tinged with gold' whom he later recognized as *Sophia*, divine Wisdom. Between the ages of 13 and 18, he went through a period of atheism, from which he emerged having acquired unshakeable faith. When he was 21, his thesis *The Crises of Western Philosophy – Against the Positivists* earned him immediate repute as a philosopher of genius whose classes at Moscow University aroused such enthusiasm that the authorities began to get worried. He was sent on a mission to London and travelled through Europe and Egypt, where he had another vision of *Sophia*. In 1881 he was definitively expelled from the university. Although he began as a fervent Slavophile, with the belief that only Russia could realize the plenitude of the 'God-man', Soloviev later promoted a worldwide Christian society, founded on the reconciliation of the Churches. He was later to give up these hopes when he began to perceive history as a tragedy whose outcome could only be eschatalogic. The

man on whom Dostoevsky based Aliosha in *The Brothers Karamazov* fascinated the Russian public by attempting to synthesize Western rationalism and Eastern contemplation on the one hand, and science, philosophy, and religion on the other.

His works

A prolific and impassioned writer, Soloviev's principal works are *The Crises of Western Philosophy – Against the Positivists* (1874), an indictment of Positivism; *Russia and the Universal Church* (1889); *The Meaning of Love* (1894); *Justification of the Good* (1897); *Three Conversations on War, Progress and the End of Universal History* (1899); and finally *A Tale of Antichrist*, an incredible prophecy published shortly before his death.

The theory

According to Soloviev the human race has reached a stage where religious differences must be settled and there must be world-wide union around *Sophia*, the 'transfiguration of matter' by the Spirit. Sophiology, which is knowledge of and through divine Wisdom, is the ultimate aim of biological evolution as well as human history (see **Bulgakov**). But, towards the end of his life, he feared that the rise of materialism would inevitably bring new forms of savagery in its wake. Bearing this in mind, the religious person is duty-bound to carry on a permanent struggle against it, motivated by ever-increasing love and devotion to art, the true 'theurgy' capable of 'illuminating and transfiguring the world'. Despite his final pessimism, even today Soloviev's works aboud with excitement for the future.

> **'Christianity** is not only a rule for everyday life, it is also the driving force behind all humanity.'

Spener and Pietism

1635 Rappoltsweiler — Berlin 1705

An awakening of Protestant religious sensibilities

Founded on the primacy of personal religious experience and encouraging charitable works, 18th-century Pietism gave new purpose to German Lutheranism.

The way had been paved for this spiritual revival by the struggle of English Puritans (like John Bunyan (1628–88) author of *The Pilgrim's Progress*) against the conformism of the official Church, as well as by the mystical tendencies which manifested themselves in the sermons of the Flemish visionary, Antoinette Bourignon (1616–80) and also, at the heart of Calvinism, by Jean de Labadie (1610–74), a French Jesuit, who became a pastor and moved to Holland.

But the true founder of Pietism was the Alsatian Philipp Jakob Spener, a Lutheran pastor at Frankfurt am Main. He formed small prayer and study groups, the *collegia pietatis*, for which he published his most famous work *Pia desideria* in 1675. Spener was an overnight success. He attacked the short-comings of the Lutheran Church, its compromises with authorities, and the growing religious indifference, highlighting the need for reform in theological study, preaching, and moral standards. This was to be achieved through the development of inner life, prayer, and charity. Appointed senior pastor at Dresden in 1686, he began to attack the lax morals and vices of the court, and was obliged to take refuge in

Berlin. It was there, under the protection of the Brandenburg elector, that he entered the most productive period of his life. By the time of his death, Spener had completed 123 theological works.

The Moravian brothers

Spener's mission was carried on by August Hermann Francke (1663–1727), a university professor at Halle. Due to him, Pietism took hold in the intellectual milieus and sent missionaries all over the world. A third German Pietist centre emerged in Württemburg. In Saxony in 1722 the Count of Zinzendorf (1700–60) gave asylum to the descendants of the Unity of Brethren, a group of Hussites who had taken refuge there in 1626. These 'Moravian Brothers' founded the village of Herrnhut ('Protection of the Lord') in which residents lived communally, devoting much of their time to prayer and song, in a spirit of union and charity. From Herrnhut, missionaries left for such far-flung destinations as Greenland and the Antilles. An offshoot of Pietism, the Moravian Society, which reached England in 1738, was to have a decisive effect on the mission of John Wesley. Widespread in 18th-century Germany, the new Pietist sensitivity prepared the way for the birth of the Romantic Movement.

Zinzendorf

'If I haven't consented willingly, I beg my Saviour to force me to suffer with Him.'

Starsi

Holy Russia's spiritual fathers

They reached the summit of their popularity in the 19th century, attracting hordes of followers; their memory is preserved in the works of Dostoevsky and Tolstoy.

The Russian word *starets* (plural *startsi* or *starsi*) is the equivalent of the Greek *geron* meaning 'elder', the name given to a monk who assumed the role of spiritual adviser. The novice, who was placed entirely in the hands of the *geron* or *starets*, believed him to represent God on earth. However, the *starets*'s role was to guide the novice on the path of prayer and enlightenment, giving him the benefit of his own personal experience. The *starsi* in Russia were very close to the people, living either in monasteries or, more commonly, in forest retreats; they used simple language which was often tempered with humour. Their teachings were not reserved solely for novices in search of vocation, but were also available to the many laypersons from all walks of life and every country in Europe who came looking for spiritual guidance.

Dostoevsky and Tolstoy at Optina Pustynye

Without question, the most revered *starets* was Seraphim of Sarov, but the actual *Starsi* headquarters were at Optina Pustynye, near the little town of Kozelsk in central Russia. It was there, in the 18th century, that the archimandrite Makarios, a disciple of Paissy Velichkovsky (see **Nikodimos**

Hagioritis), founded a monastery where the *Philokalia* or 'Jesus Prayer' was practised. The monastery soon became famous for the intensely religious character of its monks.

The best known of the monks were Macarius (died 1891), famed not only for his works on the Hesychasts but also for the remarkable conversions he was able to bring about, and above all, his disciple Ambrosius (died 1891). Ambrosius suffered from ill-health and had to spend most of his time lying down, which meant that he was unable to celebrate mass with the other monks. However, the strength of his religious conviction, his perceptiveness and gift as a healer brought him hundreds of visitors, including the writer Leontiev, who spent the last years of his life at Optina. Dostoevsky also came to ask for Ambrosius's guidance in religious matters, and was later to base Zossima in *The Brothers Karamazov* on him. He was also the model for Father Sergei in Tolstoy's short story of that name; the author had visited Ambrosius three times, looking for spiritual advice. Leon Tolstoy died shortly after his search for inner peace had convinced him to spend the last years of his life as a monk at Optina. The *Philokalia* was still practised until the eve of the Revolution, made popular through the efforts of Father John (1829–1908), curate of a parish in Kronstadt, who was famous for his miraculous curing of the sick and his prophetic gifts.

Nil Majkov, the 'Great Starets' (1733–1808)
'The monk's alms are to help his brother with words when he needs them, and to console him with spiritual reasoning in times of unhappiness.'

Steiner, Rudolf

1861 Kraljevic, Croatia — Dornach, Switzerland 1925

The founder of 'Anthroposophy'

Steiner undertook to lay down the foundations of a new Western spirituality which would develop the powers of the mind and better humankind and society.

Having studied in Croatia, then in Venice, Steiner was tutor to a retarded child whom he managed to cure. After his first book *The Fundamentals of a Theory of Cognition in Goethe* (1886) was published, he was called to Weimar to help in the preparation of Goethe's *Scientific Works* for publication. In 1894 Steiner published *The Philosophy of Freedom* which contained the elements of his future teaching. He became an extremely popular conference speaker and was appointed general secretary of the German Theosophical Society (see **Theosophists**). In this capacity, he aimed to bring about a synthesis between Christianity and Eastern mysticism. When this proved to be impossible, he withdrew from the society and in 1913 set up a new association called *Anthroposophy* which was based at Dornach near Basel where the *Goetheanum*, a vast hall for the presentation of his 'mystery dramas' was built according to his blue prints. Through his American and European conference tours, his relationships with painters, politicians, savants, and mystics, Steiner exerted a discreet but profound influence over his era, which continues today in the works of the Anthroposophical movement with its 57 centres worldwide. There are also several active Steiner research institutes and schools.

His works

The most revealing of his many works are *The Education of the Child in the Light of Anthroposophy* (1907) in which he outlines the basis for a new pedagogy; *Knowledge of Higher Worlds and Its attainment* (1904); and *Occult Science: An Outline* (1910), an impressive synthesis of anthroposophical views on the true nature of humankind and its evolution. Finally, Steiner had begun to compile his autobiography (*Mein Lebensgang*) but was unable to complete it before his death.

The theory

In the formulation of his theories, Steiner may have borrowed much from the ancient mystical tradition, but he reworked these traditions in the light of modern science. His originality lay in the practical uses to which he put them, which aimed at a blossoming of humankind and society in the most diverse areas: education and psychiatry, so-called biological agriculture and medical research, and theatre and dance (eurythmy, founded by Steiner). This diversity is perhaps why Steiner's thought is still such a rich source today.

> **'A path of knowledge** which tries to lead from the spiritual in man to the spiritual in the mind.'

Stoics

Self-knowledge as a rule

For six centuries the Stoics were an élite who later exercised a considerable influence on all Western moralists.

The Stoics owe their name to the *Stoia poikile*, the 'Painted Porch' in Athens where the first Stoic teachers gave their lessons. The Portico was founded shortly after Epicurus's 'Garden', and it too responded to specific needs which arose during a period of crisis.

Its founder, a Hellenized Phoenician born in Cyprus, called Zeno of Citium (332–262 BC), came to Athens to study under Crates the Cynic, then under Polemus, one of the leaders of the Academy (see **Plato**). Zeno devoted 20 years to study and meditation before bringing together his first followers. He was extremely successful and died a respected and honoured philosopher. The few extant fragments of his work outline the fundamental principles of his school. For 30 years after his death, the school was directed by Cleanthes of Assus, a former athlete who had been one of Zeno's followers for 19 years. We have 40 lines of a *Hymn to Zeus* written by Cleanthes, one of the few surviving early Stoic texts. After his death, the school came under the direction of Chyrsippus of Soli (c. 280–206 BC), who gave a detailed and systematic

exposé of Stoicism. Virtually all the works of the early Stoics have been lost; most of our knowledge of their doctrine is provided by Cicero and Plutarch.

The theory

For the Stoics, wisdom is primarily precise knowledge of the human race and the universe; their philosophy is also a mixture of logic and physics which leads on to ethics. Founded on the concept of *logos*, which is both language and reason, Stoic logic is extremely sophisticated and has recently been rediscovered by modern logicians. The physical element presupposes the intervention of a unique, divine cosmic principle, but the soul is only a detached and provisional parcel of 'logus' whose survival can only be relative and precarious. The supreme end of humankind consists in the accord with oneself and with universal order through virtue, which alone ensures happiness.

Roman Stoicism

In 155 BC Diogenes of Babylon, one of Chrysippus of Soli's successors arrived in Rome as part of a delegation from Athens, bringing with him the Stoic doctrine. In Rome, Diogenes enjoyed longlasting good fortune and popularity, for he corresponded exactly to ancient Roman ideals. Thanks to Panaetius of Rhodes (c. 185–110 BC), head of the Athens school who divided his time between that town and Rome,

---

Epictetus
'To blame others for our misfortunes is the act of an ignorant man; to blame oneself is the act of a man who is beginning to learn: to neither blame another nor oneself is the act of a perfectly educated man.' (*Manual*)

Marcus Aurelius Antoninus
'Death is the end of the representations which come to us from the senses, of the impulsions which dictate our movements like strings of troubled thoughts and of the servitude of the flesh.'

where he profoundly influenced the young Scipio, Stoicism reached and swiftly captivated the Roman aristocracy. The close symbiotic relationship between Greek intellect and Roman intellect that later resulted in classical culture can be traced to Panaetius.

Panaetius's successor, the great scholar Poseidonius of Apamea (135–50 BC), travelled all over the Mediterranean basin before settling in Rhodes, where Cicero came to hear him; in Rome, where he often stayed, he was a highly respected figure, whose admirers included Varro and Pompeii. With Poseidonius, Stoicism established a synthesis between contemporary beliefs and knowledge, it purported to decode the universe by recognizing the links between man and the cosmos. While it remained a distinct teaching based on doctrinal texts taught in the schools, Stoicism set itself up as a code for life, particularly in Rome where Stoic values became confused with ancient Roman virtue.

Late Stoicism

The most outstanding representation of 'Late Stoicism' are the Phrygian, Epictetus (c. 50–c. 140), a freed slave who settled at Nicopolis in Epirus and became director of an extremely popular school, and the Emperor Marcus Aurelius Antoninus (121–180), author of a kind of philosophical journal and guide to conduct, *Meditations*, which had not been intended for general publication. In it, he reflects his certainty but also his doubts, anxieties and the bitter disappointments that imperial power had brought him, power which he had dreamed

of making work for the common good of the people. Epictetus's teachings are recorded in the *Discourses* compiled by one of his disciples, the future historian Arrianus of Nicodemia, who also wrote a shorter *Manual* based on his mentor's theories which was admired by both Christians and pagans. In the 5th century, Saint Nil, a disciple of John Chrysostom, adapted it for the monks at Mount Sinai, and it also inspired Saint Benedict's rule. Epictetus's *Manual* became the breviary of the Moralists from Tertullian to Montaigne and Pascal to Kant, and also inspired writers from Corneille to Vigny.

According to 'Later Stoicism' we are only responsible for our virtues and our vices; consequently, all that is not virtue or vice is 'indifferent': this applies to sickness and death, poverty or riches, and obscurity or glory. External misfortune is only a subjective opinion which must be shrugged off; the evil man is truly unfortunate because he inflicts on himself the only damage of which man can be the victim, while the wise man adheres perfectly to cosmic order and, totally unaffected by that which does not depend on him, remains free and serene, even when beset by the most extreme difficulties. Moreover, the Stoicism of Epictetus and Marcus Aurelius Antoninus underlines the general brotherhood of man as children of God, which draws it nearer to nascent Christianity.

Simplicius

Epictetus's *Manual* 'is a weapon which must always be kept within reach, and which those who want to live well must always be ready to use.'

Sufis

Intoxicated with God

Sometimes persecuted, sometimes exalted, but always regarded with suspicion by Muslim Orthodoxy, these Islamic mystics still have a tangible influence today.

The Sufis are Islamic religious men who dressed in wool (*suf* in Arabic) to demonstrate their detachment from the world, and chose to take the path of mysticism in search of union with God. Their name could also be connected with purity (*safa* in Arabic) or even Greek wisdom (*sophia*). The movement (*tasawwuf* in Arabic) came into being during the 1st century of the hegira (7th century) as a reaction against the official cult promoted by the Umayyads, who ruled at Damascus and were more interested in conquests and material goods than religious life.

Sufism presented itself as a return to former purity, to the inner lives of believers, and was centred on a totally spiritual and even esoteric interpretation of the Koran. Sufi leaders soon emerged, the first being al-Basri (642–728), an eminent theologian renowned for his piety and asceticism, who had the courage to speak out against the accession of Yazid, a debauched drunkard, to the caliphate. Al-Basri believed him to be an unfit successor to his father, Mu'awiyyah, the founder of the dynasty. This religious opposition culminated in the overthrowing of the Umayyads by the Abassirs in 750. The latter founded a new capital at Baghdad which became a brilliant cultural centre where Christian and Muslim communicated freely, and the works of Greek philosophers, particularly the Neoplatonists, were translated, and were to mould nascent Islamic metaphysics.

Although they kept the Law of Islam and respected observances, the Sufis believed the public manifestations of the cult to be secondary to personal experience of the divine Presence of which the created world and people themselves are but the products. Experiencing God personally could be done through meditation, most often reduced to the *dhikr* technique, the incessant repetition of God's name during which the Soul 'remembers' its creator and joins with Him.

A theosophy

The ascetical movement gradually spread throughout the Muslim world and went on to become a real theosophy. Among the first representatives of Sufism as a theosophy was al-Muhasibi, the 'Conscience Examiner', an apostle of self-renunciation who lived at Baghdad (781–837). His contemporaries included the Egyptian Dhu al-Nun (died 861) and the Persian Abu Yazid (died 875), the first of the 'intoxicated' Sufis. In Baghdad there was also al-Junayd (died 910), for whom Sufism is *fana* ('death to one's self'), and the most revered leader of all, al-Hallaj, who died a martyr in 922.

Until that time the Sufis had been persecuted by Orthodox legalists, who reached the summit of their power with the scandal

---

Al-Basri
'Be with this world as if you had never been, and with the other as if you were never to leave it again.'

Al-Junayd
'Sufism is when God makes you die to yourself, in order to bring you back to life in Him.'

---

created by al-Hallaj's execution. The time had come to bring the noblest and most passionate branch of Islam back into public favour. The first Sufi theoreticians in the 11th and 12th centuries attempted to accomplish this task. These included al-Junayd and al-Quashairi, author of the famous *Letter to the Sufis* (Risala, 1046). While the *shari'a*, the religious law, was the widest path open to everyone, the *tariqa* was the narrowest, open to the select few who were to become perfect within themselves (Insankamil), to unite with God and return 'to the state in which they were before they were.'

During the 12th and 13th centuries the most eminent Muslim thinkers rallied to the Sufi flag, giving it a sound doctrinal basis.

Al-Ghazali (1058–1111) reconciled Sufism and Orthodoxy; Shihaboddin Yahya Suhrawardi (1155–91) integrated ancient Persian wisdom into Islamic mysticism; the great gnostic philosopher Ibn 'Arabi (1165–1240) confirmed the oneness of the Being; and his follower Abd al-Karim al-Jili (1366–1428), in his famous work *Al-Insan al-Kamil* (On Universal Man), explained the theory according to which 'man in his essence is the cosmic Thought incarnate who links the absolute Being to the World of Nature'.

Religious brotherhoods

It was also during the 12th and 13th centuries that the major Sufi religious brotherhoods (*tariqa*) were established, whose leaders, appointed by regular suc-

cession, guided the disciples' progress on the 'path' using careful methods. The most important *tariqa* were: the *Suhrawardiya*, from the name of its founder Shihab ad-Din al-Suhrawardi (1144–1234), to which the illustrious Persian poet Saadi of Shiraz (1208–94) belonged; the *Shadhiliya*, founded by al-Shadhili (1196–1258), a native of the Maghreb (the largest brotherhood in North Africa, including past member Ibn 'Arabi); the *Kubrawiya*, which is linked to Najm ad-Din Kubra (1145–1221) whose members included Djalal ad-Din Rumi's father Baha ad-Din Walad, and the poet Attar's mentor; the *Nagshabandiya*, which started with al-Hamadani (died 1140) and to which the Persian mystical poet Djami belonged. But perhaps the most famous and long-lasting *tariqa* is the *Mawlawiya*, or 'whirling dervishes', founded by Rumi (1207–73).

The poets

Poetry has played a fundamental role in Sufi life. The first leaders quoted erotic poetry or celebrated wine and drunkenness by giving them a spiritial meaning. Later the mystical Arabic, and especially Persian poets were to use these same allegories. Classical Persian poetry, be it didactic, lyric or even romantic, was mainly inspired by Sufism to which its most illustrious authors belonged: Sana'i (1080–1140); Attar (c. 1120–90); Nizami (1141–1209); Rumi himself; and Djami of Herat (1414–92), the last great mystical poet in Persian literature.

Najm ad-Din Kubra
'One who is absorbed in the Beloved and has renounced everything else is a Sufi.'

Al-Hujwiri
'Whoever loves anything other than God does not know himself; he who knows himself, knows the Lord with whom he joins.'

Suhrawardi

1155 north-west Persia — Aleppo, Syria 1191

'Master of Illuminationist Theosophy'

Suhrawardi reintegrated ancient Persian wisdom into Islam, and was considered to be a heretic.

Born in what used to be the country of the Medes, not far from Shiz which was home to the most important Mazdaen Sacred Fire sanctuary (see **Zoroaster**), Shihaboddin Yahya Suhrawardi was taught by a master of Islamic scholasticism which owed much to the Neoplatonists. In Isfahan he came into contact with Avicenna's successors. Then, for unknown reasons, he went to the Sunni territories of Anatolia and then Aleppo, where Shi'ites were in danger. At Aleppo he became friends with the town's governor, al-Malik al-Zahir, the son of Sultan Saladin of the Crusades. Suhrawardi came into conflict with the doctors of the Law, and was accused of having made blasphemous remarks. He was condemned to death and executed at the age of 36 on Saladin's orders, despite the pleas of the latter's son. Nicknamed 'Martyr Sheikh' and 'Master of Illuminationist Theosophy', Suhrawardi exerted a strong influence over Persian religion which is still felt today.

His works

Despite the brevity of his life, Suhrawardi left some 50 tracts by way of an introduction to his key work *Kitab Hikmat al-Ishraq* (The Book of Illuminationist Theosophy). The 'treatises in parables' as initiatory mystical narratives stand out among these tracts.

The theory

His teaching is taken from the point at which Islam, pre-Islamic Persian thought and the Platonic doctrine of ideas meet. Suhrawardi himself admitted that one of his objectives was to 'resurrect ancient Persian Sages', whose theories he intended to reintegrate into Muslim doctrine. These sages include Hermes and Zoroaster, but also the 'Imam of Wisdom, our master Plato'.

Suhrawardi's teaching revolves around the concept of the East (divine light, the world of souls) opposed to the West (darkness, the physical world of bodies) which gives birth to a cosmic system founded on a hierarchy of worlds. The most important element in this system, which is also Suhrawardi's personal contribution to philosophy, is the interworld, a place of images and archetypes, of 'subtle bodies' and of resurrection. Buried in darkness, in a burst of love, which reflects its distress, the soul attempts to go back up to the original Light. It tries to rediscover and merge with its archetype, the angel, with whose help the soul can transcend its present condition. The soul's journey, as described in Suhrawardi's narratives, was put into practice by Shi'ite spiritual groups who consider the founder of Eastern mysticism as one of their greatest leaders.

The East of the souls

'In the order of the return to the origin, the manifestation of the soul, outside the physical body, through meditation, ecstatic visions or death . . . consists in what the world of souls, which is its East, reveals to it.'

Suso

c. 1296 Constance — Ulm 1366

Champion of mystical Love

*Disciple of Meister Eckhart,
Suso favoured an internalized
and sensitive spirituality which
became the model for all ulterior
forms of devotion.*

Heinrich Seuse, better known by the Latinized version of his name, Suso, was born on the shores of Lake Constance, probably at Überlingen. His father was a draper, and a strict parent, and his mother, whose name he preferred to take, was 'fulfilled with God'. At the age of 13 he entered the Dominican monastery at Lake Constance. He devoted himself to 'divine wisdom' at an early age and attempted to subjugate his passions and pieties by a severe mode of life. In 1320 he was sent to Cologne where he became familiar with Eckhart's teachings, remaining faithful to them for the rest of his life. His first work *The Little Book of Truth*, believed to have been published in 1329, was devoted to the defence of Eckhart's ideas, but as the latter had been condemned, Suso was branded a heretic. Having renounced his excessive mortifications of the flesh, he pursued a more internal mystical path, travelling around to preach to groups of pious laypersons, who called themselves 'Friends of God', as well as to Dominican convents. Some nuns

---

One in Christ

'Man must become at one in Christ, but remain distinct, united and not united, but at one with him.'

---

professed such passionate admiration for him that on occasions he was falsely accused of misconduct. To put an end to these rumours, Suso was sent to Ulm, where he later died.

His works

Suso's writings in German are gathered into *The Example*, which includes an embellished *Biography* by one of his religious daughters, *The Little Book of Eternal Wisdom*, *The Little Book of Truth*, letters, and a number of sermons. In Latin he wrote *The Clock of Wisdom*.

The theory

One of Eckhart's disciples, but also indebted to Bernard of Clairvaux and Francis of Assisi, Suso stresses the intimate relationship between Christ and the human soul, thus paving the way for the *Devotio Moderna* (see **Imitation of Christ**). He expresses his ideas in a more personal way than his mentor, and frequently draws on his own experiences. He felt obliged to dispel the myth of the 'nameless savage' who believes himself to be free because he can 'fulfil all his desires without distinguishing between them', which had been popularized by the pantheistic heresy of the Beghards or Brothers of the Free Spirit, who purported to have found inspiration for their beliefs in some of Eckhart's more paradoxical writings. According to Suso, 'a man who has abandoned himself to God must be detached from created objects, must be formed with Christ and transformed in divinity', but, in order to find the eternal source, he must go through hardships similar to those experienced by Christ. Suso, who was one of the most popular writers of the Middle Ages, is becoming popular again today.

Swedenborg, Emmanuel

1688 Stockholm — London 1772

Explorer of the invisible

Swedenborg was a respected academic who methodically described the spiritual world, and left a strange collection of works which captivated the most eminent thikers.

A doctor of philosophy by the age of 21, Swedenborg travelled around Europe seeking out the most important scientists of his day. When he returned to Sweden in 1714, his incredible breadth of knowledge and daring scientific theories brought him fame and glory. But in 1743 he wrote 'the Lord revealed himself to me . . . and lent me . . . the power to communicate with spirits and angels'. From then on, Swedenborg gave up the secular sciences and devoted himself to describing this spiritual world which gradually unravelled itself before him, using the precision gleaned from his former training. The seeds of this change in direction had been sown as early as 1736, when he decided to write down his dreams as signs of another reality. It also appears likely that he spontaneously engaged in meditation.

Enlightenment

'Human understanding cannot grasp the religious let alone the divine unless God lights the way . . . This illumination is the sincere opening of the inner heart.'

---

exercises accompanied by breathing techniques similar to those used in *yoga*, with which he could not have been familiar. Swedenborg never lost his calm assurance, even when confronted with the unique phenomena which manifested themselves to him.

His works

Compiled in Latin, apart from scientific tracts, his works include *The Heavenly Arcana* (8 vols; 1747–58), *On The New Jerusalem and on its Celestial Doctrine* (1758), and *The True Christian Religion Containing the Universal Theology of the New Church* (1771). His mystical works were very influential; Kant was later to dedicate one of his books to them.

The theory

The visions he had during a 27-year period, led Swedenborg to construct a 'natural history of the suprasensory world', the two worlds, natural and spiritual, closely linked. His vision also informed him of the true meaning of the holy Scriptures which are essentially spiritual in nature. According to him, all pure people could reach the ecstatic state he himself had experienced providing that they were receptive to divine grace, but they must also exercise extreme caution because, 'when man delves into the secrets of spiritual things, man no longer knows how to defend himself against the tricks of hell'. Swedenborg's works made a strong impression on subsequent generations. Kant, Goethe, Balzac, Carlyle, and Emerson all recognized him as their master.

Tantrism

Late form of Hinduism and Buddhism

Tantrism claims to harness the cosmic energy contained within the human body with a view to liberation.

The word comes from the Sanskrit *tantra* meaning 'warp' or 'woof' and, by extension, a 'work' or 'book'. The tantras are vast encyclopaedic poems which, from an analysis of the component parts of humanity and the universe, provide the adept with moral and ritual prescriptions that are supposed to help them transcend their present condition. Most of the extant tracts do not date from before the 10th century, but it is believed that the first written tantras emerged at the start of the Christian era. The tantras were compiled over the centuries and are still being written today.

Tantrism has played an increasingly important role in later Hinduism because it seems better equipped to meet the evolving needs of humankind than previous religious practices, and because it advocates the full deployment of all human potential. Some great modern religious leaders have reasserted the value of its contribution, like Ramakrishna, or Sri Aurobindo who wrote 'Tantric synthesis . . . although it may be less subtle and spiritually less profound than that of the *Bhagavadgita*, is more powerful and more robust, because, by seizing the obstacles which oppose spiritual life, it forces them to become the means of a

richer spiritual conquest . . . This Tantric synthesis tries to take possession of the notion of humankind's divine perfectability held by the *rsis* (seers), but which, in the intervening years, has been pushed back into darkness, a notion destined to play such a large part in all future synthesis of human thought, experience, and aspiration'. This revival of Tantrism at the beginning of the 20th century was witnessed by an English magistrate turned initiate who was authorized by his masters to introduce important Tantric texts to the West under the pseudonym 'Arthur Avalon'.

The Bhakti

It is possible that Tantrism derived from *bhakti*, the practice of fervent individual prayer directed towards a personal God who could ensure his worshippers' salvation. The *bhakti* is primarily addressed to Siva and, above all, to Vishnu and his avatars Rama and Krishna; when the prayer is directed towards Krishna, it closely links Krihna, a rustic god, with Radha, his companion and one of the cowherds or *gopi*, with whom he indulges in erotic games that transgress the usual moral code. Although the 'orthodox' interpret these games as an image for the devotee's love for God, followers of Tantrism worship

---

Ramakrishna

'The Vedas and Puranas must be read and listened to, but one must act according to the precepts of the Tantras.'

The human body and the universe

'In the body of the seer Mount Meru rises, surrounded by the seven continents; there are the oceans and rivers, the hills and the plains, the fields and their guardians . . . There are the stars and the sun and the moon, there reside the two cosmic powers, the one who destroys and the one who creates, and all the elements, Ether, Air and Fire, Earth and Water, all of Nature.

The Shakras *of the subtle body, through which the kundalini climbs Indian miniature, Jodhpur school, Rajasthan, 18th century (Private collection)*

the almighty power of desire in Radha. Exchanges between Bhaktism and Tantrism have always occurred; they share many of their devotional practices and hymns of praise. However, one of their main differences lies in the fact that Tantrism gives greater importance to the feminine aspect of the Absolute, *shakti*, the energy force secretly at work in man and the universe which is born from the eternal union of the divine couple, *Purusha* ('Spirit') and *Prakriti* ('Nature'), in which only the female element plays an active role. This also applies to man, in whom the atman is passive and thus obliged to suffer the consequences of karman (including transmigration) until shakti awakes. Shakti, which brings about deliverance, is represented by *kundalini* (see **Yoga**), in the form of a snake coiled at the base of the spinal column which, when awoken, slithers up the subtle body to the top of the skull where it joins with the atman like a god with his shakti, and Purusha with Prakriti, the whole being enjoying the blessed state procured by perfect liberation.

Although the revival of an ancient past can be seen in the Goddess cult, Tantrism appears mainly as a reaction against the ascetical ideals presented by the renunciants (*sannyasin*) which had progressively reached the different strata of society, but which seemed incompatible with the actual political and sociological situation of the century. Tantrism was a true reversal of contemporary values. Instead of trying to weed out desire, it uses its boundless energy along with all the other forms of energy that animate human beings in a positive way 'taking people as they are and bringing

them to their fulfilment'. It was inevitable that such a subversive trend should be firmly opposed by Brahmanic orthodoxy. As a result, Tantrism has never really been practised except in specific, marginalized sects, which are uncompromisingly intolerant even of one another. These schools are only open to the initiated.

Kundalini

Arousing kundalini can be dangerous; in preparation, devotional and ritual practices including mantras and mudras, sacred formulae and gestures, must be strictly observed under the supervision of a guru. Once the cosmic energy is freed, it travels through the subtle body and finally merges with the atman like Parusha and Prakriti, recreating the original androgynous state of the being and reforming the universe in its image, while sparking off the perfect liberation.

One aspect of Tantrism which has been wrongly emphasized in the West but which, in the actual practices of the sect, is only secondary and optional, is the relaxing of the prohibitions, the usage of the five Ms, the initial of the five impurities: meat, fish, wine, fried grain, and sexual intercourse. These practices are only carried out after a long and difficult period of asceticism and are used principally as a measure of the level of detachment attained by the adept.

Buddhist Tantrism

Starting from the 8th century, Tantrism, which was spreading all over India, reached the Mahayana school of Buddhism. The principal centres of diffusion were the great monastic universities. The masters of Tantrism, the siddhas or 'faultless' ones, played a vital role in its dissemination, especially in Tibet where Tantric Buddhism became the dominant doctrine under the names Tantrayana, Martrayana (due to the use of mantras), and Vajrayana, 'Vehicle, or Way, of the Diamond'.

The central concept here is one of Emptiness, the Void (*Shunyata*), as the absolute 'non-born, non-become' developed by the philosopher Nagarajuna. From this point of view, if everything in the universe and even in humankind is stripped of essence and

---

Hymn to Durga

'You who are beyond all words . . . because you are all beings and yet give joy and freedom to all, how can we sing your praises fittingly?'

Hymn to Kali

'Ah! How can one express your majesty, O Mother? You gave birth to the world and You alone protect it, When the end of time comes, it will be reabsorbed into You.'

substance, then subduing the passions is still part of the world of illusions. Experimentally breaking the most stringently imposed rules can reveal the inanity of both the prohibitions and the person's desire, on the condition that his transgression was not motivated by selfish reasons; it must be strictly ritual, symbolic even, and accomplished with the supervision of his guru.

Moreover, Tantric Buddhism also attributes great importance to devotional figures of the Buddhas and Bodhisattvas used in worship, paying particular attention to the female powers, like *Prajnaparamita*, Supreme Wisdom, considered to be the 'Mother of all the Buddhas', or *Tara*, associated with the Bodhisattva Avalokitesvara. The iconography frequently depicts religious figures in love-making positions (*yab-youm*, 'father-mother', husband-wife') which, in the spirit of the doctrine, represent the union between complementary principles like *prajna*, wisdom (feminine), and *upaya*, active compassion (masculine), for, contrary to Hindu beliefs, in Tantric Buddhism it is the masculine

principle which plays the active role. Some of these gods are depicted in various ways, alternating between the pleasant and the more terrifying sides of their nature, which is one way of showing that the same reality can be perceived as threatening or encouraging according to the adept's level of consciousness.

The ritualism, founded on mantras and mudras, the initiatory character of the higher teachings, the role played by visualizations and the importance given to the powers of the imagination specific to Tibetan Buddhism, are all of Tantric inspiration.

The viras

Tantrism is often seriously misunderstood. Ill-informed by tendentious books, most Westerners only ever know about the rare extreme cases of magical and sexual practices which cause just as much scandal in India. It should never be forgotten that only the *vira*, the real 'men', the initiated, and not the 'cattle', common humanity, can go against the prohibitions, and even then only after a long preparatory process has allowed them to overcome their passions and instincts. It can only be accomplished with complete equanimity and detachment. Thus, the sexual act should only take place once the initiate has the ability to reproduce the divine act of creation within himself. Finally, the transgression of the taboos is usually symbolic, using substitutes that are acceptable even to orthodox Hindus.

Hymn to the White Tara

'Yes, it is I who takes you across the ocean of perils, the river of anxiety, it is I, Tara, who saves all creatures.

And this is why the saints, hands outstretched and heads bowed, prostrate themselves before me, full of respect and singing the praises of Noble Tara.'

Tariqa

Islamic mystical centres

From the 12th century to the present day, these centres have taught the path which leads to self-renunciation with a view to union with God.

This word which, in Arabic, means 'path' or 'road', refers in Muslim mysticism to the methods by which the believer passes through the psychological stages from the literal practice of the Law (*shari'a*) to divine Reality (*haqiqa*). From the 12th century onwards tariqa more specifically refers to those brotherhoods whose members are gathered together in a monastery (*takya*) around a master, the *sheikh* or *murshid*, who directs their intensive spiritual training. In the monastery, a true transmission of initiatory knowledge takes place, instigated by the *murshid* who must be an authentic link in a chain (*silsila*) which goes back to the Prophet himself.

The initiation

Entry to the 'path' or 'second birth' is an actual initiation symbolized by the donning of a habit or *khirga*. The disciple (*murid*), known as the 'son of the sheikh', owes his 'father' unconditional obedience, and treats his fellow-disciples like brothers. The murid leads an ascetical life in the community, punctuated by retreats which can last from 40 days to three years. He practises humility, charity, and sincerity, and devotes himself to the *dikhr* or repeated recitation of invocations appropriate to each stage on the path towards total purification of the soul. This 'remembrance of God', evokes the creative Word and leads to an ecstatic state in which an individual can feel the presence of God. As a basic exercise, *dhikr* engenders 'states' (*hal*), fleeting gifts which God in his generosity bestows on humankind through the disciples' efforts which are gradually transformed into permanent 'stations' (*maqam*). The *dikhr* is accompanied by meditation and occasionally by song, music, and sacred dances (*sama*) (see **Djalal ad-Din Rumi**).

The most important tariqas were founded in the 12th–14th centuries. One of them, the Mawlwiyah or 'whirling dervishes' is still active today.

The 19th century saw a revival of some Sufi brotherhoods. The *Tijaniyah* brotherhood which claims to be descended from Muhammad was founded in Algeria and spread all over Africa. Perhaps the most influential tariqa, particularly in the Maghreb was the *Darqawiyah* brotherhood founded by Abu Hamid al-Darqawi (1760–1823); more recent is the group which gathered at Mostaganem around Ahmad al-Alawi (died 1934), whose European members helped introduce Sufism in the West.

Tariqa

'The word means . . . the collection of spiritual training rights proposed by the different Muslim brotherhoods.' (C.-R. Ageron)

Tauler, Johannes

1297 (?) Strasbourg — Strasbourg 1361

Great mystical pedagogue

Preacher in Strasbourg and one of Meister Eckhart's disciples, Tauler described the various progressive stages of spiritual evolution.

Born into a rich bourgeois family, at an early age Johannes Tauler entered the Strasbourg Dominican monastery where his poor health prevented him from leading too harsh an existence. He probably heard Eckhart speak at Cologne, and later defended him after he was condemned; Tauler's ideas were so similar to those of his mentor that certain of their texts have sometimes been confused. After his expulsion from his native town with the Friars Preachers, he moved to Basel, remaining there between 1339 and 1346. It is possible that he visited Ruysbroek at Groenendaal. On his return to Strasbourg he became known for his sermons which were addressed primarily at the religious establishments but also at regular clerics and the laity.

His works

Thanks to the notes taken by listeners during his preaching career, we have Tauler's 84 *Sermons* which were published in 1498. The numerous other works attributed to him have never been authenticated.

The theory

While he faithfully reflected Eckhart's teachings, Tauler was also influenced by his in-depth study of the Neoplatonists, in particular Proclus and Dionysius the Areopagite. He distinguishes himself from Eckhart by his concern for all that is

didactic. While his master underlined essentially instantaneous nature of Go appearance in humankind, Tauler stres the need for continuous and patient eff His method is progressive for 'man is rea like three men, though remaining one'. methods deal firstly with the outwa person, the 'beginner' who must gu against his weaknesses and subdue body, then with the reasonable person 'progresser' who will ensure that his sou purified of all desire, then finally with 'deiform' who will strive to 'empty' him in order to let God work in him.

'I had to empty myself of myself . . . Si then I have been lost in this abyss. I h stopped speaking. I am mute. The divi swallowed me.' No saint has ever been a to avoid this long and difficult journey, even the Virgin Mary who could never '█ a single movement of peace or conte ment'.

Although they were appreciated in 14th and 15th centuries, the Cath Church was wary of Tauler's teachir particularly after Luther outspoke praised them. However Bossuet resto them to the favourable position they ॥ enjoy today.

Tauler
'He who has bared himself . . . need never fe again.' *(Song of Nudity)*

Luther
'As a theologian, Tauler is superior to all the doctors at all the universities.'

Bossuet
'One of the soundest, most accurate mystic

Teilhard de Chardin, Pierre

1881 Sacenat, Puy-de-Dôme — New York 1955

Evolutionary mystic

A scholar and Jesuit, Teilhard de Chardin attempted to combine science and religion; for him the glorious coming of Christ would also be the end of the evolutionary process.

Son of a well-off gentleman farmer, Pierre Teilhard de Chardin entered the Society of Jesus in 1899, was ordained a priest in 1911, and went on to study palaeontology at the Sorbonne. He was a stretcher-bearer during the 1914–18 war and later taught palaeontology and geology at the Catholic Institute in Paris. Having obtained his doctorate, he left for China in 1923 and took part in the important discovery of the 200 000-year-old Peking Man. After his return to Europe in 1945, Teilhard was elected to the Academy of sciences in 1950, but left for New York the following year, where he lived until his death. A scholar of international repute, he was nevertheless mistrusted by the church authorities who opposed the publication of his philosophical works.

His works

He produced more than 30 volumes. The publication of his *Oeuvres Complètes* (Complete Works) only began after his death. The first volume *Le Phénomène humain* (1955) (The Phenomenon of Man) created a considerable stir in public opinion, and added controversy to controversy. *L'Apparition de l'homme* (The Appearance of Man) published in 1956 was followed in 1957 by *La*

Vision du passé (The Vision of the Past) and by *Le Milieu divin* (The Divine Milieu). These books arouse less enthusiasm today than they did at the time of their publication.

The theory

A scientist and confirmed believer in evolution, Teilhard takes the most recent data on the genesis of the human race as his starting point and progresses through the stages of evolutionary biology, finally opening out on to a breathtaking, quite mystical view of the destiny of the human race, and of the whole cosmos which aims towards the ultimate convergence, the 'Omega' point. Starting from the Omega point, God reveals himself as the unique and absolute future. His theories confirm the final reign of the Cosmic Christ suggested in the writings of Paul and the Greek Church Fathers. Teilhard's passage from physics to metaphysics was well structured phenomenologically and dialectically, but as a theologian, poet, and mystic, he was also guided by his prophetic vision. In the light of these facts, the resistance his works aroused is easier to understand. However, at this stage we are unable to state with any degree of certainty whether Teilhard will be one of the great 20th century religious leaders or not.

Teilhard de Chardin's Poetic Vision

'The gigantic proportions of the universe, religious solemnity, love for matter seen as personalized . . . sense of the continuity of things, dynamism, and orientation towards the future . . . give Teilhard's lyricism unheard of tones.' (J. Van de Ghinste)

Tendai

First major Japanese school of Buddhism

Still active in Japan today, Tendai is an adaptation of a Chinese doctrine and is the origin of most of the sects which emerged after it.

Soon after Korean monks introduced it in Japan in 522, the Mahayana school of Buddhism was officially adopted by the imperial court. Prince Shotoku, architect of the centralized state and regent between 592 and 622, was the principal promoter of Japanese Buddhism. In 607 he sent a delegation to China which was the first in a long series of cultural exchanges that was to spread Chinese civilization throughout the archipelago. It was then that the different schools of Chinese Buddhism took on a distinctly Japanese character. However, Buddhism only gradually freed itself from imperial supervision to become a popular religion. At the beginning of the 9th century two monks, Saicho (767–822) and Kukai (744–835), brought two great systems of theory and practice back from China: Tendai and Shingon, which were to change the face of Japanese Buddhism and determine its evolution.

The founder of Tendai

Saicho became a monk at the age of 14 and, once he had completed his studies, he withdrew to Mount Hiei, near Kyoto, where he was won over by the theories of the prestigious Chinese master, Che-yi (538–597), who had lived on Mount T'ien t'ai ('Heavenly Terrace'). Che'yi believed that the *Lotus Sutra* was the jewel in the crown of the Buddha's teachings, and that as the Buddha nature existed in every one

of us, it was enough to understand th[e] nature to be freed. However, he also stat[ed] that this understanding could only [be] reached after a long and difficult pur[ga]tory process. In 804 Saicho went [to] China to increase his knowledge of [the] doctrine; he also studied other esote[ric] doctrines, as well as Ch'an (Zen), wh[ose] practices he incorporated into the Ten[dai] school he founded in Japan. According [to] the syncretist Tendai doctrine, the Budd[ha] is eternal but from time to time he appe[ars] in human form, as in the case of Sakyam[u]ni, in order to teach the people and gu[ide] them towards deliverance. Tendai had [its] principal temple on Mount Hiei, where monks had to undergo a strict 12-y[ear] novitiate; the majority of import[ant] religious leaders in subsequent centur[ies] studied at this monastery, which was s[een] as the 'cradle of Japanese Buddhism'. U[p to] his death, Saicho campaigned with so[me] success for the independence of the sch[ool] from secular power, and above all from older monastic communities.

Honoured after his death with the t[itle] 'Denghyo Daishi', 'Great Master of [the] Transmission of the Doctrine', the foun[der] of Tendai is still revered in Japan tod[ay]. Many Tendai disciples later went on [to] follow Shingon, but the founders of [the] Jodo and Jodo-shin schools of the Nichi[ren] sect, and of Zen were all former Ten[dai] monks.

From the Lotus Sutra

'By the countless virtues (of Avalokitesavara),
Thanks to his compassion,
All sensitive beings, no matter how many the[y]
may be,
Will be regenerated in the ocean of infinite
happiness.'

Teresa of Avila

1515 Avila — Alba de Tormes 1582

Spanish mystic and reformer of the Carmelite order

Her works transmit the ardour of her exemplary spiritual life.

Teresa Sanchez de Cepeda y Ahumada was the fifth of 11 children born to a draper of Jewish extraction. At the age of seven, she ran away from home in search of martyrdom in Moorish territory, and by the time she was 20 she had entered a Carmelite convent. Shortly afterwards she fell seriously ill, and was obliged to leave the convent for two years. During this period she read the works of the Franciscan Osuna, which introduced her to the practice of mental prayer. In 1539 she was close to death but insisted on returning to the convent where, although she eventually recovered, she remained prone to severe illnesses throughout the rest of her life.

In 1554, after a series of visions, her 'second conversion' took place. Teresa then decided to restore the Carmelite order to its former austerity, and in 1562 founded the convent of Saint Joseph of Avila, where she implemented a much stricter rule and the practice of mental prayer. Teresa's reforms were gradually applied in the 16 convents she founded, and were carried to the monasteries by Saint John of the Cross. In attempting to accomplish the task she had set herself, Teresa not only had to face a

'**Mental orison** in my opinion is nothing more than a friendly exchange during which we often converse alone with a God whom we know loves us.'

certain amount of opposition from the nuns themselves, but she also had to overcome the obstacles put in her path by the Church authorities; at one point, only the intervention of King Philip II ensured the survival of the reforms. In 1970 Teresa was declared a doctor of the Church.

Her works

Her works were all published posthumously, and are both autobiographical and didactic. In *Life*, written in 1562 on the orders of her confessor, Teresa relates her personal experiences. *The Book of the Foundations* (1577) gives a detailed account of the creation of the new convents. *Way of Perfection* (1565–70) and *The Interior Castle* (written in 1577) outline the various stages of 'mystical prayer'.

The theory

The influence Teresa exerted over the Catholic Church was partially due to her remarkable spirituality to which her works bear witness. However, she is best known for her reforms within the Carmelite movement, a religious order close in essence to Eastern monachism and linked to Old Testament mysticism through the prophet Elisha who, after Elijah's ascension, withdrew to Mount Carmel to the site where God had shown himself. Well informed on the problems inherent in spirituality and an enthusiastic supporter of inner life, Teresa remains to this day an unsurpassed spiritual guide. Orison, the key-word to Teresian teaching, is silent prayer, a direct expression of love and also the best way to help one's fellows to whom one gives more than to oneself.

Theosophists

'Those who know divine things'

Respresented by independent mystic philosophers within Judaism and Islam as well as Christianity, theosophy as a spiritual current has always existed.

In the Eastern Church, theologians have sometimes been called theosophists, but the term theosophy has come to describe esoteric interpretations of sacred texts outwith the official versions laid down by the ecclesiastical authorities. Furthermore, these interpretations do not proceed from intellectual reflection, but from inner revelation. Many theosophists in history were Sufis, particularly Persian Sufis like Suhrawardi, or Jewish Cabalists. Theosophism, as a system of non-orthodox paths leading to God, made its mark on Christianity with the Illuminatist movement led by Jakob Böhme in the 17th century, then with Swedenborg and Saint-Martin in the 18th century, and finally in modern times with the three Russians, Soloviev, Bulgakov, and Berdiaev, the Austrian Steiner, and the Frenchman, René Guénon.

The Theosophical Society

In 1875 Colonel H. S. Olcott (1832–1907) and the Russian clairvoyant, Helena Petrovna Blavatsky (1831–91) founded the Theosophical Society, about which Guénon wrote that there was 'absolutely no connection' between its doctrine and real theosophy. The doctrine, which Blavatsky expounds in her books *Isis Unveiled* (1875)

and *The Secret Doctrine* (from 1888), is in f an eclectic amalgam of Eastern religic traditions and spiritism.

In 1882 Olcott and Blavatsky mov their headquarters to Adyar, near Mad in India. On a visit to London in 18 Blavatsky met Annie Besant (1847–193 an Irish social reformer turned theosoph who was later to succeed her as the head the society. Besant was an extremely act leader, moving to India in 1891 where society became increasingly popular w the Anglo-Saxon milieu, and broaden its scope to include the issues of educat and the emancipation of women. 1908 Besant and her assistant, C. Leadbeater, tried to make a young Hind named Krishnamurti, into the 'Wo Teacher'. In 1907 the Society's m eminent member, Rudolf Steiner, spoke against Krishnamurti's anti-Christ stance and rather suspect spiritism, a left, taking with him the whole Germ contingent. Other splinter groups so followed his example. While it still surviv in Adyar and certain other countries, Theosophical Society today is no more t a centre of philanthropic and intellect activity.

The theosophist
'In truth, he seeks to gain the ultimate vision the principle of the world's reality. His work begins where rational philosophy ends, and finishes where theology begins, but the theosophist is more free and more creative than the theologian.' (A. Faivre)

Paul
'For the spirit explores everything, even the depths of God's own nature.'

Thomas Aquinas

1224 Aquino — Fossanevo 1274

The 'Angelic Doctor'

He was the greatest pedagogue in medieval Christianity, the constructor of a solid theological edifice, and a prominent religious leader.

Born in Roccasecca Castle near Aquino, Thomas studied at Naples and, despite strong opposition from his family, joined the new order of Friars Preachers founded by Saint Dominic. He was sent to Paris to the Saint James monastery, the intellectual centre of the order, where he studied under the illustrious Albert the Great, whom he followed to Cologne in 1248. Thomas returned to Paris in 1252, became a master of theology in 1256, and was appointed to one of the two chairs kept for the Preachers at the University of Paris. He went on to teach in Italy between 1259 and 1268 but was recalled to Paris to take part in the dispute on the nature of man and the relationship between faith and culture. King Charles of Anjou chose him to carry out certain educational reforms in Naples in 1272. Thomas Aquinas died on his way

'Communicating the fruit of contemplation to others is a greater thing than **contemplation** itself.'

'What I have written seems to me like a wisp of straw compared to what I have seen and what has been revealed to me.'

to the Council of Lyons. He was canonized less than 50 years after his death and nicknamed the 'Angelic Doctor' but also 'Common Doctor' for, in the interim, his theological doctrine had become that of the Church.

His works

Although he died at the age of 49, Thomas left a vast amount of works behind him. They include numerous didactic texts, like *Quodlibet* (1258) and *Quaestiones disputate de veritate* (1271), but above all his monumental doctrinal volumes *Summa Contra Gentiles* (1255–64), a critical analysis of different philosophies and earlier theology, and the huge *Summa theologiae*, written between 1266 and 1274.

The theory

Thomas understood how important the recent rediscovery of Aristotle's philosophy in the works of his Arabic commentators was to Western thought, and began methodically to review and refresh the old theology which was based on Platonic ideas. His plan was to restructure it into a strict science capable of meeting the growing intellectual needs outlined in his major work *Summa theologiae*, the point at which scholastic philosophy begins. But Thomism, which achieved great success at the end of the Middle Ages and also found favour in the 20th century with Etienne Gilson and Jacques Maritain, only reflects selected aspects of Thomas's thinking. Thomas was not only a teacher, he was also a great contemplative who made an impression on such Dominican mystics as Meister Eckhart.

Upanishads

The quintessence of Hindu wisdom

These sacred texts, whose composition is spread over several centuries, form an unequalled body of metaphysical teachings.

The *Upanishads*, which are part of the divine Revelation (*Shruti*) are the esoteric complement to the *Vedas*. Together they are the *Vedanta*, that is to say, the end or closure of the *Vedas*, a word which makes its first appearance in the *Upanishads*. It was later used to describe one of the *darshanas*, or Hindu philosophical systems, outlined in the *Brahmasutra*, the philosophical commentary on the *Upanishads* in the 3rd century BC. All the great vedantic authors, like Sankara and Ramanuja, drew on these metaphysical poems.

Many of the orally transmitted *Upanishads* come from the Vedic period and were probably compiled between 1000 and 500 BC, but the majority of the texts date from the period of crisis in Hinduism which occurred with the advent of Jainism and Buddhism (4th–3rd centuries BC). In fact, the genre survived for 2000 years, for some *Upanishads* were written in the 16th century. Traditionally there are supposed to be 108 *Upanishads*, but we already know of 225, and many others might yet be discovered. Moreover, it is not impossible that further *Upanishads* will be composed in the future. Some believe that the teaching of Ramana Maharishi could be considered as one of

them. Whatever the case may be, Hindus mainly refer to a group of about 20 *Upanishads*; 12 of them have written commentaries by Sankara, which adds to their authority. The oldest and longest *Upanishads* like the *Brihadaranyaka* and the *Chandogya* are written in prose interspersed with verse. Almost all of them are presented in the form of a dialogue between a disciple in search of the true nature of God, and his master who, in answering the former's question, reveals the supreme knowledge. This master is sometimes a god, the goddess Uma, wife of Siva, Agni, the god of Fire, or Yama, the god of Death, sometimes one of the great sages of the past, and sometimes even an animal like a bull, a flamingo or another kind of bird.

The esoteric teaching

The themes dealt with are borrowed from the ancient vedic cosmogony, but are made more profound and spiritual (like that of *Purusha*, the cosmic man offered up to the gods as a sacrifice, from whose dismembered body the world emerged), or bear witness to a metaphysical and mystical revival. Coming after the *Veda's Brahamana*, which explain the meaning of sacrifice in order to obtain material goods, the *Upanishads* provide an esoteric interpretation of inner sacrifice. This form of sacrifice can generate the supreme good, final deliverance from *samsara*, the infernal cycle of births and deaths, thanks to the destruction of *karman*. These two notions, along

---

Atman is Self

'The Self must be know here, in this life . . . if the Self is known here, there is supreme knowledge, and the aim of life will have been reached . . . If the Self is not known, then life is useless . . .' (Sankara)

'**The Upanishads** were compiled to establish the Brahman science, in such a way that ignorance would be definitively rejected, and the stream of existence stopped.'

with that of *prana*, breathing control, which is vital energy and even cosmic energy, one of the techniques taught in yoga, have become the basis of Hindu spirituality.

Atman and Brahman

But the central element and specific theme of the *Upanishads* is the concept of *atman*, which first meant 'breath', 'wind' (German *atmen* meaning 'to breathe' giving English 'atmosphere') and then came to be used as a reflexive pronoun in Sanskrit, referring to the cosmic and individual principle, 'Self'. The principal teaching thereafter was the identity of atman and of *Brahman*, the All, the Absolute, from whence came the whole universe including the gods. The atman is linked to the transitory world by illusions born of ignorance; all that human beings need to do to be forever freed, is to become aware of this basic identity.

This had already been stated in the *Aitereya Upanishad* linked to the *Rig Veda*, which describes the creation of the world and underlines the concept of the microcosm (Man) and the macrocosm (the Universe). Also very old, and of a clearly initiatory character, the *Katha Upanishad* is in the form of a dialogue between Naciketas, a pure and heroic Brahman youth, and Yama, god of the kingdom of the dead, where irritated by his comments, Naciketas's father has sent him. Yama, who has not observed the laws of hospitality, is obliged to grant the young man three wishes. The first two are accepted immediately: his father's anger will be appeased and he will return home; he also received the teaching which allows heaven to be reached. But, at the third question: 'Tell me if man continues to live after death' Yama tries to avoid giving an answer; however, Naciketas keeps on asking until he is finally obliged to answer. After declaring that the ritual practices are insufficient, he states that the only result is the identification of the migratory soul with the religious principle, which join to make a single unit, atman, which is identical to Brahman. The relatively short *Mundaka Upanishad* is dedicated to the study of the latter, while the even shorter *Mandaknaya* assimilates Brahman to the sacred syllable OM.

As subtle as they are grandiose, the *Upanishads* are the expression par excellence of the Indian metaphysical spirit. They reflect the teachings of the great *rsis*, inspired wise men and religious leaders, teachings which are always based on their experience of reality; they also express 'different phases of the same truth depending on the level of attainment of the seer'. However, the depth of the thinking and their condensed and often allusive poetic style, make understanding them very difficult. Nevertheless, some of them, translated into European languages (from 1802) have fascinated philosophers like Schopenhauer, and even poets like Victor Hugo.

Brahman, the Absolute

'Whoever in truth knows the ultimate Brahman, becomes Brahman himself. He surpasses affliction, frees himself of sin. Liberated of all ties, he becomes immortal.' (*Mundaka Upanishad*)

Schopenhauer

'In the whole world, there is no study more profitable and more edifying than that of the *Upanishads*. They have been a comfort to me throughout my life, and they will comfort me at the hour of my death.'

Vajrayana or Tibetan Buddhism

The 'Way of the Sacred Jewel'

Mahayana school and final phase in the development of Buddhist doctrine, Vajrayana, which is affiliated to Tantrism, claims to be the 'fast way' to liberation.

Although it has come to be closely associated with Tibet, Vajrayana, which has the *vajra* ('jewel', image of supreme reality, and 'lightning', the awakening to perfect wisdom) as its symbol, originated in India, where it was the result of the Tantric current which itself had emerged from the early Mahayana school. It follows on from the theories of the two great schools, Madhyamika, or 'Middle Way', and especially Yogasara, whose members believe that the world in which human beings live is but the product of their consciousness at its different levels. All effort should be directed towards eradicating these blemishes and towards the return of consciousness to its original state of purity. This can be achieved by using Tantric yoga techniques which call into play all the vital energies redeployed for this purpose.

This method generates mystical and cosmic ritualism involving the use of *mantras* and *dharanis*, sacred formulae whose powers evoke and invoke supernatural forces, *mudras*, ritualized gestures, and *mandalas*, diagrams painted or even simply traced on the ground with rice or coloured powder, for they are only intended to last the length of one ceremony. Born of emptiness, they return to it. All the same, constructing the *mandalas* is a slow and painstaking business, as they represent the component powers in the universe as well as the deities which rule over it. The adept identifies his body with the mandala and is purified; the mantra and mudra perform the same function for his words and gestures. This collection of practices characterizes Vajrayana. Vajrayana is the ultimate stage in the evolution of Buddhist doctrine and bears witness to its capacity for inner renewal and its adaptability.

Buddhist Tantras

While it first emerged in the 3rd and 4th centuries, it was not until the 7th to 8th centuries that Tantric Buddhism really began to expand, taught at the monastic universities of Nalanda and especially Vikramasila which, from the 10th century, became the main centre of Indian Tantric Buddhism. Its great leaders were the *siddhas*, or 'perfect', who played a fundamental role in spreading it to Tibet. These included Padmasambhava, who founded the first monastery there, Tilopa (988–1069) and Naropa (1016–1110), the forerunners of the first line of lamas called *Kagyu-pa*.

The *Tantras* make up a special section which is only found in the Tibetan canon. There are two collections in the Tibetan canon, the *Kanjur* and the *Tenjur*, which

---

From the Advayavajrasamgraha
'The form of the gods is but the shimmering of emptiness.'
'Perfect knowledge of the flow of things (samsara) is nirvana.'

The 14th Dalai Lama
'Vajrayana shows that, if one meets a competent master, if the candidate's faculties have reached maturity, in a matter of years of effort, one can reach the status of Buddha.'

contain roughly 4500 works. The *Kanjur* (a translation of the Buddha's words) exposes the monastic discipline (*vinaya*), the Mahayana sutras and the tantras in 5000 volumes. The *Tanjur* (translation of the treatises) contains the commentaries and teachings of the Madhyamika and Yogasara schools, and also hymns and tracts on such secondary subjects as logic, grammar, and medicine etc. This massive Buddhist encyclopaedia sums up common Buddhist doctrine, the Hinayana and Mahayana sutras as well as including the mantras which have played different roles in Tibetan religion. While the *Gelugs-pa* only tackled them after 20 years of philosophical study, they are central to the teaching of the *Nyingma-pa* who, moreover, have their own ancient tantras which are not recognized by the other schools.

However, this diversity should not be allowed to obscure the basic commonality of Buddhist doctrine in all the schools, as well as in Mahayana, from which Vajrayana adopted certain characteristics. Thus, it completes and further perfects the system of five cosmic principles personified by the Jina, still called *Dhyani Buddhi*, 'Buddha of meditation', a recent and certainly incorrect term which nevertheless underlines their true function as aids to meditation. In accordance with the *sakti* in Tantrism, Vajrayana links feminine partners to the Jina, like *Prajnaparamita*, supreme wisdom, who becomes the 'Mother of the Buddhas'.

This enlarged pantheon includes (in certain subordinate roles) some Hindu divinities and even the demons of the ancient indigenous religion, converted to the *Dharma* and, in the form of terrifying gods, presented as the defensive aspects of the good-natured bodhisattvas. In Vajrayana, the latter are more closely linked to human existence than in Mahayana, for they are incarnated in certain lamas known as tulkus.

Tibetan practices

Vajrayana teachings are not only theoretical; they are in part aimed towards practice. They stress the identity of samsara, the present condition, and of nirvana, the future condition, as well as the relationship between the macrocosm, Buddha's universe, and the microcosm, man, who is a potential Buddha. This is the true significance of Tantric rituals and symbolism. It also explains the progressively difficult meditation exercises, accompanied by 'visualization', especially the *yidam*, the deity which has become the adept's protector. This lengthy apprenticeship can only be accomplished under the supervision of a guru, in the close union of disciple and master. The various stages are sanctified by a series of 'consecrations' (*abhisekas* in Sanskrit; *wangs* in Tibetan), rites of passage to a superior level of teaching, to new practices. As an ascetical process, it takes the disciple from the relative to the absolute by encouraging him to rediscover his original participation in the limitless and allowing him to reach the ultimate goal, which is personal and universal liberation.

Samsara and Nirvana

'Samsara is the mind afflicted and obscured by countless mental constructions, coming and going like a flash of lightning in a storm and covered in the clinging filth of attachment and the other passions. Nirvana is luminous and perfectly free . . . Nothing but nirvana exists for those who, desiring freedom, wish to see endless pain disappear and to reach the happiness of Enlightenment.'

Vedas

The sacred source of Hinduism

Revealed by God, these poems make up a rich collection of esoteric symbols and have been interpreted and re-interpreted throughout history.

Veda in Sanskrit means 'knowledge', the supreme 'science', and is applied to the sacred writings of Hinduism. They are considered to be eternal, revealed by the supreme God Brahman, and 'heard' by *rsis*, or inspired wise men. For many centuries there was no written version of the Vedas, but the poems were passed down orally from generation to generation. The oldest sections date from the 13th century BC, at a time when the Aryans had invaded northwest India and were occupying the Ganges plain, and the most recent appear to have been written just before the Buddha began preaching (5th century BC). Composed of prayers (mantras), ritual or magical phrases and chants, the Vedas accompanied sacrifices and were intoned by the four classes of priests who presided at the ceremonies.

The four Vedas

The most important and ancient text in Hinduism is the *Rig Veda*, which is composed of 1028 hymns of praise to the gods; the three other Vedas are the *Yajur Veda*, which regroups the formulae recited by the acolytes, the *Sama Veda*, which supplies the music for the sacred chant, and the *Atharva Veda*, the most recent of the Vedas, which is a collection of the magic formulae reserved for the use of the nobility. Apart from the *Samhitas*, 'collections' of hymns or formulae, each of the four Vedas has a *Brahmana*, a theological commentary in prose on the *Samhita*, an *Aranyaka*, 'forest treatise', the esoteric complement to the *Brahmana*, and an *Upanishad*, a short tract containing the secret teaching. Over the centuries the Vedas have attracted a massive amount of secondary literature known as the Vedangas, tracts which are not part of the Revelation (*Sruti*), but of *Smriti*, 'memory', in other words Tradition.

Divine cosmogony

The Vedas bring into play an ordered hierarchical vision of the whole universe in which humankind, as the image of God, must participate, reflecting on earth the liturgy celebrated by the gods. A collection of beliefs and practices, the Vedas were the norm of Indian society for 1000 years, from the Indo-European invasion (c. 1500 BC) until approximately 500 BC. While respect for the Vedas continues today, and although many young Brahmans still learn them by heart, they are no longer within the reach of everyone; nevertheless, they inspired and continue to inspire all Indian mystical philosophy.

Invocations

'Listen to our songs with a favourable ear, don't say "no!"'
'If thanks to you we are happy people, it is because you let us pray to you.'
(*Rig Veda* 1, 82)

'Two oceans are Varuna's flanks—and he is also hidden in the drop of water.'
(*Rig Veda* 4, 16)

Vivekananda

1863 Calcutta — Belur 1902

Introducer of Hinduism to the West

Vivekananda spread the message of his master Ramakrishna, giving it worldwide significance.

Born in an aristocratic Bengali family, Narendra Nath Datta, the future Vivekananda, received a western-style education. He was an extremely brilliant young man, and proud of his worldly success. Although he claimed to be an atheist, he was preoccupied by questions of a religious nature. At the age of 17, in a fit of curiosity he went to see Ramakrishna who immediately recognized his great spiritual depth. Disturbed by this revelation, Vivekananda left but returned several times, gradually abandoning his scepticism. Nevertheless, it took him four years and several grave periods of self-doubt before he was ready to rejoin his mentor for good. Ramakrishna soon guided him to complete unity with God. After the latter's death, Vivekananda withdrew to the Himalayas to prepare himself for his public ministry. When he eventually took over as head of the community, he restructured it totally and, as a result of his organizational skills and preaching ability, it became much more influential.

In 1892 he left on a four-year world tour intending to spread Ramakrishna's teaching. When he spoke at the 'World's Parliament of Religions' at Chicago in 1893, he was not the only Hindu speaker present, but he was certainly the most dynamic and popular; in London he recruited a number of disciples who followed him to India. By the time of his return, news of his international fame had already reached India, and he was given a hero's welcome. Vivekananda founded the 'Ramakrishna Mission', a monastic order, in 1897. Today the order has 80 centres in India and abroad, as well as schools, hospitals, and libraries. In keeping with Ramakrishna's teaching, proselytizing has no place at the Mission, whose sole intention is to 'make a Hindu a better Hindu, and a Christian a better Christian.

His works

His books are made up of the speeches and lectures he gave all over the world, many of which were dedicated to the practice of the different yogas.

The theory

While Vivekananda intended to faithfully reproduce Ramakrishna's teaching, he nonetheless felt it necessary to make it more accessible by adding a rational formulation to the mysticism that was already present. To do so, he linked the teaching to Western science and philosophy. The general aim remained the same: union with God achieved through the techniques of yoga, but especially through *bhakti*, or passionate worship. Vivekananda's actions as head of the community enabled Ramakrishna's message to survive to the present day.

From the past to the future
'I accept all the religions of the past, and I worship God with them all. I leave my heart open to those of the future. The Book of Revelation is not yet complete.'

Wesley and Methodism

1703 Epworth, Lincolnshire — London 1791

A return to the basics of the Reformation

Wesley shook the British out of their religious apathy in the 18th century and breathed new life into the Protestant faith.

Thirteenth of the 19 children born to an Anglican priest and his wife, John Wesley was an outstanding student at Oxford. Ordained a priest in 1728, he returned to Epworth to assist his father, then moved

---

Methodism abroad

Methodism had already reached the United States, where Thomas Coke, invested by Wesley, founded the Episcopal Methodist Church at Baltimore in 1748. Despite inner strife, the religion spread to Ireland, Canada, Australia, and New Zealand. Today there are over 40 million Methodists worldwide, with 14 million in the United States, where it is the second most popular Protestant creed after Baptism, but with only one million living in Britain. In Anglo-Saxon countries, particularly among the working classes, Methodism refreshed religious sensibilities and gave rise to a powerful movement towards inner change, the effects of which continue today.

---

back to Oxford where he taught Greek and ran the 'Holy Club' with his brother Charles. Members of the Club were called 'Methodists' because of the unchanging regularity of their practices. In 1735 the two brothers left to work as missionaries among the Indians in Georgia. On his return from this ill-fated voyage, John began to frequent the community of Moravian Brethren and, on 27 May 1738, he experienced sudden enlightenment while listening to one of Luther's sermons on justification by faith alone. The following year, he agreed to take part in a mass open-air meeting organized by his colleague, George Whitfield (1714–70). These first gatherings, during which people would prostrate themselves and cry or shout out, were banned by the Anglican Church authorities, bringing about a split which Wesley had neither envisaged nor desired.

Soon Whitfield, who adhered to the doctrine of predestination taught by Calvin, and Wesley, who advocated free will and Christian perfection, had to go their separate ways. While Whitfield provoked the awakening of the British and American Churches, he did not endow them with a tenable or viable system of organization; on the other hand, Wesley, who tirelessly travelled all over the British Isles on horseback, gave such a solid structure to Methodism that after his death, the Methodists were the largest dissident community in Britain.

Wycliffe, John

c. 1328 Hipswell, Yorkshire — Lutterworth, Leicester 1384

Precursor of Protestantism

An English preacher and theologian, Wycliffe was the driving force behind an anti-establishment movement which was to lead to the Reformation, whose ideas he was the first to formulate.

Of noble birth, John Wycliffe spent many years studying at Oxford, before teaching philosophy and theology there. He was granted an ecclesiastical living, then entered the service of the Crown where he had to defend his rights against the papacy. He soon showed himself to be one of the leading opponents of the Avignon popes, defended the Scriptures against the ecclesiastic hierarchy, and maintained that the true Church was the 'community of the predestined'. From the outset, his theories supported by the nobility and a large section of the clergy, caused a stir in England, where they were spread by itinerant priests called 'Lollards' but there was public outcry when Wycliffe went on to attack the sacraments. Although he was censured by Rome, he escaped punishment in his own country because in 1378 the Great

> **Milton on Wycliffe**
> 'Wycliffe was an Englishman chosen by God to be the first preacher of a general reform in Europe: in his struggle against the harshness and violence of the clergy, he became our leader.'

Schism arose — a period when there were two rival popes — and neither pope wanted to proceed against Wycliffe for fear of alienating English opinion. He was nevertheless condemned by a council headed by the Archbishop of Canterbury. In the eyes of the Church, he was no longer a reformer, but a heretic. He withdrew to his parish at Lutterworth, and devoted himself to the composition of his works.

His works

Between 1374 and 1379 Wycliffe published several tracts in Latin: *On Civil Lordship; On the Duty of the King;* and *On the Church,* in which he defended the rights of the king against the pope. Towards the end of his life, he outlined his theological doctrine which was clearly heretical in *On the Eucharist* (1381) and *Trialogus* (1382). The last task he undertook before his death was the publication of an English language Bible produced with the help of several followers.

The theory

Wycliffe provided doctrinal justification for the outrage which the Church's decadence had provoked. In England, his work was continued by the Lollards who attacked the clergy's extravagance, the celibacy of priests, and indulgences, preparing the way for the Reformation. As a theologian, his influence was most immediate in Bohemia: his ideas were at the root of the religious and nationalist revolution begun by John Huss which tore the country apart after Huss was burnt at the stake in 1415. Wycliffe was posthumously anathematized: his remains were disinterred in 1428 and burned, and his ashes strewn.

Yoga

A systematic method for definitive liberation

While it is known in the West in popularized and moderate forms, yoga is essentially rigorous spiritual discipline.

Yoga comes from the Indo-European root which gave the English noun 'yoke' and the verb 'to join'. In Sanskrit its original meaning is 'harnessing', which corresponds to the representation of the human psyche as a carriage drawn by two spirited horses (the faculty of the senses, the passions) whom the driver (the intellect, the mind, *buddhi*) tries to control. This image is mentioned in the oldest *Upanishad*, which portrays the impotent soul rushing headling towards the void, unable to escape unless it uses yoga methods which would allow it to descend from the carriage, a metaphor for deliverance. Yoga certainly pre-dates Hinduism. Although as a technique it aims at a completely different goal from the Vedas, it was to become a fundamental part of post-Vedic spirituality. From the 6th century BC the Mahavira, founder of Jainism, and the Buddha used meditation techniques derived from yoga. The yoga method had already been described briefly in certain *Upanishads* which date from the same

time, as well as in the Bhagavadgita a little later. The oldest systematic exposé can be found in Patanjali's *Yoga-sutra* (2nd century BC) but the author merely sets down precepts that were already ancient. The text itself is extremely condensed and was probably intended as a memory-aid to accompany an oral teaching. If it had not been for several commentaries, the first of which dates from the 6th century AD, the *Yoga-sutra* would have remained largely enigmatic. The second commentary, written in the 9th century is the best extant exposé of yoga as a *darshana* (traditional philosophical system), close to *samkhya* (cosmological and psychological analysis of reality) to the extent that these teachings are often considered to be the two halves, theoretical and practical, of one doctrine.

A method of deliverance

In Hinduism, where the aim of life is to reach the spiritual maturity which halts the cycle of births and rebirths, yoga, as a method of deliverance, must necessarily play a vital role. Such an end can only be obtained through strict asceticism which leads to total control of the human mind and body, in particular those parts which are liable to transmigration after death, like the subtle body which only dissolves when the soul is finally delivered. The intellect (*buddhi*), however, survives in its true form which is absolute and unconditioned Conscience, Being-Conscience-Beautitude (*satch-tchidananda*), the individual (*jivatman*) identifying itself with the supreme Principle, *Paramatman* or Brahman. Whatever outward form the yogas may take, they all share this common goal.

Patanjali's yoga, royal yoga (*rajah-yoga*), outlines the disciples's slow progression towards the goal in eight stages under the guidance of a qualified master or guru. It begins with the observance of the five

*A **yogi*** *in meditation*

restraints (*yama*) and the five disciplines (*niyama*) which pre-suppose chastity, constancy and devotion to God. Only once the adept has consolidated his principles, can he begin the *asana* (postures), destined to recondition the organism with meditation in mind, and the *pranayama*, control not only of respiration but also of the cosmic energy of which he is the vehicle. These are only preliminaries for the next stages: *pratyahara*, withdrawal of the senses from the dominion of exterior objects; and *dharana*, concentration, the direction of all mental activity towards a single point; leading to the next stage, *dhayana*, profound inner meditation. This last stage in turn leads to *samadhi*, which is not an ecstatic state, for the yogi does not 'leave' his body, but methodically and lucidly 'establishes his residence in the lotus of his own heart'. The samadhi itself is split into various levels. At the highest degree the yogi rediscovers his identity with the Brahman, which in itself is the supreme deliverance. During this ascent all manner of supranormal powers (*siddhi*, or accomplishments) can arise, but while treating them as encouraging signs, the adept must consider them as obstacles to be overcome, the true goal being the ultimate fulfilment of deliverance.

The yogis

While rajah-yoga, as Patanjali and his commentators describe it, is considered to be classic yoga, there are other forms, particularly those outlined in some 20 *Upanishads*, termed *Yoga Upanishads*, which contain the diverse expressions of this discipline. The principal are: *karma-yoga*, yoga of action, as illustrated by the *Bhaga-*

vadgita; *bhakti-yoga*, yoga of devotional love; *jnana-yoga*, yoga of knowledge; *hatha yoga*, yoga of violent effort, and *kundalini-yoga*. These last two call dangerous forces into play, and can only be practised under the strict guidance and supervision of a guru. Of tantric inspiration (see **Tantrism**) *kundalini-yoga* aims at awakening the latent cosmic energy which lies coiled at the base of the spine. The vital energy then rises through the *sushumna* or central canal, from shakra to shakra (the centres which punctuate the sushumna along the length of the spinal cord) which open when the *kundalini* passes through allowing it to reach the *sahasrara shakra* ('lotus of a thousand petals') situated at the top of the skull. It is there that the union between female *kundalini* and male *atman*, which can be compared to Siva and his Shakti, takes place.

Thus, we can see that true yoga scarcely corresponds to the idea most Westerners have of it. What is presented as yoga in the West is mainly a degenerate form of hatha-yoga, reduced to the practice of a few *asana* and of *pranayama*, but separated from their spiritual end and, by extension, their true meaning.

From the Baghavadgita
'The yogi withdraws its sense from sensory objects like a tortoise draws its head and feet into its shell.'

From the Maitri Upanishad
'No one must teach this absolutely secret discipline to someone . . . who is not a disciple, who has not pacified himself.'

Zen

The direct way of Satori

Only recently introduced to the West, Zen put its seal on Japanese civilization and daily life.

Zen is the Japanese transcription of the Chinese word *Ch'an* which describes sitting meditation in the style of the historical Buddha. This practice gave birth to the Mahayana school of Buddhism which probably first emerged in India. It was imported to China in the 6th century AD where it adopted certain Taoist features and was very popular. Chinese Ch'an went into decline in the 12th century and was introduced into Japan by the Tendai monk Yosai (or Eisai, 1141–1215) on his return from China where he had been initiated into the practices of the Rinzai school. After his death, Zen, which was already popular with the capital's aristocracy, was mingled with other elements from the Buddhist schools of Tendai and Shingon. Dogen was believed to have spread the purest form of Zen in Japan.

Dogen was born in Kyoto in 1200. His father died when he was three, and his mother when he was eight. He was both a direct descendant of a 10th century emperor and a brother-in-law of the ruling sovereign. At the age of 14, he entered the great Tendai monastery at Mount Hiei where he was groomed for the highest ecclesiastical office. But as an adolescent, Dogen's first concern was to find self-

knowledge. He went to study and practice under the guidance of Yosai's disciple Myozen, accompanying him to China in 1223 in search of the most authentic form of Buddhism. After Myozen's death, Dogen found another master in Nyojo, leader of the Soto school, who taught the difficult technique of sitting meditation called *za-zen*. Once he had experienced the 'intuition of truth', Dogen left Nyojo in 1227, having received the teaching and been charged with its propagation. He began this task immediately after his return to Japan, preaching in simple temples at Kyoto. Faced with a growing number of disciples, in 1248 Dogen had the Eihei-ji temple built near Fukui, to the east of Kyoto, which remains the principle Soto centre. Dogen died at Kyoto on 28 August 1253.

Dogen's teachings

A resumé of his teachings can be found in (*Fukanzazengi* 1227) (The Universal Promotion of the Principles of Zen) and also in *Shobogenzo* (1231–53) (The Treasury of the Right Dharma Eye) which Dogen compiled from the sermons he gave his followers. The *Shobogenzo* occupies a central position in the Soto school and explains not only the spirit of the Law and its practice, but also the code by which monks must live. According to Dogen 'what is most important in the study of the Way is *za-zen* . . . The Path followed by the Buddha and the patriarchs was *za-zen*.' Only sitting meditation, with no hope of personal gain, can bring about

---

Dogen

'Enlightenment comes from practice,
Thus Enlightenment is limitless;
Practice comes from Enlightenment,
Thus practice has no beginning.'

Bassui

'When you practise za-zen, don't make any conjectures on good and evil!
Don't try to stop your thoughts from coming.
Ask yourself only this question: "Which is my own spirit?"'

A Zen monk in meditation in a monastery in Japan

the complete abandon of the ego which leads to *Satori* (Enlightenment). This abrupt method may appear simple, but is nevertheless extremely difficult in that it demands both selflessness and perseverance.

Zen after Dogen

The Soto and Rinzai schools soon had many followers. They were remarkable for the distinct personalities of their leaders. Keizan (1268–1325), the third Soto leader after Dogen, published a *Denko-roku* (Record of the Transmission of the Light), demonstrating the continuity of the teaching through the 53 Indian, Chinese, and Japanese leaders to follow after the Buddha. The monk Muzo (1275–1351), author of *Mucho mondo* (Dialogues in a Dream), was one of the founders of the Zen gardens, and remains one of the school's foremost theoreticians. Takuan (1573–1655) is best known for having applied Zen to swordsmanship (*kendo*), while his contemporary Suzuki Shosan (1579–1655) spread Zen amongst the laity, declaring that Enlightenment could be reached simply through exercising one's profession. Without a doubt, the most powerful and influential leader was Hakuin (1685–1768), a writer, calligrapher, and painter who restored order and unity to the Rinzai sect by systematizing the use of ancient Chinese *koans*, enigmatic words used as themes for meditation.

These monks kept the school very much alive during the five centuries it took for Zen to penetrate and change Japanese culture and daily life.

From the 13th century, several famous *samurai* became monks, following the *Bushido*, a warrior's code of honour that gave birth to many of the martial arts. With Zen, Yosai also introduced tea, which was originally intended to stop monks falling asleep; tea drinking soon developed into a ritualized event. The art of Zen gardens is spread throughout the archipelago, as is the 'way of flowers' or *ikebana*. These arts express a profound sensitivity towards nature and her symbolic significance. Above all, Zen thought and aesthetics engendered an artistic renaissance that affected architecture and pottery, painting and poetry, with *sumiye*, quick washes in black and white, and *hai-ku*, the short form poem exemplified by Basho (1643–94), both being manifestations of the spontaneity rediscovered in concentration.

Today Japan has about 10 million Zen Buddhists, divided between the Soto (6–7 million) and Rinzai (2–3 million) schools. Zen was introduced to the West by various Japanese masters after the Second World War, and has a number of followers in the United States and Europe today.

Nyojo
'Abandon body and spirit.'

When we hit our two hands together, we hear a clap. **Hakuin** asked his disciples: 'So what is the sound of one hand?'

Zoroaster and Mazdaism

c. 660 — 583 BC north-eastern Persia

Ancient Persia's great reformer

Thanks to Zarathustra, the archaic Indo-European cult of Mazdaism became a monotheistic religion in which humankind must devote itself to preparing for the final triumph of supreme Good.

From Herodotus's era onwards, the figure of the 'Magus' par excellence, Zarathustra, known by his Hellenized name Zoroaster, has fascinated philosophers from Pythagoras to Plato and Aristotle. Certain historians have gone so far as to cast doubt on his actual existence, but modern-day experts nevertheless recognize in him the reformer of ancient Persian religion and the author of the *Gathas*, 17 hymns which constitute the oldest part of the *Avesta*. For the surviving followers of Mazdaism, the Guebres in Persia and the Parsi in India, the Avesta remains a holy book in which the resonant voice of a prophet can be heard. Probably the son of a pagan priest, Zoroaster was thought to have been employed as a *zaotar*, whose functions included invocations and

oblations. However, his imperious vocation forced him to retreat into the desert where, at the age of 30, he had a powerful religious experience during which Ahura Mazda, the 'Wise Lord', creator of all things, entrusted to him the task of purifying ancient rites and beliefs. His preaching was met with the incomprehension and hostility of the existing clergy, until he converted King Vishtaspa. With the king's protection, Zoroastrian reforms were able to spread gradually throughout Persia.

The theory

Zoroaster replaced ancient ceremonial rites based on sacrifice with a cult based on the worship of one god, Ahura Mazda. One concession made to the former religion was the use of its gods, the 'Immortal Holy Ones' as assistants to the one god. Ahura Mazda's power is threatened by the spirit of Evil (*Angra Mainyu*), the antithesis of the Holy Spirit (*Spenta Mainyu*) although both of them are less powerful than the Wise Lord. This dualism is believed to date from Zoroaster himself, but did not become a definitive part of the religion until much later. Once he had prohibited animal sacrifice, Zoroaster glorified Fire worship which is still active today in Mazdaism. Under the Archaemenid and Sasanian (3rd–7th centuries) dynasties, Mazdaism became the official state religion. However, when Persia was conquered by the Muslims (7th century) it only survived in the form of isolated mountain groups, while a proportion of believers emigrated to India where they became known as Parsis. The thriving Indian community numbers c. 150 000 members today.

The wise Lord

'What help can my soul expect from anyone? On whom can I count to look after my cattle? On what, in the Invocation, if not on Your Justice, O Wise Lord, and on your Thought?'

A Mazdean altar of the sacred flame, Iran

Zwingli, Huldreich

1484 Wildhaus, Saint-Gall — Kappel 1531

Humanist reformer

Having introduced a new Christian ideal to Zürich, Zwingli went from universal pacificism to political action and died on the battlefield.

Son of an eminent citizen of a mountain district, Zwingli's education was watched over by his uncle, a well-read parish priest, who sent him to study at the universities of Vienna and Basel, and had him appointed to the living of Glarus, a position he held between 1506 and 1516. During his pastorate he read the works of the classical authors, particularly those of Erasmus and, basing himself on Humanist ideals began to campaign for reform within the Church. He opposed the Pope's recruitment of Swiss mercenaries and the alliance with France. By 1518 his eloquence had earned him the position of preacher in the Zürich cathedral. From then on, following Luther's example, he began to be drawn towards the Reformation. In dispute with the Bishop of Constance, and with the backing of the town council, Zwingli denounced the celibacy of priests and advocated that church teaching should be based on the Scriptures alone. By the end of 1523 the split was definitive; the churches were pillaged, convents knocked down, and

mass abolished. In 1524 Zwingli married a widow with whom he lived for two years. In Zürich, the Church depended solely on the jurisdiction of the civil authorities; certain of Zwingli's followers broke away from these authorities and rose against them: this group, later known as the Anabaptists (see **Müntzer**), was absolutely crushed by Zwingli and the government of Zürich. Soon Zwingli opposed Luther on the subject of the Lord's Supper, which for him was purely symbolic, and the colloquy of Marburg of 1529 was unable to reconcile their differences. By this time, the Reformation had taken over Basel, Berne, Saint-Gall, and Schaffhausen, but the seven other Swiss cantons remained Catholic; Zwingli sent the Reformation army against them. The first clash ended in the Kappel peace treaty, but during the second battle, his troops were defeated and he was killed.

His works

He wrote several books on the new faith. The most important are *On True and False Religion* (1525), one of the first dogmatic tracts to appear during the Reformation, and *On Providence* (1529), Zwingli's most daring text.

The theory

Zwingli's conception of the Reformation, which he put into practice in Zürich, was more radical than Luther's in that, following on from Erasmian rationalism, he rejected all ancient traditions as superstitious and in terms of his doctrine, he relied less on Lutheran justification by faith alone than on 'the invincible will of God' and on personal sanctification.

The divine

'Therefore I dare to call what we have received from the Gentiles divine, if it is Holy, religious and unquestionable.'

Glossary

Generally speaking, the lay person has little or no knowledge of the vocabulary concerning religion and spirituality. For this reason, although the terms which might present any problems have been defined in the text, we thought it appropriate to list and define some of the most frequently used terms which may require further explanation.

Adventism A prophetic current founded in 1831 in the United States by William Miller who announced the 'second coming' of Christ predicted in the Book of Revelation. Today, the representatives of this American sect are the Jehovah's Witnesses (see **Protestantism**).

anchorite (Greek *ana* 'apart' and *khorein* 'to withdraw'). One who retreats into solitude in order to devote himself to contemplative life.

apocrypha (Greek *apokryptein*, 'to hide') This refers particularly to certain books or parts of books in the Old and New Testaments which have not been authenticated, and as such are excluded from the canon or the official list of the books of the Bible, either by Jews or by Christians.

apophatic (Greek *apo*, 'distance, 'outside' and *phemi*, 'to say') A theological attitude of refusal to reduce the mystery of God to any conceptual formulation considered to be limiting. Apophatism is a characteristic of the teachings of the Church Fathers, but can also be found in Hinduism and Buddhism.

apophtegm A memorable sentence attributable to an illustrious figure – the apophtegms of the Desert Fathers.

Bodhi (Sanskrit *Buddhi*) The highest level in the mind at which the absolute Being is reflected. In Buddhism, the Awakening to fundamental Reality normally concealed by the illusion of the world of appearances.

Bodhisattva One destined to become Enlightened and a future Buddha, but who postpones entry to *Nirvana* in order to help others reach the same stage.

Buddha More of a state of being, than a proper name, Buddha means 'Enlightened', denoting someone who has knowledge of Absolute Reality. According to the doctrine this name which is usually applied to the historical Buddha, Sakyamuni, can also be applied to all those who have reached a state of Enlightenment.

canon (Greek *kanon*, 'rule') A catalogue of books recognized by ecclesiastical authorities as being divinely inspired.

Charismatic (Greek *charis*, 'grace') Seen as a manifestation of the Holy Spirit comparable to that visited on the Apostles at Pentecost, charisma is said to endow those it touches with the miraculous gifts enjoyed by the Apostles, in particular the power to heal the sick.

contemplation In its religious sense this describes the mystical state in which the soul is emptied of its content and awaits the presence of God.

cosmogony (Greek *kosmos*, 'world' and *gonos*, 'generation') A theory explaining the origins of the universe.

cosmology The science of the general laws which govern the universe.

cosmos (Greek *kosmos*, 'order') The order which governs the universe.

dharma Sanskrit term used in both Hinduism and Buddhism, which is impossible to translate because of the number and subtlety of its meetings. From the root *dhr* 'to carry' it indicates all that is implied by material or moral reality; it is the law and norm of everything that exists and also the law which maintains and governs the whole universe. In Buddhism, *dharma* also refers to the Buddha's teachings which allow absolute reality to be reached.

dualist This refers to any doctrine which puts forward two distinct and irreconcilable principles like Good and Evil, spirit and matter (see **Mani** and **Manichaeism, Zoroaster**). In non-dualist philosophy these same elements are seen as indissociable and complementary.

eschatology (Greek *eschatos*, 'last' and *logos*, 'a discourse') The doctrine of the end of man and the universe. It includes beliefs concerning life after death on the one hand and the end of the world on the other. According to Revelation, at the end of time Christ will return in glory (parousia); he will resurrect the good and reign with them for one thousand years (millennium) at the end of which the Day of Judgement will take place. In the first centuries of Christianity, much hope and faith was invested in the millennium as a reward for the good, a theory which re-emerged in the Middle Ages, during the Reformation, and is still active today, with the Adventists (see **Revelation, Joachim of Fiore, Müntzer and the Anabaptists, Protestantism**).

Exegesis An interpretation of texts in holy books, particularly the books of the Bibles – Christian and Judaic.

Guru In Hinduism, this refers to a spiritual adviser who is considered to be a divine incarnation and must be obeyed as such (see **Ashram**).

heresy A religious opinion opposed to the authorized teaching of the Church, and thus condemned by it.

homily A simple teaching on religion, consisting of a commentary on the holy texts given in a sermon by a Christian preacher.

hypostasis A term describing each of the three persons of the Christian Trinity and also, less specifically, divine principles, as in the works of Plotinus.

immanent In philosophical and religious terms, it means that which is indwelling and not a result of exterior action. Defined this way, immanent is the opposite of transcendent.

karma (Sanskrit 'action') In Hinduism and Buddhism, it refers to the positive and negative consequences of acts, accumulated during present or former existences (see **Bhagavadgita**).

Logos (Greek 'word') It is used in reference to the creative divinity, Creation being assimilated to words spoken by it. In Christian doctrine, the Logos or Word is the second person of the Trinity, identified with Jesus Christ.

mandala In Hinduism and Buddhism, it is a mystical circle or cosmic diagram used as a meditation aid, particularly in Tantrism.

mantra A sacred phrase in Hinduism and Buddhism.

meditation It means deep thought. In the vocabulary of Christianity, it is the application of the mind to an examination of religious truths. In Hinduism and Buddhism, meditation (*dhyana*) is of particular importance. Corresponding to profound inner concentration, it dismisses deceptive mental processes and allows the individual to reach freedom, thanks to a penetrating vision of absolute Reality (see **Ch'an, Yoga** and **Zen**).

mudra (Sanskrit 'seal') A ritual and symbolic gesture used in Hinduism and Buddhism.

nirvana (Sanskrit 'end of suffering', 'of attachments and the passions,' 'cessation of individual existence' and 'return to the absolute Principle'.) Sometimes wrongly translated as nothingness, in Buddhism and Hinduism the word not only means deliverance from the cycle of births and deaths (*samsara*) but also the perfect blossoming of the being.

orison An invocation or prayer addressed to God and his saints. In mysticism, mental prayer is an act of worship and love, through which the soul opens itself completely to God (see **Teresa of Avila**).

orthodox (Greek *orthos*, 'right,' and *doxa* 'opinion') It is applied to that which conforms to Church dogma and doctrine. More specifically, the words orthodox and orthodoxy are applied to the Eastern Christian Church as opposed to the Western, termed Catholic Church.

parousia The glorious return of Christ at the end of time.

rabbi (Hebrew *rabbi*, 'master') A doctor of the Jewish law, religious leader of a congregation in the synagogue (see **Judaism**).

samsara In Hinduism and Buddhism this refers to the endless cycle of births and deaths in which the quality of actions in former lives (*karma*) affects the progess of the living on the path to final deliverance (*nirvana*).

sannyasin In India, this refers to one who has renounced wordly life in order to dedicate himself to religion (see **Ashram**).

schism (Greek *schisma*, 'a split') An act of separation from the Church previously adhered to. The Eastern Schism in 1004 ratified the separation between Eastern (Orthodox) Christians and Western (Catholic) Christians.

sheikh (Arabic word 'old man') It is used in particular to denote the religious leader of a Muslim brotherhood (see **Tariqa**).

sura (Arabic *surah*, 'chapter') A chapter of the Koran.

syncretism A philosophical or religious doctrine which attempts to reconcile different beliefs by drawing out their commonalities, often through artificial or superficial means.

theology (Greek *theos*, 'god,' and *logos*, 'a discourse') The science of religion and divine things.

tradition (Latin *traditio*, 'transmission') An oral transmission of doctrine over a long period of time. According to some authors, a single Tradition of which all other doctrines are more or less distorted reflections, is said to exist (see **Guénon**).

transcendent In its purest meaning, that which rises above. In the language of philsophy and religion, that which goes beyond the sensory world.

Index

Note: Entries in **bold type** refer to item headings on the pages referred to in the book.

INDEX

INDEX